DATE DUE

DEMCO 38-297

Tennessee Studies in Literature

Persons interested in submitting manuscripts should address the Editor, *Tennessee Studies in Literature*, McClung Tower 301, University of Tennessee, Knoxville, Tennessee 37916. Contributions from any qualified scholar, especially from this state and region, will be considered. Return postage should accompany manuscripts. Papers (ribbon copies on non-erasable bond paper) should be no longer than five thousand words. Other inquiries concerning this series should be addressed to the University of Tennessee Press, 293 Communications Building, University Station, Knoxville, Tennessee 37916.

CONTENTS

Abstract. The failure of Mario Praz to include the work of William Wordsworth in *The Romantic Agony* (1936) must be accounted an oversight. Primarily a study of the appearance in Romantic literature (largely under the influence of the Marquis de Sade) of algolagnia, a sexual pleasure derived from suffering or inflicting pain, the book deals with Coleridge, Byron, Shelley, and Keats but does not mention Wordsworth. The literary symptoms of algolagnia, however, such as the confusion of pleasure and pain or the gratuitous dwelling upon human cruelty and suffering, are clearly apparent in Wordsworth's play *The Borderers* and in many of his poems. The inseparability of pleasure and pain, upon which Wordsworth strangely insists in *The Prelude*, is raised to a kind of aesthetic principle in the Preface to *Lyrical Ballads*. Because of the focus of Wordsworth's work on English rusticity, it is possible that Praz failed to perceive there those symptoms which he discovered in the more familiar climates created by the other major English Romantics.   (CRW)

Abstract. "Hart-Leap Well" has been passed off by most critics as a minor "curse" poem that tells the simple pedantic story of a duke who mindlessly slays a hart and thereby offends the spirit of nature. But a closer reading reveals an elaborate analogy between the hart and Christ. There are a number of parallels that cannot be missed: the hart's death occurs at Easter time, a cross of aspens grows up over the site, and of course the hart itself is an animal representative of Christ. There are also a number of minor parallels. But what is startling is not the analogy but the savage scorn Wordsworth seems to be holding for those men whose brutal actions in nature daily recrucify Christ.   (JBT)

iv

Abstract. Keats had Shakespeare the sonneteer as well as Shakespeare the dramatist in mind when he formulated his theory of Negative Capability during the winter of 1817. The primary way that Shakespeare's narrator poet of the sonnets copes with the problems which confront him is his use of Negative Capability. He uses his ability to identify completely with another consciousness, to yield himself completely to an experience, and to exist "in uncertainties, mysteries, doubts, without any irritable reaching after fact and reason" to thwart all his attackers. T. S. Eliot charged that Shakespeare was incapable of manipulating his emotion into art in the sonnets and that he lacked an objective correlative. If one reads the sonnets straight through, he can perceive the pattern of attack on the narrator and response by the narrator through Negative Capability. The pattern is a chain of action and reaction sufficiently consistent to be considered an objective correlative.   (FPK)

Abstract. "Ode on Indolence" reveals the way in which Keats's poetic imagination operates under apparently unpoetic circumstances. The poet transforms an indolent fit, the initial stimulus for the poem, into a heightened state of consciousness, a state of mind which inspires more imaginative acts. The epigraph from Matthew 6.28 ("They toil not, neither do they spin") prefigures the unusual artistic growth in the poem; the unself-conscious growth of the lilies corresponds to Keats's imaginative growth in the poem. The poet's ultimate submission to indolence, after initial self-conscious resistance to this shadow world, leads to his discovery of unexpected richness in an experience which orthodox minds would think barren. Keats's entrance into the complexities of indolence is in accordance with the implications of "Negative Capability." A selfless poet receives and then records the amplitude of an indolent fit. "Indolence" is finally a study of a seemingly ordinary state of mind, made extraordinary by poetic sensitivity. Even indolence is generative for Keats.   (HHH)

Abstract. The crisis of the novel, when Becky is caught with Lord Steyne by her husband, has aroused much conflicting interpretation of her behavior. Actually, rather than pronouncing her innocent or guilty of misconduct, Thackeray purposely leaves the question of her guilt open. The crisis occupies a crucial point in the plot: there the pattern of punitive comedy, in which Becky exploits the vanity of others, gives way to punishment for Becky herself, a punishment increasingly demanded by the shift in her objectives and victims after the Waterloo chapters. Because Becky herself acquires the social vanity characterizing her earlier victims, she comes to deserve some humiliation. However, by treating ambivalently her behavior with Steyne, Thackeray depicts her banishment by Vanity Fair as perhaps excessive, thus sustaining residual pity for Becky and permitting a return to the view of Becky as certainly no worse than those whose egos she has offended. Such a view preserves the complex comedy of the novel.   (BKM)

Abstract. In *The Princess* Tennyson effectively uses imagery of growth to advance the serious theme of the poem: one can fulfill himself, know himself, only in relationship with others. When incorporated in the speeches of the women, this imagery provides an ironic commentary on the women's futile attempts to exclude love from their lives, thus creating a metaphorical and ironic counterpoint to the literal growth of the Prince, narrator and central character of the poem. In the final canto, which unites the metaphorical and literal emphases on growth, the Prince makes use of the growth image to affirm his self-fulfillment and maturity through union with Ida.   (KES)

Abstract. Contrary to the opinion of most Browning commentators, Mr. Sludge adopts a dishonest pose throughout the poem; thus the ending is no more of a "give-away" than the rest of the poem, and Sludge's condemnation of the creative imagination in the supposed "truth section" must not be equated with Browning's own attitudes. Using the "rule-of-reverse," Sludge creates a series of contradictory images in the desperate attempt to exonerate himself. Through the manipulation of religious terminology, he describes himself as a penitent, Christ, or whatever is most expedient at any one time. In addition he manipulates moral standards so that actions deemed undesirable for his followers are acceptable for his own use. While early arguments are undercut by open admissions of guilt, arguments in the later "truth section" are further undercut by continued utilization of manipulatory techniques previously established. The medium's ultimate failure to distinguish between acceptable use and the misuse of creative imagination emphasizes his dishonest pose even in the "truth section." The entire poem is thus an ironic series of contradictory images and Mr. Sludge's own exploitation of tactics he condemns in others. (BBN)

Abstract. A careful reading of *The Ring and the Book* does not support the position taken by some critics that Guido will be saved because he experiences moral regeneration. Although Pope Innocent hopes that the villain will see the light in the instant before death, he provides for the possibility that Guido will die unregenerate. Guido's second monologue is not an exercise in self-illumination, but an admission of the truth that he has always known—an admission demanded by Browning's scheme for the poem. Guido's final line, "Pompilia, will you let them murder me?" is a cry for life, not salvation. Ironically, however, Guido will be saved despite himself because Browning's version of spiritual economics can allow no soul, not even the blackest, to be damned. (BL)

Empedocles, Omar Khayyám, and Rabbi Ben Ezra
By Edward C. McAleer   76

Abstract. Many readers have felt that Browning's "Rabbi Ben Ezra" (1864) is a reply to Edward FitzGerald's *Rubáiyát of Omar Khayyám* (1859), basing their opinion on the antithetical philosophies in general and in particular on the metaphor of the potter's wheel found in both poems. There is no evidence, however, that Browning knew the *Rubáiyát* before 1864; his philosophy may be considered a reply to any presentation of hedonism; and he himself used the metaphor of the wheel long before FitzGerald did in the *Rubáiyát*. On the other hand, it is likely that Rabbi Ben Ezra replied to Matthew Arnold's *Empedocles on Etna* (1852). Browning knew *Empedocles* well; over the years he and Arnold made similar veiled replies to each other; the stanzaic form of "Rabbi Ben Ezra" is remarkably like that of Empedocles' chant; and not only is there a point-by-point reply to Empedocles' philosophy, but there are almost too obvious verbal echoes. (ECM)

Rossetti's "Absurd Trash": "Sir Hugh the Heron" Reconsidered
By Michael E. Greene   85

Abstract. Dante Gabriel Rossetti later described "Sir Hugh the Heron," a narrative poem which he wrote when he was twelve, as "absurd trash"; although "Sir Hugh" can hardly be described as good poetry, it is nonetheless interesting because it defines themes and techniques which Rossetti explored in much the same way in later work. Many of Rossetti's mature preoccupations—his refusal to be either consistently abstract or concrete, his interest in the magical, his ambivalence about the sacred and the profane, and his fascination with the saintly but romantic heroine—are present in the early poem in much the same form in which they appear in his later work. A reading of "Sir Hugh" demonstrates that Rossetti's mental and emotional patterns were defined with extraordinary fullness at age twelve; thenceforth he was to work primarily refining an already established set of responses rather than growing and changing as he encountered other stimuli. (MEG)

Abstract. Henry James and George Meredith were unique in their day for insight into the nature of women, their strengths, their possibilities, and their repression. The two writers expressed essentially the same ideas about women, ideas foreign or distasteful to most of their contemporaries. In James's *The Portrait of a Lady* and Meredith's *The Egoist*, the characters Isabel Archer and Clara Middleton are revealed as intelligent and charming women who form their own opinions and maintain their independence in spite of pressure from society and from the men in their lives. Both Isabel's husband and Clara's fiancé, though egoists of the first order, are unable to quell or alter their indomitable spirits. Isabel and Clara illustrate James's and Meredith's perception of how women could be intelligent, independent, and strong, yet retain their femininity.   (ASP)

Abstract. Hardy's frequent use of the designation "dramatic" to describe his poetry, once it is understood, provides a useful context for studying much of his verse. When he insists in his prefaces upon the dramatic quality of his poetry, Hardy means that his poems, while often personal utterances, do not reveal him fully and permanently; they are almost always in some important sense incomplete renderings of his vision. In some poems he effaces the persona so that the experience in the poem is incomplete because it is presented without a context; in others he binds the narrator's vision to the particulars of time and place in the experience so that the vision cannot be generalized beyond those particulars. In neither case can the poem be said to represent Hardy wholly and directly. Hence, while many of his poems are transparently personal, most are at the same time dramatic in that they present only partial visions of experience. As partial visions they may be and often are inconsistent with one another.   (WWM)

Abstract. Hardy's verbal irony becomes a more important and more frequently used tool in his writings over his quarter-century as a novelist. Four branches of verbal irony that he uses are denotative, connotative, tonal, and referential. Denotative and connotative ironies serve *en masse* to add depth and meaning to dramatic situations. Often detachable and unimportant in context in the early fiction, these ironies contribute to theme, interpret character, and provide insight into plot as they become integral parts of the later works. Tonal irony also complements the ironic themes of these novels and soon becomes integral to style as Hardy uses sounds to add to his ironic sense. Referential irony is weak in the early novels in that it is often extraneous and detachable. By the last ironic novels, however, the ironic references help to establish scene, character, and symbolism.   (LHP)

Abstract. The purpose of this article is to clarify the crucial roles which the literary critics William Archer and Edmund Gosse played in facilitating the acceptance of Henrick Ibsen's work in Britain and to explore the complex personal relationship between Archer and Gosse. More than any of their contemporaries, Archer and Gosse were responsible for "creating Ibsen's reputation in the English-speaking world. . . ." This essay, based in part on some unpublished correspondence among Archer, Gosse, and Edward Tyas Cook, explains the relationship of Archer, the dramatic critic, and Gosse, the literary critic and essayist, by clarifying their "acrimonious behind-the-scenes battles" in 1890–91 and their subsequent collaboration to bring Ibsen's work before the British public. (JOB)

Abstract. During his lifetime Rudyard Kipling's reputation as a poet was dominated by the sterile debate carried on between hostile critics and undiscriminating cultists. As a result, only two critics, Robert Bridges and T. S. Eliot, reviewed his poetry with original and independent judgments, and his growth as a poet, evident in his final volume of verse, *The Years Between* (1919), was largely unnoticed. The obituaries that followed Kipling's death in 1936 reflected this stalemate in Kipling criticism and dramatized the conflict between critics, cultists, and poet-critics.   (MH)

BOYD LITZINGER

KENNETH LESLIE KNICKERBOCKER

Professor Knickerbocker retired in May 1974, having completed twenty-eight years of magnificent service to the University of Tennessee, to the larger community of academics, and to the English department which his timeless efforts helped to make distinguished. That career was richly varied, as the man himself is.

He was born May 19, 1905, into a Dallas, Texas, family which respected and encouraged mental discipline and hard work. His father was an active Methodist minister; one of his brothers was to become an administrative executive at Southern Methodist University, another a well-known and widely read war correspondent. By age twenty-two, he had earned A.B. and A.M. degrees at S.M.U. and had gotten a year of college teaching under his belt as an instructor at Texas Technological College. Now a comprehensive university, Texas Tech in 1926 was a newly founded small college intended to educate young West Texans— mainly in engineering and the technological skills required by the growing oil and natural gas industry. There one learned the art of combining the useful and the good in one's teaching. Liberal learning, yes—and so one taught literature; but applied learning as well, and so one taught what is now called technical writing for engineers.

The sense of being in at the beginning of a new institution—set on the high plains of Texas, where the hot dry wind whips incessantly down from the Panhandle, rolling tumbleweeds and sandstorms before it— together with the excitement every natural teacher feels as he enters his true vocation must have combined to help overcome serious difficulties for a young teacher and aspiring scholar: a library that hardly merited the name, a college with no established tradition of learning, an isolated small town with all its development yet to come. The next few years were to be decisive.

In 1929, provided now with a charming and talented young wife, Dorothy, he entered Yale as a doctoral student. The intellectual atmosphere must have been heady, and the faculty certainly was distinguished. Browning studies were represented by "Billy" Phelps, an old-time enthusiast and popularizer, and by a very methodical and serious young scholar, William Clyde DeVane. It was the latter who directed Mr. Knickerbocker's dissertation on Browning and who was to become a lifelong friend and important collaborator. One feels that Yale meant other things as well. If in all the years since, Kenneth Knickerbocker has been keenly aware of the financial needs of doctoral students, one suspects that his years at Yale (during which the young couple struggled to make ends meet and Dorothy earned many of their meals by playing the violin in New Haven's better restaurants) confirmed that spirit of sympathy he has always shown toward the student with ability (and often a family) but without adequate means.

Three years later—the Great Depression at its deepest, his dissertation in hand, and his first scholarly article in print—he returned to Texas Tech. In 1933 Yale awarded him the Ph.D., and a year later he accepted a position at the University of Rhode Island where, with time out for World War II (during which Lt. Kenneth L. Knickerbocker, USNR, commanded the V-12 unit at Ohio Wesleyan), he remained until 1946, progressing from assistant professor to professor and department head. In 1946 he accepted the offer of a professorship at the University of Tennessee, thus beginning the distinguished tenure that would last until his retirement.

One of the jobs that fell to him in Knoxville was directing the freshman English program, which had swollen rapidly with the massive enrollment of veterans eager to use their G.I. Bill benefits. To bring some kind of order out of potential chaos, to maintain a reasonably even standard of instruction, and to raise the level of writing for large numbers of students with uneven preparation and disparate career aims were no easy tasks; and, if the "Tennessee system" became a kind of model from which other institutions learned, that fact was due in large part to Professor Knickerbocker, who has never viewed the teaching of composition as a necessary evil. To teach a student to write well is also to teach him to think logically, and to break the psychological barrier between thought and the written expression of thought is to begin the student's liberal education.

Dissatisfied with the available textbooks, he conceived *Ideas for Writ-*

ing, which was to become one of the most widely used, admired, and imitated "readers" in a competitive market. It was based upon sound principles, the first being "That a student paper undisturbed by an idea is a clod and, no matter how precise the grammar, need not have been written." It assumed that college freshmen were mature enough to study all sides of controversial subjects and to form their own judgments, and so it included sections on atheism, communism, and segregation. Today it is only a matter of historical curiosity (but then it was a sign of the times) that the book was attacked as subversive by a well-known professor at Tennessee's other great university, in a letter written on behalf of an ultra-conservative political group to the University's Board of Trustees. The attack was a mistake. Dr. Knickerbocker's reply to Professor X (it is merciful not to use his name) was devastating. A little logic, spiced with a bit of humor, demolished objection and man alike; for not only had Professor X argued poorly but he had also set a trap in which he himself could be caught: he too was the author of a freshman text, in the preface of which he stressed the value of a freshman's studying topics from different points of view. "Apparently," concluded Dr. Knickerbocker, "Mr. X has his own notions concerning the questions upon which it is permissible to diverge." *Ideas for Writing* went into several editions and was followed by other successful and useful textbooks: *Interpreting Literature* (with H. W. Reninger in 1955, and going to five editions), *Readings and Assignments* (with Bain Tate Stewart in 1961), and *How to Write About Poetry* (1967).

Through these textbooks, his development of the freshman program, and his involvement with a myriad of professional associations his influence upon undergraduate English instruction extended far beyond the Knoxville campus. But U.T.'s English department was building solid graduate programs as well, and Professor Knickerbocker was active at every level of instruction.

As a scholar-teacher, he was always more interested in the pursuit of ideas than in mere fact-grubbing; but unlike the fashionable followers of the "new critics," whose emphasis upon the poem as artifact misled so many students into believing that a firm grasp of literary history, biography, and patterns of thought was unnecessary, he saw—and taught—poetry as part of the larger human drama, the experience of man. Ideas moved the world; it was essential to grasp these ideas if one was to understand it. As a teacher he did not eschew *explication de texte*, but in the relaxed and informal classes he conducted, one came to feel that the best explication was a thoughtful reading, done in a rich, flexible, modulated voice (flavored always by that soft Texas drawl), not an actor's performance proceeding from long practice, but a scholar's interpretation rising out of a deep and comfortable knowledge of the poet and his mind. One became aware of hidden subtleties; verbal and grammatical difficulties vanished.

His scholarship was of a piece with his teaching, moving always beyond and behind Browning's poetry into the sources of his ideas and their implications. The titles of a few selected articles will themselves suggest as much: "Browning's *Cenciaja*," disclosing the original source of the poem (*Philological Quarterly*, 1934); "Browning and His Critics," opening a topic which has since occupied a large place in Browning studies (*Sewanee Review*, 1935); "Browning's Letters to Isabella Blagden," practically forcing a re-edition of the most important body of the poet's letters to a single correspondent other than Elizabeth (*PMLA*, 1939); "A Tentative Apology for Browning," challenging long-accepted views of Browning as a "thinker" (*Tennessee Studies in Literature*, 1956); and "Robert Browning: A Modern Appraisal," laying the groundwork for future estimates of Browning's philosophical poetry (*Tennessee Studies in Literature*, 1959). Further, his introduction to the Modern Library edition of Browning's poems (published in 1951) still offers the general reader one of the best entries to the poet and his poetry; and *The Browning Critics* (University of Kentucky Press, 1965), which he coedited, has proved a springboard for Browning scholars ever since.

In addition he could and did do exact scholarship of the most laborious kind, as *New Letters of Robert Browning* (edited with DeVane and published in 1951 by Yale) beautifully demonstrated. But even in the years of painstaking work that went into that fine volume, he and his collaborator kept in mind a broader purpose: not simply to present a mass of letters and new information to Victorianists (as valuable as that object was), but also to do the work so exactly that future scholars would have a rigorous model from which to work. Perhaps only those familiar with the development of Browning studies (which had, for decades, been a mixed bag indeed—with impressionism, appreciation, and special pleading the rule rather than the exception) can appreciate the impact *New Letters* had and has upon workers in the field. It would no longer be possible for "editors" to ignore textual difficulties, to delete names or fail to identify persons referred to by the writer, to reprint published letters without having seen the originals, or to "correct" the poet's distinctive spelling and punctuation.

Nor did the new example remain unfollowed. Having shown in 1939 (see above) that Browning's letters to Isabella Blagden were both incomplete and badly edited, Dr. Knickerbocker had gotten permission to do the job properly. However, instead of reserving them to himself as he had every right to do (and as many other scholars actually have done in similar cases), he generously turned them over to his first doctoral student, Edward C. McAleer. This act was typical. For Kenneth Knickerbocker, scholarly publication has never been a selfish matter or one that admitted of needless delay for personal reasons. If there was a good job of work to be done and if he recognized in his student a talent for the job, then it was only logical for him to bring the two together. This is, no doubt, why so many of his students have published good work.

In any case, his choice of Ed McAleer was excellent. *Dearest Isa*, published by the University of Texas Press a year after the appearance of *New Letters*, confirmed the editorial standards of the latter and set McAleer on a brilliant career as scholar and editor. This first dissertation must still be considered one of the very best to have come out of the University of Tennessee and helped, no doubt, to establish the value of its doctoral programs.

This incident is one of many which could be cited to underscore a happy fact: a fine scholar himself, Kenneth Knickerbocker has also been the cause of scholarship in others. It was only natural, then, that when *The Browning Newsletter* (now *Studies in Browning and His Circle*) embarked upon a policy of honoring scholars for distinguished service to Browning studies, Kenneth Knickerbocker was chosen as the first such person to be "profiled."

Many a scholar-teacher now active entered the field of Victorian studies as a result of his influence. Did you want to write a dissertation under his direction? Fine. But there was a streak of practicality in the man's advice to his students: choose if possible an important topic dealing with a major Victorian figure. It would, of course, be a holy and a wholesome thing to learn all that can be known about punctuation in Thomas Lovell Beddoes; however, you will become a scholar-*teacher*, and how often will you have the opportunity to teach punctuation in Beddoes to your future students? Advice was followed by practical assistance: introductions to department chairmen, established scholars, publishers, and foundation officers; letters of reference, recommendation, and practical support unlimited. Was a teaching assistant in temporary financial need? Well, perhaps an extra section of freshman English could be found for him. Was there a (temporary, it was hoped) oversupply of young Ph.D.'s? Perhaps the University could supply some post-doctoral teaching and research fellowships to help young people get on their professional feet (U.T. did), and perhaps other large universities could be persuaded to follow suit (some did).

To get back a seminar paper or a thesis chapter after he had marked it was to realize that he had entered enthusiastically into a joint intellectual venture. Sometimes too enthusiastically. On at least one occasion, a graduate student got back a paper literally cut up: Professor Knickerbocker had expressed himself so vigorously in marginal comments that he found it proper to excise most of them with the help of a pair of scissors.

In 1958 Dr. Knickerbocker took on broader administrative responsibilities, becoming Dean of the College of Liberal Arts. It was inevitable that the five ensuing years would see the college expand rapidly, but to supervise orderly growth was only part of the administrator's role. The other and more important role was to use every opportunity to strengthen the college, not simply to add numbers to the faculty, but to add numbers of superbly qualified men and women to it. So Dean Knickerbocker did much to build upon real strengths and to repair weaknesses.

As always, he kept an eye on the general well-being of the University and the community. Did the Knoxville Symphony Orchestra (of which he became a director and in which Mrs. Knickerbocker and her violin held a valuable spot) need a first-rate oboist, or the Carousel Theatre a director of children's productions? Well, out there among the qualified aspirants for teaching positions, there must be someone (or someone's spouse) with an unusual talent.

Nor was it enough for him to act merely as an arm of the central administration or as an intermediary in faculty-administration disputes. One had to lead, and this occasionally led to the championship of right causes. One of these was the repeal of the notorious "monkey law," which remained on the books long after the Scopes trial of 1925, obsolete and intellectually indefensible, but technically denying all teachers the right to "teach evolution." Unanimously the faculty of the college had voted to ask the trustees to join the faculty in an effort to repeal the law. It was Dean Knickerbocker's duty, of course, to forward the petition, and he did so. And, being a political realist, he also knew that the trustees would not be particularly receptive to reopening an emotionally charged subject. But expediency held no attractions when principles were involved. In the letter advising the president of the University, and through him the board of trustees, of the faculty's action, Mr. Knickerbocker wrote:

The more one thinks of the issue involved, the more one is convinced that our University must take a stand in favor of repealing this bad law. In my mind, I have asked: what would other universities do with this issue? The answer from every university would be the same, I think: any law which denies the right to explore, to examine any theory or system, or sincere attempt to discover truth strikes at the foundations of the learning process and must be opposed.

To oppose any law, or thing, or attitude that strikes at the foundations of the learning process is a principle more honored in the breach than in the observance, one fears, but not so in this case.

In 1963 Dr. Knickerbocker voluntarily resigned the deanship to return to the English department, where he was now to serve as chairman and Distinguished Professor. Needless to say, his activity was not in the least reduced, and his influence upon the teaching profession continued to grow. He was elected president of both the Tennessee College English Association and the South Atlantic Association of Departments of English. In addition he was named to the Executive Committee of the National Association of Departments of English. With all of these activities he still found time to read and advise on manuscripts submitted not only to *Tennessee Studies in Literature* (of which he was coeditor for ten years) but also to a host of other journals and a number of university presses.

In 1971 he was asked once more to take on full-time administrative work, and in September of that year he agreed to serve, for two years only, as Academic Vice President of the University of Tennessee's statewide system. And so, at a time of life when most men are content to take in sail and to glide toward retirement, Kenneth Knickerbocker was willing to undertake new responsibilities and to face new challenges; for the late sixties and early seventies saw the rise of new enemies of promise—the cults of "do your own thing" and of the downward-levelers who call for "universal higher education." In an address to the 1973 graduates of the University of Tennessee at Martin, Dr. Knickerbocker demolished the pretensions of the anti-intellectuals. The word *elitist*, he pointed out, is used as a weapon against higher education by those who seem to believe that all will be well if everyone achieves the equality of a college degree. But, he showed, this theory is based not upon democratic principle but upon sheer sentimentality and, in practice, makes higher education a meaningless and futile exercise. "Higher education," he asserted, "should be more difficult, more demanding, more varied, and more specialized than lower education. I can hear the reproving cry: 'Elitist!' If higher education is to have any meaning—if it is to do its job at all—it must be elitist." A harsh conclusion? Not at all, but a forthright expression of the philosophy held by a man who had spent a lifetime wrestling with difficult questions, a man who respects man and man's mind.

And this, one feels, is a fair indication of the quality of Professor Knickerbocker's mind, the mind of a scholar-teacher who thinks things through. Reading his books, articles, and addresses, one is struck not only by his command of fact and power of argument, but more by his respect for logical thought and its accurate expression, both of which must lead to principled action. "The unexamined life," said Socrates, "is not worth living." One feels that it is an appropriate motto in this case.

It is fitting that Dr. Knickerbocker chose to spend his last year at the University teaching, not administering. For practically the first time in thirty years he was free to teach his students and pursue his research to the exclusion of all other professional duties. One would like to have been a student in that last class. It is entirely characteristic of him that, in a letter to one of his former students, he should write simply: "I am working harder than ever." It is difficult to believe that he will work less hard in retirement. One can hope that, as he enjoys at greater leisure some of the pleasures he has always loved—watching the progress of his daughter, Alzada, his son, Robert, and their families; keeping a watchful and philosophical eye upon the body politic; traveling to interesting places in the company of interesting people; and, yes, playing a bit of golf surprisingly well—one can also hope that he will find the time to expand that modern appraisal of Browning and to write down some reflections on the academic world as he saw it through a long, varied, interesting, and distinguished tenure.

In the meantime his friends, colleagues, and students are delighted and proud to have this opportunity to honor him, to wish him and his gracious wife long years of health and happiness, and to hope that the years ahead prove to be the rich and fruitful time that should cap a rich and fruitful career.

Saint Bonaventure University

CHARLES R. WOODARD

WORDSWORTH AND THE ROMANTIC AGONY

In compiling a descriptive bibliography of the Wordsworth collection at Amherst, published in 1936, Cornelius Howard Patton made the following comment concerning Mario Praz's *The Romantic Agony*,[1] which had first appeared in English translation three years earlier: "By means of a wealth of scholarly quotation and reference, Dr. Praz undertakes to show that the romantic movement in Europe, after 1800, became permeated with a sickness that turned rapidly to decadence. . . . Wordsworth receives the compliment of not even being mentioned." [2]

Patton's comment is suggestive, in a mild way, of the criticism which Praz's book at first frequently encountered. Gradually, over the years (a second English edition appeared in 1951), the work has won a steadily growing acceptance, to the point where Edmund Wilson could refer to it as being, "in its field of comparative literature, . . . one of the most fascinating works of our time."[3] Wordsworth, however, continued to go without mention in the second edition; and so far as one may judge by the critical silence on the subject, Patton's assumption that Wordsworth is outside the scope of Praz's inquiry continues to be accepted without question. On its very face, however, even without an examination of Wordsworth's work, the proposition seems somewhat unlikely. Was Wordsworth unmoved by the forces, largely emanating from the works of the Marquis de Sade, which had such a strong influence, according to Praz, on the works of Wordsworth's contemporaries, both in England and on the Continent? Was he alone unaffected while Byron, Keats, Shelley, and even his close friend and collaborator Coleridge fell under the spell of that influence?

Praz's book, entitled in Italian *La Carne, La Morte e Il Diavolo*, is a

1

study of the growth of a literary tradition, dating from the eighteenth century, which has been succinctly described by Wilson as one "of erotic cruelty, hysterical enjoyment of horror and perverse admiration for crime" (152). It should be added that the enjoyment of horror and the admiration for crime have the same erotic base as the cruelty; Praz says that his book is an investigation of Romantic literature under the aspect of "erotic sensibility" (Foreword, vii). More specifically, it is primarily a study of the appearance in literature of algolagnia, defined in psychiatry as sexual pleasure derived from inflicting or suffering pain. The literary symptom is any apparently perverse confusion of pleasure and pain, or the derivation of the former from the latter, in circumstances where conditions of human cruelty or suffering may seem to be unduly or gratuitously dwelt upon. Here perhaps we have the major reason for Wordsworth's continued exclusion from the ranks of his fellows in this regard. Who is likely to think in such terms of the poet whom we regularly associate with libertarianism, humble life, and the highest moral principles? And yet if we reread the poetry with *The Romantic Agony* in mind, it is difficult to avoid the conclusion that Praz's failure to include Wordsworth in his study must be attributed to an oversight.

Appendix I of Praz's book is entitled "Swinburne and 'Le Vice Anglais.'" The "vice" is sexual flagellation, coupled with "a morbid attraction for sights of suffering" (415). In this connection Praz refers to "the French legend of the Englishman whose greatest pleasure was to attend executions, a legend which was developed during the Romantic period and received a new stimulus from the Goncourts" (416). Evidently Praz was unaware of or did not think worthy of mention Wordsworth's reputed statement to Carlyle that he witnessed the execution of the Girondist Gorsas in Paris in October 1793.[4] The fact that Wordsworth's biographers generally agree that his presence in France at this time is unlikely merely adds to the interest of Carlyle's statement. F. W. Bateson says that Carlyle may have misunderstood Wordsworth but concedes that it is more likely that Wordsworth may have been "romancing,"[5] a rather surprising word to use in this context. Bateson seems unaware of the implications of such an invention on Wordsworth's part. Hangings are described in "Guilt and Sorrow" and in *The Prelude*, and Wordsworth wrote a series of sonnets in support of capital punishment. Such concerns serve to remind us that we are dealing with a poet who spent part of his wedding day with his bride reading the inscriptions on the gravestones in a churchyard[6] and who wrote three short works on epitaphs.[7]

These are minor matters perhaps, but from such considerations it is only a step to an awareness of the extent to which Wordsworth's poetry is concerned with the mad, the blind, the crippled, the outcast—with almost every conceivable form of human suffering. A glance at the Wordsworth concordance is suggestive in this connection. The entries for the word *death* take up two columns, as does the word *sorrow* in its various forms. The word *grave*, mostly the noun, takes up two columns; the various forms of *pain* require two and a half columns, as does *sad*, with its variations. *Suffer* in its different forms, *blood*, and *sick* each occupy a column. The entries for the word *poor* take up almost three columns; and, perhaps most notable of all, *fear* takes up more than four.[8]

Wordsworth's poems in which physical suffering, deformity, and death appear come quickly to mind: "Ruth," "The Thorn," "Guilt and Sorrow," "Vaudracour and Julia," "The Idiot Boy," "The Old Cumberland Beggar," "Resolution and Independence," "Simon Lee," "To a Sexton," "Andrew Jones," "The Convict"—one could multiply the list almost indefinitely.[9] Wordsworth's *Somersetshire Tragedy*, never completed and destroyed by his grandson, apparently as unsuitable for publication, was a tale of murder and hanging (Bateson, 130–32). Madness, like hanging, is a staple of Wordsworth's works; occasionally the preoccupation with death exhibits a discomfiting attention to wormy circumstance, as in the early "Dirge":

> List! the bell-Sprite stuns my ears
> Slowly calling for a maid;
> List! each worm with trembling hears
> And stops for joy his dreadful trade.

"All through the literature of Romanticism," Praz writes, "down to our own times, there is an insistence on . . . [the] theory of the inseparability of pleasure and pain, and, on the practical side, a search for themes of tormented, contaminated beauty" (28). Wordsworth's growth, he tells us, was "fostered alike by beauty and by fear,"[10] a remarkable combination of stimuli whose significance Wordsworth may not have fully understood but which is surely relevant to the literary tradition under discussion.

Chapter III of *The Romantic Agony*, entitled "The Shadow of the Divine Marquis," is devoted primarily to the theme of "the unfortunate, persecuted maiden." Praz sees her modern prototype in Clarissa Harlowe, who, "ensnared and seduced by the libertine Lovelace and persecuted by her implacable parents, becomes ill with grief and fades slowly away amid the funeral pomps of an exemplary death" (95). Wordsworth uses this theme or a variation frequently; one thinks particularly of "Her Eyes Are Wild," about an abandoned mother suffering from incipient madness; "Ruth," in which Ruth is deserted by her American lover and driven mad; "Vaudracour and Julia," which concludes with their child dead, Julia driven by her family into a convent, and Vaudracour "an imbecile mind"; "The Thorn," in which Martha Ray is abandoned by her lover ("She was with child, and she was mad") and thought to have killed her child; "Guilt and Sorrow," whose female vagrant has lost her husband and three children after unnumbered hardships; and "The Widow on Windermere Side," in which the widow loses all her children while laboring to pay off the indebtedness left by her dead husband. Of these poems, "The Thorn" is of especial interest because of a comment upon it made by Swinburne, who, in addition to being the subject of an appendix in *The Romantic Agony*, as already mentioned, is frequently cited in the body of the book. If we are to believe him, the author of "Dolores" was shocked and horrified by Wordsworth's poem: "A subject of such naked and untempered horror as he attempted to manage in his semi-dramatic idyll of *The Thorn*—one of the poems elected by himself for especial mention as a representative example of his work, and of its guiding principle—instead of being harmonised by his genius into tragic and pitiful and terrible beauty, retains in his hands the whole ghastliness and dreadfulness of a merely shocking hideous reality."[11]

More to the point is Swinburne's comment earlier in the same essay on Wordsworth's play *The Borderers* (1796–97):

[*The Borderers*], in the moral conception and development of its leading idea, is, I suppose, unparalleled by any serious production of the human intellect for morbid and monstrous extravagance of horrible impossibility. Some invention perhaps might be recovered from the earliest and most frantic romances of Eugène Sue, written in what Dumas has indicated—borrowing a favorite reference from the pure-minded Sainte-Beuve—as the Sadique stage of that novelist's youthful inspiration, which if set beside this young imagination of Wordsworth's might seem, in point of sheer moral monstrosity, to come as near it "as moonlight unto sunlight, or as water unto wine."   (207)

In a concluding broadside, Swinburne says, "From the purely ethical or moral point of view, I should really be curious to see its parallel, in any branch of any literature, as a sample of the monstrous and the morbid" (208).

Even when we remember that Swinburne was less easily shocked by the "monstrous extravagance" of his favorite Elizabethan dramatists, these are remarkable comments. From what we now know of Swinburne's life, as well as of his writings, he must be regarded as no mean authority in such matters, and it is surely worthy of note that he connects the play with the spirit of his own avowed master, the Marquis de Sade.

Quite apart from the action of *The Borderers*, the "prefatory essay" which Wordsworth wrote for it is sufficiently remarkable. "Let us suppose," he begins, "a young man of great intellectual powers yet without any solid principles of genuine benevolence," who "is betrayed into a great crime" (*Works*, I, 345). The characterization continues,

> In his retirement, he is impelled to examine the unreasonableness of established opinions; and the force of his mind exhausts itself in constant efforts to separate the elements of virtue and vice. It is his pleasure and his consolation to hunt out whatever is bad in actions usually esteemed virtuous, and to detect the good in actions which the universal sense of mankind teaches us to reprobate.
>
> . . . .
>
> It will easily be perceived that to such a mind those enterprizes which are most extraordinary will in time appear the most inviting. His appetite from being exhausted becomes unnatural . . . . He is like a worn out voluptuary—he finds his temptation in strangeness, he is unable to suppress a low hankering after the double entendre in vice. . . .   (345–47)

The description, of course, is of Oswald, a figure reminiscent of Iago, dedicated to "the wholesome ministry of pain and evil," who without motive deceives the younger Marmaduke into bringing about the death of an innocent man. Oswald is clearly in the long line of satanic figures whom Praz traces back to Tasso, Marino, and Milton; it is difficult to understand why, particularly in view of Swinburne's overheated reaction, Oswald is not included in Chapter II of *The Romantic Agony*, entitled "The Metamorphosis of Satan," devoted in large part to the Gothic novel and to Byron. If one did not know better, in fact, he might assume Wordsworth's description of Oswald to be intended for one of Byron's characters rather than one of Wordsworth's. It is impossible, too, as Swinburne surely perceived, to miss in Oswald's character correspondences to Sade's customary inversion of virtue and vice, set forth in his Preface to *Justine*: "Nous allons peindre le crime comme il est, c'est-à-dire toujours triomphant et sublime . . . et la vertu . . . toujours maussade et toujours triste . . ." (quoted in Praz, 80).

Although students of Wordsworth have always been aware of the prevalence of human suffering in his works, they have attributed it usually to his concern for the poor and downtrodden, as seen in his stated intention in Book XII of *The Prelude* (1850) to be the poet of humble persons and humble circumstance. Bateson's comment is typical: "He was profoundly sorry for the world's failures, the unwanted, the unloved . . . because he had known the bitter humiliation of social failure himself" (128). No doubt Bateson is at least partially right, but his explanation does not adequately account for either the frequency with which suffering appears in the poems or the remarkably detailed way in which Wordsworth tends to dwell on it. A peculiar experience which he underwent during his visit to Salisbury Plain, later recorded in *The Prelude* (1805 version, XII, 320–26; 1850 version, XIII, 321–35), sheds an odd light on the position occupied by the humble class in at least the unconscious portion of his mind. The experience took the form of a hallucinatory "vision" of human sacrifice carried out by Druids. The event is to be found in almost identical form, testifying to its importance to Wordsworth, in the earliest manuscript version of "Guilt and Sorrow," where again appear "long-bearded forms with wands uplifted" and "the sacrificial altar fed / With living men" (*Works*, I, 104n., ll 27–34). What is remarkable is the fact that Wordsworth seems somehow to connect these imagined sacrificial victims of pagan Britain with the impoverished class of his own age. The "monuments and traces of antiquity," he wrote in his "Advertisement" to "Guilt and Sorrow," "led me unavoidably to compare what we know or guess of these remote times with certain aspects of modern society, and with calamities, principally those consequent upon war, to which, more than other classes of men, the poor are subject" (*Works*, I, 95).

It may be argued that libertarian and humanitarian feelings are at work here, but it is equally appropriate to question the impulses which led Wordsworth to conceive a comparison of such violence and horror. If his intention is merely to call attention to the plight of suffering humanity, he may be said to protest too much. Praz remarks on the way in which the "unctuous pietism" of Richardson's novels is overwhelmed by the detailed descriptions of the vice against which it is ostensibly directed, resulting in a "contradiction of intention and result" (96–97). By repeatedly describing as he does the most minute physical details of age, infirmity, and suffering, Wordsworth suggests that he is unconsciously more interested in the condition than in its cure. There is frequently a remarkable detachment in these descriptions, incidentally; the narrator of "The Old Cumberland Beggar," for example, although he details at length the virtues of charity, is content to leave its specific application to his neighbor, who, "though pressed himself," gives the beggar food. Although he dwells upon the infirmities of the decrepit leech-gatherer in "Resolution and Independence," "perplexed and longing to be comforted," the narrator sees him not as an object of pity but as a means of reassuring his own faltering confidence.

When charity is extended by the speaker in one of the poems, there is often a self-congratulatory tone which is distinctly unpleasant. "Alice

Fell, or Poverty" is a case in point. After dwelling at length on the miseries of a little orphan girl whose coat has been caught in the wheel of a coach and made into "a miserable rag indeed," the narrator relates how he gave money to the host of a tavern and directed him to purchase her a new coat, concluding in a somewhat lordly manner,

> "And let it be of duffil grey,
> As warm a cloak as man can sell!"
> Proud creature was she the next day,
> The little orphan, Alice Fell!
>   (ll. 57–60)

One hardly knows what to make of the poem. The girl's despair at the loss of her coat is what is dwelt upon, not her pride in the possession of a new one. Although she has a new coat, she remains an orphan, with all her other miseries unchanged. The speaker's awareness of having committed an act of benevolence is perhaps more warming to him than the new coat is to Alice Fell. The same ambiguity of intention may be seen in "Simon Lee, the Old Huntsman," in which Simon, "poorest of the poor," is described as follows:

> And he is lean and he is sick;
> His body, dwindled and awry,
> Rests upon ankles swoln and thick;
> His legs are thin and dry.
>   (ll. 33–36)

After describing again Simon's swollen ankles the narrator recounts an episode when he came across Simon attempting to grub a rotten stump out of the ground:

> The mattock tottered in his hand;
> So vain was his endeavour,
> That at the root of the old tree
> He might have worked for ever.
>   (ll. 77–80)

The narrator takes the mattock and "with a single blow / The tangled root I severed," to Simon's profound gratitude:

> The tears into his eyes were brought,
> And thanks and praises seemed to run
> So fast out of his heart, I thought
> They never would have done.
>   (ll. 89–92)

Although the narrator concludes that "the gratitude of men / Hath oftener left me mourning" than their coldness, the incident is an unpleasant one. Whatever Wordsworth's intention may have been, the poem, by dwelling so insistently on Simon's weaknesses, serves to degrade the infirmities of age while celebrating the vigor and strength of youth. The tone approaches smugness; humanitarian impulses have been strangely confused with other motives, to the point where suffering, rather than its alleviation, may be the primary concern.

Finally it must be seen that the relationship between pain and pleasure in Wordsworth is not to be inferred from the poetry alone but that it came, over the years, to play an important part in his concept of poetic development and of the aesthetics of poetry. Many of the episodes of *The Prelude* are intended to show the contributions of fear, as well as of beauty, to the "growth of a poet's mind"; frequently, in fact, the sense of beauty is indissolubly connected with fear or even seems to derive from it. It is as if the enjoyment of beauty must be paid for in the coin of emotional pain and suffering. It is in the Preface to *Lyrical Ballads*, however, several times revised, that we are given the best insight into the way in which Wordsworth's mind habitually made associations between pain and pleasure. It is notable that he cannot long write on the subject of the "passions," the feelings which he sees as the poet's proper subject, without those passions metamorphosing under his pen into "pain" or "suffering." Thus he remarks in one paragraph on the difficulty of the poet's maintaining the force of "that which is uttered by men in real life, under the actual pressure of those passions" (*Works*, II, 394). In the next paragraph he writes, "However exalted a notion we would wish to cherish of the character of a poet, it is obvious that while he describes and imitates passions, his employment is in some degree mechanical, compared with the freedom and power of real and substantial action and suffering" (394).

Again, writing on the poet's "one restriction," to give pleasure to his readers, he says, "It is a homage paid to the nature and naked dignity of man, to the grand elementary principle of pleasure, by which he knows, and feels, and lives, and moves. We have no sympathy but what is propagated by pleasure: I would not be misunderstood; but whenever we sympathize with pain, it will be found that the sympathy is produced and carried on by subtle combinations with pleasure" (395).

Further on in the Preface, after his discussion of the identity of the language of poetry and the language of prose, his explanation of his reason for employing meter in his writings takes on a very interesting form. Poetry, he says, has as its aim the production of excitement and pleasure, but "if the words . . . have an undue proportion of pain connected with them, there is some danger that the excitement may be carried beyond its proper bounds" (399). The regularity of meter, he says, serves to temper this excitement, and he concludes, "There can be little doubt but that more pathetic situations and sentiments, that is, those which have a greater proportion of pain connected with them, may be endured in metrical composition, especially in rhyme, than in prose" (399).

Thus, in Wordsworth's mind, "poetic situations" inevitably suggest suffering or pain, pain is indissolubly joined with excitement, and excitement is interchangeable with pleasure. He appears at one point, indeed, to be saying not so much that meter helps to alleviate the pain of suffering as that it helps to keep pleasure and excitement within bearable emotional limits for the reader.

Edmund Wilson has pointed out that the first reaction of many readers—Croce, for example—to Praz's book is "to protest that Signor Praz has ignored all the generous emotions, the noble libertarian ideals, that were also given expression by the Romantic Movement" (156). Such qualities are certainly present; the fact that Praz does not discuss them does not constitute a denial of their existence. They are, in fact, more consistently present in Wordsworth's poetry than in that of any of his English contemporaries; the fact that they are sometimes found in combination with the syndrome which is the subject of Praz's study merely suggests the complexity of that subject. To say all this is in no way to denigrate the work of the most original of English Romantic poets. In the same way that it is not to be taken as a compliment to Wordsworth that he was omitted from *The Romantic Agony*, it is not defamatory to suggest that he should have been included. It is perhaps because of Wordsworth's humanitarianism, as well as his determined avoidance of the overtly sensational and the flamboyant exoticism of some of his contemporaries, that Praz was misled. His poetry was animated by the same forces which acted upon the other Romantics treated by Praz; but in Wordsworth, for the most part, these forces are more firmly controlled, less easily discerned in the homely affairs of the rustics whom he believed to be the proper subject of poetry. *The Borderers* aside, there are no Manfreds in Wordsworth, no Geraldines, no Belles Dames Sans Merci. The symptomatic confusion of pain and pleasure is present, even, as we have seen, in the Preface to *Lyrical Ballads*; but it is a form of confusion peculiar to Wordsworth—the algolagnia of rusticity, so to speak—and we may surely forgive Praz for having overlooked it.

NOTES

[1] Trans. Angus Davidson (London: Oxford Univ. Press, 1933).
[2] *The Amherst Wordsworth Collection* (Amherst, Mass.: The Trustees of Amherst College, 1936), 214.

3 "Mario Praz: *The Romantic Agony*," in *The Bit Between My Teeth* (New York: Farrar), 152.

4 James V. Logan, "Wordsworth in France," *TLS*, Nov. 20, 1937, p. 891.

5 *Wordsworth: A Re-Interpretation*, 2nd ed. (London: Longmans, Green, 1956), 116–17n.

6 Dorothy Wordsworth, *Journals of Dorothy Wordsworth*, ed. E. de Selincourt (1941; rpt. Hamden, Conn.: Archon, 1970), I, 176–77.

7 *The Prose Works of William Wordsworth*, ed. A. B. Grosart (London: Moxon, 1876), II, 27–75.

8 *A Concordance to the Poems of William Wordsworth*, ed. Lane Cooper (New York: Dutton, 1911).

9 E. de Selincourt and Helen Darbishire, eds., *The Poetical Works of William Wordsworth*, I, 2nd ed. (Oxford: Clarendon, 1952). All subsequent citations of the poems, except for *The Prelude*, will refer to this edition, designated as *Works* in the text.

10 *The Prelude*, ed. E. de Selincourt, 2nd ed., rev. Helen Darbishire (Oxford: Clarendon, 1959), 1850 version, I, 303.

11 "Wordsworth and Byron," in *The Complete Works of Algernon Charles Swinburne*, Bonchurch Edition, XIV (London: William Heinemann, 1926), 226–27.

University of Alabama in Huntsville

JAMES B. TWITCHELL

"HART-LEAP WELL": WORDSWORTH'S
CRUCIFIXION POEM

Although "Hart-Leap Well" is now making its return to the classroom reader by way of such anthologies as Perkins' *English Romantic Writers*, it has still been overlooked by most scholars. Its almost nursery-school story line of an evil duke who kills a young stag is cradled in such a lilting ballad that most have considered it too childish for comment. Add to this the pedantic and obtrusive moral that is tacked onto the end—"nature loves all the little animals"—and one can understand why it has so often been passed off as one of the "curse" poems and forgotten.[1] But like all of Wordsworth's poems that have simple surfaces, this one too is deceptive. Hazlitt's warning about Wordsworth's *Lyrical Ballads* ("Fools have laughed at, wise men scarcely understand them") is equally fitting for "Hart-Leap Well."[2] For if the cover is pulled aside, this may be one of the most trenchant and evocative pieces of pantheism ever written. And it may also be Wordsworth's most bitter poem.

Although on first reading the poem may seem almost simple-minded, two biographical facts should make the reader pause before too quickly turning the page. One, the poem is based on a story Wordsworth had heard while making his way from Sockburn to Grasmere. There is the possibility that he is paralleling the almost "preternatural strength of [the hart's] homing instinct with his own."[3] For like the stag, he is returning to the heart's home in, as he says in "Home at Grasmere," a kind of "awful trance." And two, "Hart-Leap Well" was written in the winter of 1799–1800, at the same time Wordsworth was writing *Michael*.[4]

Now aside from certain pastoral similarities, "Hart-Leap Well"

11

shares little with *Michael*. The two poems are dissimilar in all but one aspect—they are both based four-square on a Biblical story. In *Michael*, it is the story of Abraham. For just as Abraham had to give Isaac up to God as part of his covenant, so Michael has to give up Luke to the city as part of his covenant. Paradoxically, of course, these covenants are based on different grounds: Abraham makes his with God, Michael makes his with lawyers and "society." This point, along with a number of references such as the villagers' calling Michael's house "The Evening Star," the characters' names (Michael and Luke, instead of the shepherds' names common in the pastoral genre), and the repeated use of the word "covenant," makes it obvious that Wordsworth was trying to create a religious tone in the poem. He is using a Biblical story as the symbolic analogue for his own tale in order to deepen the feelings of the reader. He wants the reader to recognize the differences between the two stories, to see that society has an almost godlike power, and that every day young men are sacrificed to its laws.

Perhaps Wordsworth is doing the same with "Hart-Leap Well." In this case, however, it is the story of the crucifixion of Christ that is used as the symbolic keystone. It seems clear that Wordsworth wants us to compare the killing of the stag with the killing of Christ. Here is Part I of Wordsworth's story: once upon a time, a knight spent all day chasing a hart, until it finally bounced over a hill to its death beside a spring. Full of reverential joy, the knight knelt beside the dead animal and vowed to "build a pleasure house upon this spot. / And a small arbor made for rural joy" (ll. 58–59). The house would be a place for entertainment for him, a refuge for pilgrims, and "a place of love for damsels that are coy." He pledged to have a basin, or a font, built around the spring, and three stone pillars erected near the top of the hill where the stag had leapt to his death. Three months later, so the story continues, this had been done. The knight had indeed built a "house of pleasure" on the exact spot where the hart died; he had erected the stone pillars and had planted an arbor near the well. Here Part I of the poem, as told by Wordsworth, concludes.

In Part II a different poet, Wordsworth's foil, enters and tells a story that has happened to him in the recent past. Like a ghost-story teller who starts his tale by saying, "Now this won't be scary at all," and then proceeds to scare the wits out of us, the poet starts his part of the tale by saying:

> The moving accident is not my trade;
> To freeze the blood I have no ready arts:

> 'Tis my delight, alone in summer shade,
> To pipe a simple song for thinking hearts.
> (ll. 97–100)

But what follows is no "simple song." The poet tells us that while passing from Hawes to Richmond he has seen three crumbling pillars and the remains of an arbor: "It chanced that I saw standing in a dell / Three aspens at three corners of a square; / And one, not four yards distant, near a well" (ll. 102–104). Could it be that these trees are in the form of a cross? The question is never asked, but it is obvious that Wordsworth would like it to be, for he has the poet say, "What this imported I could ill divine" (l. 108).

All life around these trees has ceased, as if "Nature here were willing to decay" (l. 116). The only explanation that the poet can find for this wasteland is given by a shepherd who appears at that moment and says that the spot is cursed. The good shepherd explains (after making sure that the poet knows that these trees are aspens, not beeches or elms), that

> "There's neither dog nor heifer, horse nor sheep,
> Will wet his lips within that cup of stone;
> And often times, when all are fast asleep,
> This water doth send forth a dolorous groan."
> (ll. 133–37)

Pressed farther by the poet, the shepherd guesses that this spot is cursed because here long ago a duke ran a hart to death. He proceeds to tell the same story we have heard in Part I, adding only that the heinous killing of the hart may have occurred in April. The poet presumably has not heard this story before but immediately recognizes it as being more than just a "simple song for thinking hearts." And so he congratulates the shepherd:

> "Grey-headed Shepherd, thou has spoken well;
> Small difference lies between thy creed and mine:
> This Beast not unobserved by Nature fell;
> His death was mourned by sympathy divine."
> (ll. 161–64)

Here begins the implied analogy between God, who lets no sparrow fall unnoticed, and nature, who lets no beast fall unobserved. In the next stanza this bromide grows into obvious pantheism.

> "The Being that is in the clouds and air,
> That is in the green leaves among the groves,
> Maintains a deep and reverential care
> For the unoffending creatures whom he loves."
> (ll. 165–68)

In the remaining stanzas, Wordsworth brings the various parts and personae of his poem together into one moral—man must learn from nature that even the smallest creature has feelings. And so

> "One lesson, Shepherd, let us two divide,
> Taught both by what she [Nature] shows, and what conceals;
> Never to blend our pleasure or our pride
> With sorrow of the meanest thing that feels."
>
> (ll. 177–80)

Still, for just a second the same Wordsworth who was later to accuse Keats of writing "a very pretty piece of paganism" in Endymion's Hymn to Pan lets out all the stops. God is the spirit not above nature, but in nature. He is the "Being . . . in the clouds and air . . . [and] in the green leaves" who loves all life. Still, Wordsworth very carefully never forces the Duke's action over the crucifixion story. Instead he lets the reader ask the questions. Might it be that if God is the "Being" in nature, Christ might be the pursued deer? Might not the cross formed by the aspens be symbolic of the crucifixion? Could the cross of aspens that stands out in the blasted landscape be a living testament that God or the "Being" has "deep and reverential care" for all life? Isn't it strange that we are told once by the poet (l. 103) and once by the shepherd (ll. 125–26) that these trees are aspens, not beeches or elms. Could it be because the aspen was thought to be the tree from which the cross was made? "In Christian tradition [the aspen is] a tree of mourning, pride, and sinful arrogance. According to the legend the cross was made of aspen wood and thereafter the aspen trembled."[5] And why is it a "hart" that is pursued instead of a hind, a fawn, or a doe, which would have added to the pathos? Could it be that the hart is the only deer commonly associated with Christ?[6] And why are we told that this heinous act occurs in the spring, once by Wordsworth in Part I (the pleasure house is built in the summer, three months after the killing), and again by the good shepherd (the killing may have occurred in April)?

The crosslike shape of the trees, the repeated mention of aspens, and the springtime death of the hart—these are the strongest suggestions that the poem is tied to the crucifixion. But there are other details that reinforce this impression. For one thing, might not the three stone pillars marching in a line along the hill be symbols of the crosses of Calvary, particularly since the poet is so careful to note that they are located "four roods" above the pleasure house? A "rood" is rarely used as a linear measure; its more common usage is a "cross." Furthermore we are told that when the knight first saw the hart lying dead, he "leaned against a thorn," and this thorn is mentioned again in the next stanza. Even the strangely ritualistic way that the knight, standing on a hill above the dying hart, circles his quarry suggests the three upper points of the cross:

> Sir Walter walked all round, north, south and west,
> And gazed and gazed upon that darling spot.
>
> (ll. 47–48)

And what of two other interesting occurrences? First, the "chase" lasted thirteen hours (l. 145), which is exactly the time elapsed between the Last Supper and the "Coenaclum" and the Crucifixion at Calvary.[7] And second, the hart dies of thirst and exhaustion (ll. 41–45), just inches from the spring. It may be more than coincidence that, according to Luke 16.24, Christ's last words were "I thirst."

If these pieces do fit, if Wordsworth was superimposing his story of the death of a deer on the story of the death of Christ, why did he do it? What depth does it add to the reading of the poem? Are we really meant to react to the death of a deer/hart with the same awe and woe that we usually reserve for such cataclysmic events as the death of God's son? Are we ready to see that a dumb beast, in fact a "beast of sport," is in any way analogous to the Savior? If the analogy within the poem is to be taken seriously, then the answer must be yes. The symbolic reading becomes hyperbolic, for then the poem is more than an outburst of pantheism; Wordsworth seems deeply bitter about how man has perverted and destroyed the divinity he has found in nature. For the knight who "stares upon the spoil [the hart-Christ] with silent joy" (l. 36) vows to build a pleasure house on the very spot, a house that will be refuge for pilgrims (l. 59), or in other words, a church. The knight promises to have "A cunning artist [brought in] to frame / A basin for that fountain in the dell" (ll. 62–63). The fountain is just at the mouth of the stag, and is it stretching the imagination too far to see his basin to be built from this natural well as a font of holy water? If the church is to be built on the site of the dead animal, the font would be at the door. But the font represents a perversion of nature and God by man, a dead artifact: "A cup of stone received the living well."

If this reading is valid, and there seems to be much internal evidence to support it, Wordsworth is doing something very similar to what he did in *Michael*. He is using the Biblical story as more than a mechanical allusion; he is showing how the most potentially dreadful acts of God, his covenant with Abraham and his allowing his son to be crucified, are nothing compared with the really dreadful acts of man. Luke is sacrificed because Michael is trapped in the greed and hypocrisy not of himself, but of others. It is his nephew's debt that he is paying. The hart is sacrificed not for its venison, but for man's pleasure. Then as if to celebrate this perverse act, a cathedral is built on the spot and pilgrims come to be baptized in its holy water. But the baptism results only in decay and death.

This sounds most un-Wordsworthian, more like Thomas Hardy or Stephen Crane. Yet critics have spotted this strain in Wordsworth's poems of 1797–1800, although no one has commented upon how deeply his bitterness ran. "Hart-Leap Well" is indeed, as Charles J. Smith and W. Strunk, Jr., have claimed, a member of the "curse" poems.[8] But even these critics do not realize how deeply the curse goes. It reaches far deeper than the curse in "Peter Bell," "Goody Blake," "The Thorne" or "The Danish Boy." It is a curse that extends to a great portion of mankind. To be sure, there are good people like the shepherd, but he is the exception. There is the implication, especially at the end of the poem, that most of mankind would have frequented the Duke's chapel as revelers, travelers, or pilgrims. Man killed Christ and now celebrates the killing of Christ by building a cathedral. If this implication is the conscious intuition of the poem, then "Hart-Leap Well" must be the bitterest poem Wordsworth ever wrote.

NOTES

1 Although this grouping did not originally include "Hart-Leap Well," the category was suggested by Thomas Hutchinson in his edition of the *Lyrical Ballads* (London: Duckworth, 1898), 255.

2 P. P. Howe, *The Complete Works of William Hazlitt* (London: J. M. Dent, 1930), XI, 87. Hazlitt thought so highly of "Hart-Leap Well" ("one that has always been a favorite with me") that he quoted it in full in his "Lecture on the Living Poets," V, 157.

3 Geoffrey H. Hartman, *Wordsworth's Poetry, 1787–1814* (New Haven: Yale Univ. Press, 1964), 142.

4 *The Poetical Works of William Wordsworth*, ed. E. de Selincourt and H. Darbishire (Oxford: Clarendon, 1940–49), II, 514–15; V, 319–20 (Appendix A).

5 Gertrude Jobes, *Dictionary of Mythology, Folklore and Symbols* (New York: Scarecrow Press, 1961), I, 141–42. Also the aspen leaf "is said to tremble because Christ's cross was made of aspen wood, or because at the hour of the Passion the plants and trees of the world trembled and bowed their heads all except the aspen which asked, 'why should we weep and tremble? We have not sinned.'" (Maria Leach, *Funk and Wagnalls Standard Dictionary of Folklore, Mythology and Legend* [New York: Funk and Wagnalls, 1946], I, 83.)

6 Jobes, I, 729.

7 Henry H. Halley, *Halley's Bible Handbook* (1924; rpt. and rev., Grand Rapids, Mich.: Henry H. Halley, 1963), 443.

8 Charles J. Smith, "Wordsworth and Coleridge: The Growth of a Theme," *SP* 54 (1957); and W. Strunk, Jr., "Some Related Poems of Wordsworth and Coleridge," *MLN* 29 (1914), 201–205.

University of Florida

FLORENCE PHYFER KRAUSE

NEGATIVE CAPABILITY AND OBJECTIVE CORRELATIVE IN SHAKESPEARE'S SONNETS

It has apparently escaped critical attention that when T. S. Eliot coined the term "objective correlative," he was thinking of Shakespeare's sonnets as well as of *Hamlet*:

> Hamlet, like the sonnets, is full of some stuff that the writer could not drag to light, contemplate, or manipulate into art. And when we search for this feeling, we find it, as in the sonnets, very difficult to localize. . . . The only way of expressing emotion in the form of art is by finding an "objective correlative"; in other words a set of objects, a situation, a chain of events which shall be the formula of that *particular* emotion; such that when the external facts, which must terminate in sensory experience, are given, the emotion is immediately evoked.[1]

Anyone who has tried to find his way through the jungle of commentary that has overgrown the sonnets during the last two centuries might, on tripping over Eliot's criticism neatly tucked away in a prepositional phrase, be tempted to regain his composure and forget what he saw. But there is an objective correlative in the sonnets.

The primary emotion that Shakespeare is concerned with in the sonnets is love—what the emotion does to the narrator and what fruit it produces. If one reads the sonnets at a single sitting, he perceives a story made up of a series of attacks upon the narrator. The chain of events which is a consistent pattern in the sonnets is the way in which the narrator poet copes with these attacks, the manner in which his love emerges victorious. This chain of reaction is forged by the poet's Negative Capability, which is, of course, Keats's term. An examination of its formulation and an analysis of its working in the sonnets will do much to establish the objective correlative that Eliot found missing.

Keats's formulation of the concept of Negative Capability took place during the months of November and December 1817, when he was

17

reading Shakespeare's sonnets, working on *Endymion*, going to the theater to see Edmund Kean and publishing critiques of his performances, and writing letters about Shakespeare and poetry. One can see the theory of Negative Capability emerging in all his writing at this time.

On November 22, Keats was alone at Burford Bridge, having left Hampstead to work on *Endymion* in seclusion. He wrote two letters that day. To John Hamilton Reynolds he mentioned what he was reading:

One of the three Books I have with me is Shakespear's Poems: I neer found so many beauties in the Sonnets. . . . He overwhelms a genuine Lover of Poesy with all manner of abuse, talking about—

"a poet's rage
And stretched metre of an antique song."
Which by the by will be a capital Motto for my Poem, won't it?[2]

The quotation, which Keats did use on the title page of *Endymion*, is from Sonnet 17. This sonnet, along with those immediately surrounding it, was still in Keats's mind when he wrote Benjamin Bailey on the same day. He speaks of "the holiness of the Heart's affections and the truth of Imagination—What the imagination seizes as Beauty must be truth —whether it existed before or not. . . ." A little later he mentions " 'a Vision in the form of Youth' a Shadow of reality to come." Then he speaks of "having what we call happiness on Earth repeated in a finer tone and so repeated. . . . The simple imaginative Mind may have its rewards in the repeti[ti]on of its own silent Working coming continually on the Spirit with a fine Suddenness."[3] This idea one finds in the sonnets, when Shakespeare speaks of his friend the fair youth as a shadow or prefiguring of the reality of beauty which will blossom in his own (Shakespeare's) poems in time to come (Sonnet 15).

Going on with his letter to Bailey and possibly turning the "stretched metre of an antique song" over in his mind, Keats asks,

Have you never by being Surprised with an old Melody—in a delicious place— by a delicious voice, fe[l]t over again your very Speculations and Surmises at the time it first operated on your Soul—do you not remember forming to yourself the singer's face more beautiful that [for *than*] it was possible and yet with the elevation of the Moment you did not think so—even then you were mounted on the Wings of Imagination so high—that the Prototype must be here after—that delicious face you will see.[4]

This is a variation of the phenomenon Shakespeare describes in Sonnet 17, which Keats mentioned in his other letter written the same day:

Who will believe my verse in time to come
If it were filled with your most high deserts?
Though yet, heaven knows, it is but as a tomb
Which hides your life and shows not half your parts.

If I could write the beauty of your eyes
And in fresh numbers number all your graces,
The age to come would say, "This poet lies—
Such heavenly touches ne'er touched earthly faces."
So should my papers, yellowed with their age,
Be scorned, like old men of less truth than tongue,
And your true rights be termed a poet's rage
And stretched meter of an antique song.
　　But were some child of yours alive that time,
　　You should live twice—in it and in my rime.[5]

A few lines later in his letter to Bailey, Keats again pursued the happiness theme and spelled out two of the conditions that would emerge in his theory of Negative Capability—necessity of living in the present moment and immersion of the self in another consciousness: "I scarcely remember counting upon any happiness—I look not for it if it be not in the present hour—nothing startles me beyond the Moment. The setting Sun will always set me to rights—or if a Sparrow come before my Window I take part in its existence and pick about the Gravel."[6]

By the middle of December, Keats was back in London, watching Edmund Kean as the Duke of Gloucester in *Richard III* at Drury Lane. In his review of the play, which appeared in *The Champion* on Sunday, December 21, he mentions Kean's ability to "deliver himself up to the instant feeling, without a shadow of a thought about anything else." This is the same ability that Keats had spoken of in his phrase "picking about the Gravel" with the sparrow. Of Kean he goes on to say, "Although so many times he has lost the battle of Bosworth Field, we can easily conceive him really expectant of victory, with a different termination of the piece."[7] Kean's identification with his character was so complete, his rendering of emotion so intense, that he created for his audience a sense of present time, of immediacy, sufficient that they forgot what the outcome of the play was to be. Kean's performance was Negative Capability in action.

Keats wrote the review of *Richard III* sometime after Monday, December 15, the night he saw the play. It is significant that on December 21, the same day on which his review appeared in *The Champion*, Keats wrote the letter to his brothers, George and Thomas, in which he coined the term "Negative Capability," the quality that "went to form a Man of Achievement especially in Literature, and which Shakespeare possessed so enormously—I mean *Negative Capability*, that is when a man is capable of being in uncertainties, mysteries, doubts, without any irritable reaching after fact and reason. . . ."[8]

The next week Keats saw Kean again at Drury Lane in *Richard Duke of York*, an adaptation of Shakespeare's three plays about Henry VI, and again his praise was glowing. Of Kean's stage death, Keats wrote: "Kean always 'dies as erring men do die.' The bodily functions wither up, and the mental faculties hold out till they crack. It is an extinguishment, not a decay. The hand is agonized with death. . . . The very eyelid dies. The acting of Kean is Shakespearian—he will fully understand what we mean."[9] In this critique Keats is noting Kean's possession of Shakespearean Negative Capability, his capacity to lose his own identity, to live the moment in the character's life so intensely that he is for the moment that character. It was the same quality that Shakespeare exhibited when he created the character.

Keats added to his definition of Negative Capability in a later letter to Richard Woodhouse. He again referred to the poet as a being having no identity, as a chameleon, who "is continually . . . filling some other Body" and who relishes "the dark side of things" as much as "the bright one; because they both end in speculation." [10] Again he had Shakespeare in mind, observing that the poet has "as much delight in conceiving an Iago as an Imogen."[11]

Keats's concern with Negative Capability was evident in his poetry as well as in his letters and critiques, and the emotion of happiness always appeared as a part of the concept. During the winter months of 1817, when he was formulating his theory, he was finishing *Endymion*, which contains a passage to which he referred as the "pleasure thermometer."[12] Here, by identifying himself with objects and finally with other human beings, he expresses poetically the principle of "filling another body," "picking about the gravel" with the sparrow. Love is always the emotion which triggers the pleasurable experience. Even when Keats identifies with the objects of nature, he uses love metaphors: first he suggests folding a rose leaf around a finger to soothe one's lips; next a kiss impregnates the winds and elicits "Aeolian magic from their lucid wombs: / Then old songs waken from enclouded tombs." Among the "richer entanglements" are friendship and, highest of all on the scale, love, in which our "souls interknit . . . wingedly." His metaphor for this highest degree of pleasure is the union of the mother pelican with her brood, which she was believed to have fed with her flesh and blood, giving up life as a result of her maternal love.[13] Keats's final image in the passage is that of the nightingale, singing "but to her love."

All the characteristics of Negative Capability are here: complete surrender of oneself to an experience, identification with another object or person, and willingness to exist in a situation "without any irritable reaching after fact and reason." In this supreme "fellowship with essence," Keats writes, men "fan / And winnow from the coming step of time / All chaff of custom, wipe away all slime / Left by men-slugs and human serpentry." They are "content to let occasion die."[14] These are the same qualities which Keats admired in Edmund Kean, whose acting Keats called "Shakespearian," and whose performance led Keats to this remark: "Shakespeare was the only lonely and perfectly happy creature God ever formed."[15]

It is apparent from Keats's letters and critiques, and from *Endymion*, that at this period in his life he was very much concerned with the process of mind which he called Negative Capability and that Shakespeare was the supreme possessor of the characteristics inherent in his theory. It is easy to see these characteristics in Shakespeare the dramatist; they are also at work in Shakespeare the poet of the sonnets, though in a different way. In the plays, Shakespeare, through his own Negative Capability, creates characters who come to life, but these characters are not themselves necessarily endowed with Negative Capability. In the sonnets, Shakespeare has created a narrator poet who does possess Negative Capability. It is this set of qualities—ability to fill another body, ability to yield completely to an experience, and ability to live exclusively in the moment—that conditions his response to the various problems that confront him.

Of the different kinds of attack to which the poet of the sonnets was prey, by far the most serious is the assault of time, which appears as a "bloody Tyrant" who not only can obliterate one's physical being, but also can remove every shred of evidence that one has even existed. Shakespeare uses one of the characteristics of Negative Capability as a thwarting device: filling another body. In the beginning sonnets, the technique is suggested on a physical level—the friend can recreate himself in the person of his own child. The poet soon moves to a more permanent, abstract level, the imaginative recreation of his friend in the lines of the poems. Through this device the friend inhabits the poem. He is, furthermore, recreated afresh each time a person reads the poet's verses, and he thereby fills the bodies of the readers of the sonnets. The attack of time is allayed "So long as men can breathe or eyes can see" (Sonnet 18).

Another way in which Shakespeare uses the same technique to defy time is to pour his own identity into that of his friend:

> My glass shall not persuade me I am old
> So long as youth and thou are of one date;
> But when in thee time's furrows I behold,
> Then look I death my days should expiate.
> For all that beauty that doth cover thee

> Is but the seemly raiment of my heart,
> Which in thy breast doth live, as thine in me:
> How can I then be elder than thou art?
> (Sonnet 22, ll. 1–8)

The complete identification with another consciousness enabled the poet to defy the attacks not only of time, but of adversities brought on by sickness, poverty, and ill repute:

> So then I am not lame, poor, nor despised
> Whilst that this shadow dost such substance give
> That I in thy abundance am sufficed
> And by a part of all thy glory live.
> (Sonnet 37, ll. 9–12)

So fully does the poet immerse himself in his friend's identity that he is able to withstand scorn, even that of the friend, and to hate himself with equanimity: "Such is my love, to thee I so belong, / That for thy right myself will bear all wrong" (Sonnet 88), and "For thee, against myself I'll vow debate, / For I must ne'er love him whom thou dost hate" (Sonnet 89). He manages to tolerate an affair between his own mistress and his friend, though his suffering is obvious. He conquers jealousy through his complete identification with his friend: "But here's the joy: my friend and I are one; / Sweet flattery! then she loves but me alone" (Sonnet 42).

Expression of the poet's identification with his friend perhaps reaches a peak in Sonnet 62, when he confesses a feeling of guilt at praising himself: "Sin of self-love possesseth all mine eye / And all my soul and all my every part." He ends the sonnet with a statement of his oneness with his friend: "Tis thee (myself) that for myself, I praise, / Painting my age with beauty of thy days."

Shakespeare's most explicit delineation of Negative Capability, furnishing an example for the characteristics that Keats defined, may be found in Sonnet 116. Here is the complete fusion of one personality with another, the complete yielding of oneself to the experience of love, and the capability "of being in uncertainties, mysteries, doubts, without any irritable reaching after fact and reason":

> Let me not to the marriage of true minds
> Admit impediments; love is not love
> Which alters when it alteration finds
> Or bends with the remover to remove.

An understanding of Negative Capability makes clear the meaning of those lines which Yvor Winters found blurred:[16] "It is the star to every wand'ring bark, / Whose worth's unknown, although his height be taken." "Height" here is a known fact, perhaps the only known fact about the star. "Worth," which Winters questioned, stands for everything about the star that is unknown—all the uncertainties, mysteries, doubts. The bark can exist on stormy seas because the star "looks on tempests and is never shaken." The lover in the sonnets is able to weather even the ravages of time because the characteristics of Negative Capability are inherent in his love.

To say that the narrator in the sonnets did not suffer because of his love would be an untruth. He suffered when he himself transgressed as well as when his friend went astray. The poet's love demanded complete loyalty on the part of both, an ideal which both fell short of occasionally. though not permanently. Sonnets 110, 111, and 112 recount experiences which the poet regards with a sense of shame. Exactly what his transgressions were cannot be deciphered. The phrases "vulgar scandal" (112), "made myself a motley to the view" (110), and "Fortune . . . / The guilty goddess of my harmful deeds" (111) might lead one to believe that his trouble involved activities on the stage. Whatever the cause, he regards his shame as reflecting on his friend; he apologizes —"Mine appetite I never more will grind / On newer proof, to try an older friend" (110)—asks forgiveness, and says that his friend's pity is his cure (111).

The last twenty-seven sonnets, those commonly called the "Dark Lady" sonnets, bring out the narrator's ability to dwell in "uncertainties, mysteries, doubts." It would be a mistake to call his attitude one of indifference, because he is thoroughly involved with the lady. The problems differ from those emanating from his relationship with his friend. The attraction between the poet and the lady is primarily a physical one, but it is of sufficient strength that he regards her as beautiful, though he is conscious on another level that she is not and that her appearance belies the ideal image of the beautiful woman of that day. Sonnet 138, which begins "When my love swears that she is made of truth / I do believe her, though I know she lies," is a perfect example of humorous treatment of that aspect of Negative Capability which enables a man to dwell serenely in mysteries. The poet is able to tolerate his lady's infidelities, and she, his less than youthful appearance. Sonnet 141 is a more serious treatment of the same theme. The poet notes the lady's faults and is able to live not only with them but with his own guilt for loving her, because the pain of his sin atones for his action. At the core of his being, he does not deceive himself about his feelings nor about the immorality to which they have led him. He maintains existence in a balance of desire and repugnance. There is sorrow that he is captivated by an evil force, but there is no record of escape or of serious attempt to escape, nor of any vow not to repeat the experience. The poet knows exactly what he is doing: "No want of conscience hold it that I call / Her 'love' for whose dear love I rise and fall" (Sonnet 151). As Keats said, the poet relishes "the dark side of things" as much as "the bright one; because they both end in speculation."[17]

The sonnets attest to the fact that Shakespeare understood love and suffering. Yvor Winters called his attitude in the face of mistreatment "servile."[18] T. S. Eliot charged that he was incapable of manipulating his emotion into art. How can these opinions be reconciled with the great admiration that Keats expressed for the sonnets? Keats felt as he did because he understood the characteristics of Negative Capability in Shakespeare not only in the dramas but also in the sonnets. The pattern of attack on the poet and response by the poet through Negative Capability forms a consistent chain of reaction sufficient to form an objective correlative which is the formula of the particular emotion Shakespeare sought to express, the emotion of love. Shakespeare's sonnets are probably as complete a testament of love as the world is likely to get, unless it is the thirteenth chapter of St. Paul's First Epistle to the Corinthians. Possibly there are those who would call a man who "beareth all things, believeth all things, hopeth all things, endureth all things" servile. The poet of the sonnets is an actual example of that ideal. Even when he feels extreme revulsion or agony, he is in control of the situation; there is a level at which he accepts himself and the circumstances surrounding him. His Negative Capability enables him to be a thorough-going participant in all the delights and adversities that love can bring, with such an immediacy and intensity that the reader is held at knife-edge. When one has read the sonnets straight through at one sitting, the poet narrator emerges as the Shakespeare Keats understood, a man who was "capable of being in uncertainties, mysteries, doubts, without any irritable reaching after fact and reason," and as the "only lonely and perfectly happy creature that God ever formed."

NOTES

[1] "Hamlet and His Problems," *The Sacred Wood* (London: Methuen, 1920), 100.

[2] *The Letters of John Keats*, ed. Maurice Buxton Forman (London: Oxford Univ. Press, 1935), 65, hereinafter cited as *Letters*. It is not known whether the book Keats refers to is his copy of Shakespeare's poems which is now in the Keats Museum at Hampstead. This copy, in which the sonnets are more heavily marked than any of the other poems, was given to Keats by Reynolds. The inscription "John Hamilton Reynolds to John Keats 1819" is in Keats's handwriting, not Reynolds' as Caroline Spurgeon says in her book *Keats's Shakespeare* (London: Oxford Univ. Press, 1928), 38. The signature of Keats in the inscription is iden-

tical to his signature on his letter of November 1817 to Charles Wentworth Dilke. Mrs. Christina Gee, librarian at the Keats Museum, set the letter and the title page bearing the inscription side by side, and we agreed that the signatures were identical. The writing of Reynolds is quite different from that of the inscription. The fact that Keats, not Reynolds, wrote the inscription suggests that Keats had the volume in his possession before 1819, and conversely, that Reynolds did not inscribe the volume and send it to Keats in 1819.

3 *Letters*, 67–68.

4 Ibid.

5 William Shakespeare, *Sonnets*, ed. Douglas Bush and Alfred Harbage (Baltimore: Penguin, 1961), 39. Subsequent citations to Shakespeare's sonnets in the text are from this edition.

6 *Letters*, 69.

7 "On Edmund Kean as a Shakespearian Actor," *The Poetical Works and Other Writings of John Keats*, ed. H. Buxton Forman (London: Reeves & Turner, 1889), III, 5, hereafter cited as *Works*.

8 *Letters*, 72.

9 John Keats, "On Kean in 'Richard Duke of York,'" *Works*, III, 11.

10 *Letters*, 228.

11 Ibid.

12 John Keats, *Endymion, The Poetical Works and Other Writings of John Keats*, ed. H. Buxton Forman (New York: Scribners, 1939), II, 60–63, ll. 777–842.

13 M. H. Abrams, ed., *Endymion, The Norton Anthology of English Literature* (New York: Norton, 1968), II, 511 n. 3.

14 *Endymion*, p. 63, l. 822.

15 "On Kean in 'Richard Duke of York,'" *Works*, III, 12.

16 Yvor Winters, "Poetic Style in Shakespeare's Sonnets," *Discussions of Shakespeare's Sonnets*, ed. Barbara Hernstein (Boston: Heath, 1965), 109.

17 *Letters*, 228.

18 Winters, 107.

William Woods College

HOWARD H. HINKEL

GROWTH WITHOUT TOIL:
GENERATIVE INDOLENCE IN KEATS

Keats's poem on indolence had the misfortune of having been written as an ode in Keats's remarkable spring of 1819. Because of its form and date of composition, "Ode on Indolence" is usually judged alongside the Great Odes, and judged to be comparatively weak. A cursory examination of the scholarship demonstrates the relatively low critical opinion of the poem. Ian Jack considers "Indolence" a postscript to the "Grecian Urn" which has "the air of being the work of some gifted imitator of Keats."[1] Walter Evert says that it is "unlikely that the 'Ode on Indolence' has ever been anyone's favorite poem."[2] Douglas Bush finds mostly "verbal echoes" of the better odes.[3] Walter Jackson Bate thinks that "its value is primarily biographical."[4] Aileen Ward says that the poetic attempt to recreate Keats's daydream vision of three figures on a Grecian vase "was not a success."[5] Kenneth Muir considers "Indolence" "less highly wrought" than the other odes.[6] The poem indeed suffers from such comparison and contrast. "Indolence," though, needs to be read as an independent poem with its own peculiar structure and its own particular statement. So read, the poem reveals unexpected riches and adds another dimension to Keats's outstanding achievement during his most productive period.

Although Keats rarely uses Biblical allusion, a direct Biblical quotation stands prominently as the epigraph for "Ode on Indolence." Keats tersely quotes the gospel writer: "They toil not, neither do they spin." This epigraph prefigures an extraordinary artistic growth which Keats has recorded in the poem itself. This growth results in significant changes in Keats's poetic consciousness at a time when he had begun

26

to suspect that he was stagnating. What Keats records in this ode is the way in which the poetic imagination operates under seemingly unpoetic circumstances. The changes occur as Keats gradually surrenders himself to the unexpected rewards of an indolent fit that serves as the initial stimulus for this particular poetic expression.

The entire sixth chapter of Matthew suggests the sort of unselfconscious surrender, the selfless immersion in the moment, that led to this particular ode. The key verse, verse twenty-eight, reads: "And why take ye thoughts for raiment? Consider the lilies of the field, how they grow; they toil not, neither do they spin." Christ then exhorts the multitudes to "Take therefore no thought for the morrow; for the morrow shall take thought for things of itself" (6.34). Christ's example of the lilies suggests that men, like lilies, should be free of debilitating preoccupations with living, and release themselves, thereby, to fuller immediate life. "Ode on Indolence" is, in Keats's own terms, a poetic adaptation of Christ's wisdom. The poet's emerging determination to make any moment valuable and rich, whatever its nature, will mature in the Great Odes where it recurs as a major theme. "Ode on Indolence," though, is the prelude which prepares Keats for the better poetry written in the spring, summer, and early fall of 1819.[7] Ironically the agnostic Keats adopts the paradoxical wisdom of "The Sermon on the Mount" as a source of poetic salvation. In the poem he toils not, but grows substantially.

The seeming paradox of this poetic expression is the paradox of the Biblical exhortation originally. Keats, though, transforms religious orthodoxy and offers an interpretation of the Christian message more in keeping with his poetic sensibility. There is energy in the poem, but of a kind much different from the usual energy of man's toils. Rather than continue his self-conscious quest for fame and success (a quest which he had outlined for himself as early as "Sleep and Poetry"), Keats immerses himself in an experience which, to common minds, seems unproductive and lazy—an ordinary fit of indolence. But poets find the extraordinary in the ordinary; Blake discovers a world in a grain of sand, heaven in a wild flower. In indolence and in withdrawal from the everyday world, Keats rediscovers his most fecund world, the world of imagination. This is the real importance of the poem to Keats. By surrendering himself to a world of shadows, by entering an element which others might judge unfruitful, Keats finds unexpected richness and inspiration to accept life and create from its varied substance.

The key to understanding Keats's generative indolence is the dreamlike movement which provides the structure of the poem. Although most critics have censured the apparently haphazard structure of the "Ode," Keats actually has deliberately provided a loose, mesmerizing movement which draws him and the reader steadily toward the center of indolence where the mood can be explored in all its riches.[8] Once this apparently loose structure is appreciated, there is easy entrance into Keats's world of shadows. The indifference and passivity which pervade the first stanza provide an unusual starting point for a Keats poem— no passionate Porphyro storming across the moors toward Madeline, no Endymion in frantic quest of Cynthia. Instead, Keats asks that we regress rather than progress. The apparently indifferent "One morn," the soft "placid sandals," and the pallid "white robes" are gentle and subtle invitations to join the poet in a deliberate withdrawal from the ordinary world. Whereas Endymion ascends to the heavens for his apotheosis, the poet here descends into a remote world of shadows where is rediscovered his imaginative capacity to enter empathically any experience in any moment. The descent into indolence finally reawakens Keats's sensitivity to sensations around him. Indolence then becomes generative.

In the first stanza the "three figures" appear twice. Their second appearance dramatizes the extraordinary moment which Keats is entering, for they "were strange to me, as may betide / With vases, to one deep in Phidian lore." Phidias and the Parthenon represent a world of classical rigor and structure which is antithetical to the remote, shadowy world of this special indolence. Keats is slowly immersing himself in indolence whose full meaning he has not yet discovered in the second stanza. As the "Shadows" confront him for the second time, he suspects a conspiracy ("muffled," "hush," "deep-disguised plot," "steal"—all make the figures seem sinister). This, though, is only initial rationalistic resistance to the unknown world into which he descends. Entrance into this world of shadows at first disturbs the poet, and stanza two appropriately poses a series of questions which suggest anguished uncertainty. The "three figures" of the first stanza have become "Shadows" apparently involved in some kind of subterfuge:

> How is it, Shadows! that I knew ye not?
>   How came ye muffled in so hush a mask?
> Was it a silent deep-disguised plot
>   To steal away, and leave without a task
> My idle days?

Progressive withdrawal into the realm of shadows brings him face to face with abstract figures which are unrecognizable because he is not viewing them in their usual disguises. Indolence leads the poet out of the commonplace into a world where poetry, love, and ambition will lose the tormenting emotional impact they had upon him before his descent. Despite the disruptive questions, the fit of indolence grows, and the absence of commonplace sensations becomes more appealing; the poet now asks to be left alone in the midst of "summer-indolence":

> Ripe was the drowsy hour;
> The blissful cloud of summer-indolence
> Benumb'd my eyes; my pulse grew less and less;
> Pain had no sting, and pleasure's wreath no flower;
> O, why did ye not melt, and leave my sense
> Unhaunted quite of all but—nothingness?

Indolence at first is desirable because it eliminates contraries and anesthetizes the poet to the pains of life. Languidity, no longer feared, is now cherished, and the "Shadows" betray not by stealing away, but by lingering and disturbing his special "nothingness." Fear of involvement and activity, of confronting the anxiety of consciousness, supplants fear of idleness.

A state of numbness, a moment free of sensations, though, is alien to Keats. The poem instead moves to satisfy his cry in a letter to Benjamin Bailey (November 22, 1817), "O for a life of sensations rather than of thoughts."[9] But the poem takes Keats one step further by making the sensations of indolence the very foundation for future poetic thoughts. In the third stanza the figures appear for a third time, and now it is clear that the visit is actually Keats's sinking deeper into indolence, not the shadows getting closer. Here the dreamlike movement of the structure best serves Keats's intentions. The apparent looseness of the poem is really carefully controlled movement on the part of the artist. The poet moves free from the cares of the world, and this freedom is achievable only when he is not spinning. As the ode develops further, as Keats surrenders to the moment of the poem, the indolent fit grows. And paradoxically as his easy indolence becomes a full experience in itself, as it widens and expands, it becomes less languid, and the poet's emotions correspondingly become more troubled:

> A third time came they by;—alas! wherefore?
> My sleep had been embroider'd with dim dreams;
> My soul had been a lawn besprinkled o'er
> With flowers, and stirring shades, and baffled beams.

Sleep is energized as the dreamer slips farther into the center of indolence, and the scenery of the vision becomes more colorful; the poet finds himself in the midst of an indolence which is increasingly rich in sensation. Surrender, then, brings increased sensitivity to sensations.

The world outside as well calls for a full response to this special "noth-ingness" and forecasts the growth which is taking place:

> The morn was clouded, but no shower fell,
> Tho' in her lids hung the sweet tears of May;
> The open casement press'd a new-leav'd vine,
> Let in the budding warmth and throstle's lay.

The "throstle's lay" recalls the thrush's song in the sonnet, "O thou whose face hath felt the Winter's wind" wherein the thrush concludes,

> He who saddens
> At thought of idleness cannot be idle,
> And he's awake who thinks himself asleep.

Indolence is indolence, not nothingness. The thrush's song is the first intrusion of sound into the poet's consciousness, and it adds another dimension of sensory awareness to the poet's languidity. By withdrawing from the everyday and the harsh sounds of "the voice of busy common-sense" (l. 50), the poet becomes more receptive to the sensations which comprise his indolence. This gradual expansion of his conscious-ness is complemented by the "morn" which, itself inactive, promises "budding warmth" and a long withheld shower, the "'sweet tears of May." Growth is promised, but growth in accordance with the peace-ful, unself-conscious growth of the lilies of the field. Indolence is no longer a means of escape but has become a frame of mind, a widened state of consciousness, which affords both pleasure and pain, tranquil-ity and sensation.

The fourth and fifth stanzas focus upon the expanding vision that further stimulates sensations. The result of this persistent stimulation is an increased energy of thought and feeling. On the third appearance the poet is so thoroughly immersed in the vision that he can see beyond the shadows the actual faces of the shadow figures. In this state of in-tense perception the poet yearns for further involvement. The intensity of this desire for further immersion in the dream is recaptured by the poetic reconstruction of that moment:

> A third time pass'd they by, and, passing, turn'd
> Each one the face a moment whiles to me;
> Then faded, and to follow them I burn'd
> And ach'd for wings because I knew the three.

The desire to escape with the three figures subsides, however, in the fifth stanza as he evaluates Love, Ambition, and Poesy. Love is easily dis-missed as a maid who is undefinable and unpredictable. Ambition is written off as a disease, something which springs from "a man's little heart's short fever-fit." The rejection of Poesy, though, is more hesitant, indeed more difficult:

> For Poesy!—no,—she has not a joy,—
> At least for me,—so sweet as drowsy noons,
> And evenings steep'd in honied indolence. . . .

This is the crucial moment in the poem, for it is the moment in which Keats realizes that only by abiding in the richness of this experience at hand will he grow as a poet. The intellectual commitment to Poesy as an abstraction must be sacrificed so that poetry, more naturally and organically, can grow from Keats's full experience of the sensations allowed him by a fit of indolence. In a remarkable passage from the second book of *Milton*, Blake writes:

> There is a Moment in each Day that Satan cannot find
> Nor can his Watch Fiends find it, but the Industrious find
> This Moment & it multiply. & when it once is found
> It renovates every moment of the Day if rightly placed.[10]

Northrop Frye has called this moment "a moment of eternal life which no death-principle can touch, a moment of absolute imagination."[11] Keats's Satan and Watch Fiends differ from Blake's, of course, but the two poets share the general opposition of imagination and "death-principle" which is reductive ratiocination and abstraction. In "Ode on Indolence," the satanic powers of Love, Ambition, and Poesy (abstractions rather than Blake's "minute particulars") threaten but cannot penetrate finally the moment which Keats enters and celebrates. Poesy, an abstract intruder from the outside, calls in vain. The "honied indolence" of the earlier stanza, now even more attractive because it has evolved into a fruitful moment of rich sensations, again envelops the poet. Keats has entered a timeless moment of imaginative participation in indolence. What earlier had seemed "nothingness" is now recognized as a fully developed fit of indolence, judged "nothingness" only by those who think growth comes solely from spinning.

In the final stanza the three figures are again reduced to "Ghosts" which have haunted Keats. These "Ghosts," though, have made him aware of the richness of the moment at hand. The speculation and self-consciousness stop, and the poet relaxes in his fit of indolence. The mission of the three figures has failed to raise his "head cool-bedded in the flowery grass," and the last six lines celebrate the victory of indolence:

> Fade softly from my eyes, and be once more
> In masque-like figures on the dreamy urn;
> Farewell! I yet have visions for the night,

> And for the day faint visions there is store;
> Vanish, ye Phantoms! from my idle spright,
> Into the clouds, and never more return!

The poem has come full circle as these last lines recreate the dreamlike atmosphere of the opening stanzas. The "Phantoms" must be dismissed, for Keats ultimately is not attracted to ghostly abstractions. There has been a movement from easeful languidity, to fitful and uneasy speculation as the figures become identifiable, and finally there is a return to an enriched state of indolence. Keats is alone again at the end of the poem, free to recline in the "flowery grass" and enjoy still more "faint visions." Yet growth has occurred; indolence has become much more than tranquil numbness. The poet, by immersing himself in the moment that Satan cannot find, has multiplied that moment, indeed renovated "every Moment of the Day." Relaxed acceptance, deliberate withdrawal from "the voice of busy common-sense," has led to the growth of more visions. Without spinning and toiling, the poet has grown.

Kierkegaard's analysis of the same text from Matthew 6.24–34 suggests that Keats's experience in "Ode on Indolence" is available to anyone who is capable of unself-conscious meditation on apparently ordinary phenomena which most men take for granted. In the first section of his discourse, *What We Learn From the Lilies of the Field and the Birds of the Air*, Kierkegaard says that the lilies (and the "fowls of the air," in Matthew, which "sow not, neither do they reap, nor gather into barns") can teach, "only if the troubled one really pays attention to the lilies and the birds, forgets himself in considering them and their life, while in this absorption with them, he subtly learns through himself something about himself."[12] As does Keats, Kierkegaard understands the implications of the Biblical paradox, that rich and unlabored growth requires a submission of the self to the moment and experience at hand. Ironically what Keats learns about himself is really only a rediscovery of the implications of his own theory of "Negative Capability" which he stated as early as December 1817. A poet, he believes, must be capable of negating his own ego so that he might enter, participate in, and ultimately expose the complexity of his subject. In the "Ode" Keats struggles but finally succeeds in annihilating his own ego. The three figures on the urn would lure him to his frequent self-conscious state of mind in which Love and Ambition make worldly demands on him and Poesy seems demonic because it requires that he escape such worldly concerns before it can be written. The poet as man must achieve a state of "nothingness'" before his creative faculties can begin to operate. Keats's rejection of "the voice of busy common-sense" and his submission to the pleasurable sensations of indolence lead to artistic creation.

The growth of the lilies, then, objectifies naturally the unlabored growth of the poet in the fertile setting of a totally relaxed mind. This generative indolence proves to be vital to Keats's poetic development because it reinforces his earlier trust in his creative imagination as it develops from an open acceptance of the present moment. Although Keats did not state a formal theory or definition of the imagination, he often equated dreams with imaginative perception. The letters of 1817 unequivocally proclaim the validity and reliability of the imagination as an informing power for the poet. There is especially the letter to Bailey (November 22, 1817) avowing "the holiness of the Heart's affections and the truth of the Imagination" and then asserting that "The Imagination may be compared to Adam's dream—he awoke and found it truth" (I, 84–85). One year later, though, the "Epistle to John Hamilton Reynolds" expresses stark doubt about the imagination:

> Or is it that imagination brought
> Beyond its proper bound, yet still confin'd,
> Lost in a sort of Purgatory blind,
> Cannot refer to any standard law
> Of either earth or heaven? It is a flaw
> In happiness, to see beyond our bourn,—
> It forces us in summer skies to mourn,
> It spoils the singing of the Nightingale.
>   (ll. 78–85)

Here the imagination perceives truths, but truths which are disruptive because the mind and emotions cannot assimilate, balance, and accept them. The imagination disturbs the poet by allowing him to see more than most men see. Happiness, it seems, is denied the imaginative poet who would see beyond the commonplace.

"Ode on Indolence," then, is a transitional poem for Keats because it represents a newly attained state of mind in which he can accept an imaginative experience, whatever its nature, without fear of its being deceptive, illusory, or destructive. In the Great Odes this capacity for acceptance matures, and acceptance of things (pain, sorrow, melancholy, even death) becomes a recurring theme. The better odes, as Richard H. Fogle has said, reveal "an exquisite awareness of the existence of joy and melancholy, pleasure and pain, and art and life. They express a feeling that these are inseparable, although not identical, and they express acceptance of this inseparability of the elements of human experience."[13] "Ode on Melancholy" insists upon our recognition and acceptance of the transience of the beautiful if we are to know fully the feeling of melancholy; and of course melancholy itself, like indolence, is accepted as a full, rich, human experience. "Ode on a Grecian Urn" demands that we accept the urn and its legend not only as an inspiring expression of love, beauty and spring, but also as a "Cold Pastoral" which teases us mortals with thoughts of eternity, or as a beautiful artifact which also may be one of Yeats's "self-born mockers of man's enterprise." "To Autumn" demands that an autumnal scene be accepted for what it is unto itself, and what it is can be discovered only after the poet surrenders to the seasonal beauty and refuses to see autumn as a cold harbinger of spring. "Ode on Indolence" has prepared Keats for this resolute acceptance of experience by insisting that Love, Ambition, and Poesy will not deter his enjoyment of easy indolence; he will peacefully accept the "faint visions" which grow from quiet, relaxed meditation. The imagination, then, need not be only the vehicle for an urgent, energetic quest for philosophical truths. Indeed, it may be a creative power which works gently, easefully, and—paradoxically—passively. Wordsworth's "wise passiveness" resembles the imaginative act of "Indolence," though Keats's setting for "wise passiveness" is not Wordsworthian nature, but the unself-conscious mind. The poetic mind is nurtured by its own capacity to create "faint visions," and like the lilies of the field, it finds pleasure and contentment in its own unlabored growth.

This theme of acceptance of present experience is also indebted in part to the Matthew text, though again Keats has adjusted orthodoxy until it fits his poetic needs. Having called upon men to witness and learn from the oblivious growth of the lilies, Christ urges our acceptance of the ways of God even in times of want. Verse thirty-one in particular reads: "Therefore do not be anxious, saying, 'What shall we eat?' or 'What shall we drink?' or 'What shall we wear?' For the Gentiles seek all these things; and your heavenly Father knows that you need them all." Man should accept experience with faith that God will ultimately provide and that man is prepared for God's "kingdom and his righteousness" (6.33) by the suffering endured in his life. In the early spring of 1819 Keats reached a position of acceptance of life with its myriad antinomies; ironically his resolution resembles very much the Christian faith in Providence. In the April 21 section of the journal-letter to George and Georgiana Keats (perhaps only two weeks before "Ode on Indolence" was written), he writes in the famous "vale of Soul-making" letter: "Do you not see how necessary a World of Pains and troubles is to school an Intelligence and make it a soul? A Place where the heart must feel and suffer in a Thousand diverse ways!" (II, 102). In his own terms the agnostic Keats has adopted an essentially Christian justification of optimism and trust. The poetry and letters in the early months of 1819 show that Keats had become most disillusioned with life, but the letter, and the poetic expression in "Indolence" of the need to submit to and accept life, led to his reawakening in the spring. In short, the earlier disillusionment and unhappiness proved to be generative, for out of his suffering came the best of his poetry. Keats knew that suffering nurtured poetry. In a letter to Sarah Jeffrey, June 9, 1819, he writes that "One of the great reasons that the English have produced the finest writers in the world is, that the English world has ill-treated them during their lives and foster'd them after their deaths. They have in general been trampled aside into the bye paths of life and seen the festerings of society" (II, 115). Man and poet are shaped by the suffering and pain of living. Failure "to see beyond our bourn," to pretend that the commonplace and orthodox are sufficient, is to stagnate. But acceptance of life and celebration of its various experiences, including indolence, is to come alive as a poet. "Ode on Indolence," with its indebtedness to the paradoxical wisdom of Christ, gave Keats the peace of mind and the courage to write.

A final irony arises from Keats's having written a poem about indolence, and Karl Krober has thus exposed this irony: "does it take more energy to write an 'Ode on Activity' than to write an 'Ode on Indolence'? Keats's very celebration of indolence and rejection of poetry in a fine poem is an expression of energy and a validation of poetry."[14] In this respect "Indolence" resembles Coleridge's "Dejection: an Ode" which laments the loss of the imaginative power which simultaneously creates the poem. The "demon Poesy" seems to have disappeared, but its influence persists, and out of the "nothingness" which is the subject of the poem comes the poem itself. "Indolence" shows us the poet or "soul" born of suffering. More important, the poem is a study in indolence in which Keats achieves an acceptance of a moment for whatever that moment offers. He has found what Kierkegaard calls "contentment with our common humanity." But contentment requires submission to life and process rather than resistance, and in such submission there is generated a power to celebrate each moment for whatever it brings.

NOTES

[1] *Keats and the Mirror of Art* (London: Oxford Univ. Press, 1967), 244.

[2] *Aesthetic and Myth in the Poetry of Keats* (Princeton: Princeton Univ. Press, 1965), 305.

[3] *John Keats: His Life and Writings* (London: Weidenfeld and Nicolson, 1966), 148.

4 *John Keats* (New York: Oxford Univ. Press, 1963), 528.

5 *John Keats: the Making of a Poet* (New York: Viking, 1967), 280.

6 "The Meaning of the Odes" in *John Keats: A Reassessment*, ed. Muir (Liverpool: Liverpool Univ. Press, 1969), 65.

7 Although the precise date of composition is uncertain, my reading presupposes that "Indolence" antedates the Great Odes. Two scholars have argued convincingly for this early date. Aileen Ward says that "Indolence" echoes Keats's two sonnets on fame (written well before the Great Odes) and "Ode to Psyche" and that its last lines "closely parallel a sentence from *The Golden Asse* . . . which Keats was reading at the time he wrote 'Psyche.' " See *John Keats: the Making of a Poet*, 432–33 n. 15. Robert Gittings argues that "Indolence" was written on May 4, immediately after "Psyche" and before the other odes. In "Indolence" Keats describes a May morning between showers. Gittings has discovered that May 4 "was the only day of such weather in a three week's fine spell," and for evidence he cites *The Gentleman's Magazine* (1819), I, 494. See *John Keats* (Boston: Little, Brown, 1968), 313. More important, whenever the poem actually was written, it obviously began to take shape in Keats's mind as early as March 17, 1819. See the journal-letter to the George Keatses, March 17–19.

8 I have accepted the stanzaic order proposed by H. W. Garrod. Citations from Keats's poetry in my text are to Garrod's *The Poetical Works of John Keats* (London: Oxford Univ. Press, 1956).

9 All passages from the letters are from *The Letters of John Keats*, ed. Hyder E. Rollins (London: Cambridge Univ. Press, 1958). As has Rollins, I have simply accepted the irregularities and inconsistencies in Keats's spelling and mechanics.

10 *The Poetry and Prose of William Blake*, ed. David V. Erdman (Garden City, N.Y.: Doubleday, 1970), 135, ll. 42–45.

11 *Fearful Symmetry* (Princeton: Princeton Univ. Press, 1947), 387.

12 *The Gospel of Suffering and The Lilies of the Field*, trans. David. F. and Lillian M. Swenson (Minneapolis: Augsburg Publishing House, 1948), 171–72.

13 *The Imagery of Keats and Shelley* (Hamden, Conn.: Archon, 1962), 210.

14 *The Artifice of Reality* (Madison: Univ. of Wisconsin Press, 1964), 82.

University of Missouri

BRUCE K. MARTIN

VANITY FAIR: NARRATIVE AMBIVALENCE AND COMIC FORM

Much critical discussion on *Vanity Fair* has concerned Thackeray's powers of creating characters. Not surprisingly, Becky Sharp has been singled out as his consummate triumph of characterization. Interestingly, though, there has been little agreement over Becky's behavior toward her husband and Lord Steyne culminating in her fall from grace in Chapter 55. While tacitly assuming Becky to be guilty of something, more critics disagree sharply on what she is guilty of and on Thackeray's rationale for the degree of guilt assigned to her.[1] This diversity of critical interpretation suggests the complexity of Thackeray's presentation of the crisis and the need for further examination of it.

The present essay will argue that Thackeray is ultimately noncommittal about Becky's guilt and that his inconclusiveness serves a definite structural objective. He judges Becky's guilt as "not proved," in accord with the novel's complex design. The possibility of her being guilty of something very serious adds to the mounting pressure for punishment of Becky after the Waterloo chapters, while the continuing possibility of her innocence and the harsh aftermath of her discovery by Rawdon create pity for Becky in her banishment and permit her to resume her initial role as rogue heroine. Thackeray's indefiniteness at this stage reinforces the complexity of action and character demanded by the comedy of the novel.

I

Perhaps the most striking aspect of Becky's crisis is the extent to which Thackeray raises, without resolving, the question of her guilt. No

37

critic who claims that Becky is innocent of adulterous sex with Steyne
has demonstrated her innocence. The narrator's questions following the
catastrophe—"What *had* happened? Was she guilty or not?" (517)[2]—
presumably refer not to the altercation between Becky, Steyne, and
Rawdon upon his return home—this Thackeray has given in objective
detail—but to what occurred between Lord Steyne and Becky before
her husband's return. Steyne's informing Becky of Rawdon's appointment the night before the ball in no way dispels the possibility of a tryst
after the party once Rawdon has been detained. Presumably Steyne's
ardor for Becky is at its height at the party,[3] while the news of Rawdon's
appointment plus his removal by Moss might make Becky more ready
to comply.

At the same time, while Steyne may be wise to many of Becky's
tricks, she is his equal in trickery. That she would risk much before
cementing a permanent bargain seems doubtful. Steyne's immediate
suspicion of a trap suggests that she has not made such a bargain by the
time Rawdon returns, for it would be a strange and amusing trap were
the wife already to have given in to her suitor before the husband's discovery. Steyne's protestation of Becky's guilt seems directed more
toward the supposed scheme between husband ("the bully," Steyne
calls him) and wife to blackmail him, than toward her sexual activity.
Furthermore her resistance to pressure from Steyne long after Rawdon's
arrest may signify that she never intends sex with the Marquis. Obviously Steyne expects it, but her awareness of the impracticality of ever
giving him the ultimate prize surely remains. Her regrets the next day
after Rawdon discovers them—"Good heavens! was ever such ill luck
as mine? . . . to be so near and to lose all. Is it all too late?" (529)—
refer to some further concession which she had hoped to win, presumably with the promise of sex. Whether Becky intended to fulfill that
promise remains an open question.

Thackeray's ambiguity regarding Becky and the sex issue can be
related to his treatment of the entire crisis and to the novel's overall
structure. More to the immediate point, however, is his apparent desire
to shift the question of her guilt from sexual fidelity to general loyalty of
motive. After establishing sex as the lure used by Becky, Thackeray
deftly turns the issue away from sex to the broader issue of vanity. His
refusal to confirm Becky as an adulteress reflects not simply a prudish
aversion to explicit sex in his novel,[4] but also the recognition that his
audience might become preoccupied with the sexual question and lose
sight of the wider social and moral issues surrounding *Vanity Fair*. But

in so shifting his novel's emphasis Thackeray moved only from one ultimately unanswered question to another, since by the end of the novel the reader feels even more uncertain of Becky's fidelity of motive than of her sexual fidelity to Rawdon. All the evidence in Becky's favor Thackeray manages to qualify but not to refute entirely. Her claims of innocence to Pitt in Chapter 55—the references to Rawdon's poverty and the appointment she had secured for him—are undercut by her exaggerations of her affection for her husband and by her obviously fake appeal to Pitt's ego. In the same scene her blaming Steyne for the detention of Rawdon appears questionable in view of her earlier falsely blaming Rawdon to Steyne for misspending money the Marquis had given her (Chapter 48). Her claim to Rawdon in Chapter 52—"I have your interests to attend to, as you can't attend to them yourself" (505)— similarly seems dubious in its context, where Thackeray describes how Rawdon, Jr., and Briggs were gotten out of the house through collusion between Steyne and Becky.

The most substantial fact in Becky's favor is the appointment which she secures for Rawdon. As early as Chapter 48 we see her telling Steyne to get her and Rawdon "a place." Yet even this is subject to the hardly very favorable interpretation that she may have an ulterior motive in pursuing a colonial appointment for her husband. While Becky can eliminate Rawdon temporarily as an obstacle to her progress with Steyne, any more profitable bargain demands more permanent removal. Though no such motive is indicated by Thackeray, it seems as plausible as the notion that Becky, with her acquired taste for London social life, would very readily accompany her dull husband to a colonial outpost. Thus the appointment, though benefiting Rawdon financially, might work to his ultimate disadvantage.

Especially when combined with other evidences of her disregard for Rawdon, an ulterior motive on Becky's part appears to explain her seeking the appointment for him. The most damning indication of her desire for freedom from Rawdon is, of course, the money given her by Amelia which she hides in the desk. In addition, Becky increasingly mistreats Rawdon, causing him to fear her independence and to tighten his watch on her. Her disloyalty is further suggested by Steyne's sudden willingness to befriend Pitt, whom he previously has snubbed, and by Steyne's secret purchase of diamonds and other gifts for Becky. Such things reinforce the impression of Becky as a totally selfish schemer, who confides her real intentions to no one.

In light of thoughtful scrutiny, though, these "proofs" of Becky's disloyalty appear inconclusive. The financial independence she gains from Rawdon by hiding money may be the means of protecting both of them from his irresponsible spending or from his many creditors. And, given Rawdon's increasing bent toward policing Becky, his detention at Moss's may be expedient if Becky is to receive concessions from Steyne conducive to both her and Rawdon's further security. Though she may be using sex only as a false lure for Steyne, Rawdon would hardly countenance her pursuing their common benefit in this way, for Steyne, unlike George Osborne, is dangerous game. Becky's neglect of Rawdon may signify only the intensity of her pursuit of the Marquis, and her exclusion of Rawdon from that pursuit may indicate merely her recognition of Rawdon's dull-wittedness. Thus it can be argued that Rawdon's desperate resistance to her more shrewd, if less honorable, design on Steyne forces her to resort to Wenham and Moss as a way of keeping her husband quiet.

The opinions of other characters concerning Becky's treatment of Rawdon reflect both the general unreliability which Thackeray attributes to the society of the novel and the biases of particular commentators. The satire of *Vanity Fair* aims, among other things, at fashionable society's propensity toward gossip. Such satire is reinforced in Chapter 47, at the height of Becky's overtures to Steyne and shortly before her fall, by Thackeray's introduction of Tom Eaves as a representative of the curious, obsequious, and untrustworthy gossips who regard Mrs. Crawley as a dangerous upstart. They supply the basis for the suspicions of the Becky-Steyne relationship felt by Pitt, who himself, despite his awareness of Steyne's black reputation, is not above patronizing the wealthy Marquis. And Thackeray attributes Lady Jane's dislike for Becky largely to jealousy over Pitt. Even Macmurdo, the most objective and disinterested of Becky's critics, relies on the countless rumors of the social and military sets, both bent on destroying Becky from a selfish desire to preserve caste, and admits, "She may be innocent after all. . . . Steyne has been a hundred times alone with her in the house before" (524). If Wenham's weak excuses for Steyne and Becky arouse Macmurdo's suspicion, that suspicion depends partly on the same scandalmongers characterized by Thackeray as most unreliable. At the close of the crisis section of the novel, Thackeray again undermines the guilt pronounced against Becky by a society disposed, for reasons of vanity, to believe the worst of her: "Was she guilty or not? We all know how charitable the world is, and how the verdict of Vanity Fair goes when there is a doubt" (538). And Rawdon himself unwittingly echoes this judgment when he says, "If she's not guilty, Pitt, she's as bad as guilty" (537), for like Vanity Fair he equates appearance with fact.

Hence the reader cannot be certain either of Becky's innocence or of her guilt. Thackeray tells us that she may or may not be guilty. At the same time we see that despite the paucity of evidence society will find her guilty. The ambiguity of the narrator's final verdict, plus the power of rumor in Vanity Fair, suggests that Becky need not be guilty for punishment to fall. But whether guilty or not, she merits Rawdon's anger, for there is no question but that he has been deceived and, for whatever reasons, cruelly treated by her. Yet the shallowness suggested by the most favorable interpretation of Becky's behavior is lost on a society bent upon the most unfavorable interpretation. Becky thus stands convicted of the wrong charge.

II

The key to the inconclusive treatment of Becky's guilt, as well as the mixed feelings aroused in the reader by her crisis, can be found partly in the structuring of events before her downfall. Becky's whole experience with Steyne represents the final step of a progression beginning with her departure from Miss Pinkerton's academy, where Thackeray sets up the comic paradigm to be repeated, with important variations, until she departs from Curzon Street, at the end of Chapter 55. In the context of Miss Pinkerton's pompous farewells to her pupils, Becky's greetings in French and her refusal of the hand so condescendingly offered her appear most appropriate humiliations for the vain school-mistress. Becky climaxes her jibes at the expense of "the Semiramis of Hammersmith, the friend of Doctor Johnson, the correspondent of Mrs. Chapone herself," by throwing the revered dictionary out the coach window. In the first chapter Thackeray indicates Becky's position as a social outsider, her consequent reliance upon her wit, and her ability to expose and exploit fraud. Becky is thus cast as the nemesis of vanity, determined and able to survive in Vanity Fair by preying on the conceit of others.

Her subsequent adventures represent attempts, with varying success, to improve her position against a society at best indifferent to her welfare. Her predicament as a penniless orphan becomes the rationale for her brazen pursuit of Jos Sedley, whose comically disastrous "courtship" constitutes the first phase of action involving Becky. Miss Sharp's near-conquest of fat Jos constitutes an attack not only on the vain young Sedley, but also on the would-be gentility of the merchant class to which his family belongs. Jos's heavy drinking represents a necessary "accident" in the plot. As with the need for keeping Rawdon Crawley away from his aunt,[5] Thackeray could not allow Becky to triumph here, for he intended her to move elsewhere in search of security. So brilliant is his handling of Becky and so amusing the predicament of the drunken Jos that the reader detects no authorial manipulation. Rather, the entire episode reinforces the picture of Becky as keenly alert to the vanity of others and able to exploit their egoism.

Each of the later phases of her experience corresponds to the first. Becky moves from the London merchant class to the old landed aristocracy, but again we see her preying on the vanity of those she meets by turning their comic weaknesses against them. In attacking the Crawleys, she continues to seek a secure marriage. Our amusement stems from her clever advances upon Sir Pitt, Pitt, Jr., and Miss Crawley, each of whom displays a particular brand of vanity: old Pitt in his boorishness; Pitt, Jr., in his pious worldliness and personal vanity; and Miss Matilda in her paradoxical combination of radical political views and tyrannical personal behavior. Moreover Becky's victims expose each other's vanities; Pitt implicitly uses his father's greed to subdue the old man while Miss Crawley's wealth inspires an uncharacteristic amiability among her relatives. And most important, Thackeray here casts Mrs. Bute Crawley as an antagonist to Becky and an indirect victim of Miss Sharp's comic strategy. Mrs. Bute's indignation at the upstart Becky's advance is depicted as sordid greed hiding behind concern for class and respectability.[6] Becky appears much more knowing about herself and others, for in telling Amelia, "Revenge may be wicked, but it's natural . . . I'm no angel" (19), she acknowledges the impurity of her motives. Because she establishes herself among people with equally impure motives but without her clear-sightedness, her humiliations of her victims delight the reader.[7]

The second phase of the Becky plot ends, of course, with the disclosure to Miss Crawley of her marriage (Chapter 15). Here again Thackeray introduces an "accident," the death of Lady Crawley, to force Becky to show her hand and precipitate a failure, and thus shift her story to its next phase. After marriage Becky's objective continues to be security, or more particularly cash, and this she seeks from two sources, Miss Crawley and George Osborne. The possibility of securing funds from Miss Crawley is virtually terminated at the end of Chapter 25, while the assault on Osborne's capital ends abruptly with the third "accident" of the novel, his death at Waterloo. As Becky next exploits family connections, Thackeray again makes her actions laughable by providing her not only with vain victims, but also a comic antagonist, the amusing Countess Southdown, whose spirited opposition to Becky reflects religious hypocrisy.[8] The final phase of Becky's activities before her downfall is her relationship with Steyne, which, though beginning in Chapter 37, does not take precedence over her relationship with the Crawleys until Chapter 47. Even here Becky's success remains partly tolerable through the presence of snobbish adversaries, headed by the haughty Lady Bareacres.

As suggested earlier, Thackeray alters the basically comic pattern in Becky's adventures to retain the reader's interest and to conform to the broader structure of the novel. One most obvious alteration is the social shift, whereby Becky moves from the merchant class of the Sedleys to the old gentry, represented by the Crawleys, and finally into the upper echelon of London society. But in moving Becky up the social scale Thackeray committed himself to a pattern which carried with it the danger of tiring the reader; he could not afford too many steps in Becky's progress into upper society. Given the need to extend his novel twenty full numbers, he at some time in the writing of *Vanity Fair* must have sensed the inadequacy of the social structure as the basis for plotting.[9] Despite its appropriateness for social satire and picaresque variety, Thackeray utilized this pattern for only two-thirds of the novel, ultimately subordinating it to a more complex structure.

Of crucial relevance to such complexity are the moral implications of Becky's social rise. Her exploitation of the socially vain people she meets can only temporarily offset the fact that she herself, for whatever motives, is on the social ladder and infected by the climbing disease. But for most of the novel Thackeray, like Becky, chooses to ignore the implications of her climb.[10] Not until her episode with Steyne does Thackeray explicitly show that Becky herself is subject to the social vanity on which she has so readily capitalized. Up to this point the reader has observed Becky pursuing, in succession, marriage, money, and "credit." With the advent of Steyne, however, Thackeray makes it clear that she is operating in a quite different sphere, with a presumably different objective. The narrator assumes a different tone in the initial description of Steyne from that employed in first describing Sir Pitt:

The candles lighted up Lord Steyne's shining bald head, which was fringed with red hair. He had thick bushy eyebrows, with little twinkling blood shot eyes, surrounded by a thousand wrinkles. His jaw was underhung, and when he laughed, two white buck-teeth protruded themselves and glistened savagely in the midst of the grin. He had been dining with royal personages, and wore his garter and ribbon. A short man was his lordship, broad-chested, and two-legged, but proud of the fineness of his foot and ankle, and always caressing his garter-knee.   (366)

Compared with the earlier picture of Sir Pitt—"a man in drab breeches and gaiters, with a dirty old coat, a foul old neckcloth lashed round his bristly neck, a shining bald head, a leering red face, a pair of twinkling grey eyes and a mouth perpetually on the grin" (68)—the description of Steyne is notably grim. The ensuing dialogue between Becky and Steyne, who joke in mock-pastoral terms about Becky's "moral shepherd's dog," lacks the lightness of tone with which old Pitt's rascality is treated. Similarly the lengthy history of Steyne's family given in Chapter 47 differs in both content and tone from the amusing sketch of the Crawleys in Chapter 11. The taint of hereditary illness, the mystery of imprisoned relatives, and Steyne's ruthlessness toward his wife inspire a profound revulsion wholly unrelieved by the comic elements dominating Thackeray's treatment of the Crawleys.

This change in Thackeray's treatment of Becky's would-be lovers corresponds to a change in Becky's objectives in pursuing them, or at least to Thackeray's belated acknowledgment of her total motives. Thus the hypocrisy of her social ascent becomes apparent in her pursuit of Steyne, who represents to her more than simply wealth. Not until she is about to be presented at court do we learn that "to be, and to be thought, a respectable woman, was Becky's aim in life. . . " (460). Her appearance at court is a watershed in the development of her snobbery, a point after which she can no longer function principally as a punitive comic agent. In shifting from the Crawleys to Steyne, Becky has come to regard herself not merely as shrewdly opportunistic, but as inherently more deserving than others. She comes to equate social position with virtue, something she has never done before, and to believe in social respectability as an end and not simply the means to a material end. Hence her reaction to being presented to George IV, whom Thackeray castigates elsewhere as a "contemptible imposter":[11] "This may be said, that in all London there was no more loyal heart than Becky's after this interview. The name of her king was always on her lips, and he was proclaimed by her to be the most charming of men" (463). Becky comes not only to profit by the social system but to believe in it. Her change from economic to social values marks her as deserving the humiliation she earlier had meted out to others.

Accompanying Becky's shift of values after the Waterloo chapters is a shift to a more innocent class of victims, whom she injures more seriously than she did George Osborne or Lady Southdown. In working for "credit" instead of cash, she begins to trample on honest, simple people. This new class of victims includes the landlords, milliners, and nurses cheated by Becky as she leaves Paris. Upon returning to England she and Rawdon continue to bleed merchants of their hard-earned funds. The most sustained portrait of an innocent victim is that of Raggles, the ex-butler to Miss Crawley, who rents Becky and Rawdon the house in Curzon Street and supplies their food; "a good man; good and happy" (359) is Thackeray's description of Raggles, whose loyalty to the family of his former mistress results in imprisonment for him and poverty for his family. Unlike Briggs, another well-meaning victim of Becky's thoughtless financial schemes, Raggles is no foolish sentimentalist but simply an honest tradesman who mistakenly attributes honesty to Miss Crawley's family. After Becky's downfall the cry of honest Raggles, "I little thought one of that family was a goin' to ruing me— yes, ruing me" (528), underscores the indiscriminateness of Becky's later victimizings.

Perhaps the most pathetic victims of her increased ruthlessness in the second half of the novel are her son and husband. By giving Becky a son shortly after Waterloo, Thackeray set up another cause of pressure for the downfall she later suffers, as her mistreatment of Rawdon, Jr., further disqualifies her for the tolerance sustained so long by the punitive comedy in which she is the central agent. Equally important here, as several critics have noted,[12] is the growth of responsibility undergone by Rawdon, whose new-found maturity centers on a concern for the boy, in marked contrast to Becky's neglect. And nowhere is Thackeray's strategy in placing his chapters more evident than in his placement of the chapters devoted to Amelia after Waterloo and before Becky's downfall, in which Amelia's devotion to George, Jr., despite hardship forms a sharp and damning contrast to Becky's mistreatment of her son amid prosperity. Through direct portrayal of little Rawdon's distasteful treatment by his mother, and through more oblique indications—references to the elder Rawdon's affection for the boy or Amelia's sacrifices for Georgy—Thackeray, in virtually every chapter between Rawdon's birth and his final separation from his mother, presents Becky's failure as a mother as the least tolerable of her mounting offenses.

III

Through these cumulative pressures—Becky's acquired snobbery, her growing tendency to inflict pain on undeserving victims, and her increasingly apparent shortcomings as a wife and mother—Thackeray causes the reader to demand some type of punishment. But, while the developing crisis with Steyne at first appears to be such a punishment, Thackeray's ambivalent treatment of Becky's behavior toward Steyne renders her punishment less than comic. Despite the ironic appropriateness of her being turned out by the society she has duped for so long, Vanity Fair's escape without punishment creates some pity for Becky.

The partial injustice of her punishment becomes apparent in Chapter 64, where Thackeray shows Becky wandering through Europe, hounded by rumors of her past. Instead of describing her vices on the Continent, he concentrates on the mistreatment of Becky by people with mixed motives: on Wenham's slandering her to Pitt, on the desire of fashionable society to have her deported, and on the rumors which foil her attempts to establish herself in Europe. Significantly Thackeray climaxes this persecution with Becky's meeting Steyne, who threatens her life. To the reader Becky is partly redeemed by her helplessness at his hands. Given the sharp fall she has suffered and her precarious relationship with a society indisposed, for reasons of vanity, to allow her even a modicum of security, the independence Thackeray grants her in the end appears an appropriate affront to the citizens of Vanity Fair, while the prohibition against her re-entering high society sufficiently punishes her for her earlier errors of egoism.

The justness of Becky's final position is suggested also by her actions during the crisis between Amelia and Dobbin. Dobbin's outcry against the sentimental Amelia's unqualified reacceptance of Becky works in both his favor and Becky's. On the one hand, since his initial appearance Dobbin has seemed as alert as Becky to the vanity of others, yet totally lacking in the ambition which drives Becky up the social ladder. Further the reader can see that despite Dobbin's reliance upon undependable rumor, Becky is certainly not what she claims; her protest to Amelia of devotion to Rawdon, Jr., for example, confirms Dobbin's distrust as well founded. In view of his many years of patient devotion, his objections to Becky's quick readmittance into Amelia's favor seems reasonable, while Amelia's seeming indifference to his ultimatum appears unreasonable. At the same time, despite Becky's roguery in dealing with Amelia, her misadventures after leaving Rawdon have marked her as deserving the minimal security Amelia would offer. Thackeray conveniently resolves the reader's conflict of sympathies at this point by having Becky intervene in Dobbin's behalf. Her intervention seems to assure his winning the long-sought Amelia, but, more important, it suggests the element of fair play in Becky's character and further qualifies her for the limited success she achieves in the end.

The conclusion of the novel finds Becky with friends, but also with enemies, financially secure, but only on the fringe of polite society. Thackeray defines this final situation as the degree of success to which her keenness of wit and mistreatment by vain society, as well as her moral limitations, entitle her. Lest the reader become overly sympathetic with Becky after her heroic defense of Dobbin, Thackeray inserts the briefly described episode involving the death of Jos Sedley, to remind us that Becky continues to be "no angel."

The ambivalent treatment of this final Sedley episode[13] preserves the balance inherent in the "unheroic" view of life sustained throughout the novel and in the comic form in which Thackeray chose to embody that view. The same principle operates in his treatment of Becky's crisis, with which this discussion has been chiefly concerned, for there he avoided creating too much or too little sympathy for Becky. The crisis represents a pivotal point in the novel, where the pattern of punitive comedy gives way temporarily to humiliation for Becky herself, before returning to the view of Becky as certainly no worse than those whose egos she has offended. Had Thackeray pronounced her guilty of disloyalty to Rawdon, the novel might have moved out of the comic sphere; at any rate, it might have seemed unnecessary to continue the novel beyond Becky's punishment. To pronounce her innocent, on the other hand, would detract sharply from the carefully developed demand for punishment of some sort and also would remove the novel from comedy by creating largely unalloyed pity for Becky.

To be sure, the completed novel hardly resulted solely from adherence to a formal type or from the author's non-heroic perspective. Of the many extrinsic factors governing its composition, the demands of serialization especially helped dictate the shape and size of *Vanity Fair*. That some looseness resulted cannot be denied. Clearly, though, Thackeray's ambivalent treatment of Becky at key points in the novel, and particularly his noncommittal attitude toward her activities immediately before her crisis, helped minimize unavoidable looseness by keeping the novel from what, in terms of serialization, would be a premature conclusion. The narrative ambivalence surrounding Becky's fall permits a combination of both types of comedy—that in which Becky is punisher and that in which she is punished—while allowing, indeed requiring, the novel to extend beyond the crisis with Steyne. Narrative ambivalence thus helps sustain both the comedy and the unity of *Vanity Fair*.

NOTES

[1] For example, Kathleen Tillotson, *Novels of the Eighteen-Forties* (London: Oxford Univ. Press, 1956), 250, implies Becky's responsibility for Rawdon's arrest, but skirts the question of her ultimate objective: whether in consorting with Steyne she envisioned an adulterous relationship which would give her independence from Rawdon or, as she claims, she acted principally in Rawdon's interest

to secure him the appointment. On the other hand, F. E. L. Priestley, "Introduction" to *Vanity Fair* (New York: Odyssey, n.d.), xvi, asserts that Becky's claim of innocence "at least means that she had not yet rendered to Steyne the services as mistress for which he had paid so extravagantly, and obviously in advance." Without indicating why we are to assume that Steyne and Becky have not consummated their relationship earlier in the day or even after the charade party of the night before, Priestley, by his phrase "at least," raises without resolving the important questions of whether Becky may not be innocent of more than adultery and why Thackeray permits her to retain even this much innocence. A view somewhat different from Priestley's is taken by Frank Chandler, *The Literature of Roguery* (Boston: Houghton, 1907), II, 465, who maintains that "Becky's mendacity is indeed so unusual that the reader does not know whether to believe her protestations of innocence at the critical moment." But where Chandler attributes the reader's uncertainty over the crisis of Becky's cleverness, Andrew Von Hendy, "Misunderstandings About Becky's Characterization in *Vanity Fair*," *Nineteenth-Century Fiction* 18 (1964–65), 283, sees the questions posed by the narrator at the close of Chapter 53 as reflections of Becky's own moral confusion. Assuming that Becky had contemplated adultery all along, he concludes that "Her moral bankruptcy, rather like Bulstrode's, prevents her from being honest even with herself." Finally, G. Armour Craig, "On the Style of *Vanity Fair*," in *Style in Prose: English Institute Essays, 1958*, ed. Harold C. Martin (New York: Columbia Univ. Press, 1959), 104, after allowing that Becky is guilty of preparing for adultery, insists that Thackeray's final questioning of her guilt reflects his inability or unwillingness to face squarely the implications of her behavior. "Thackeray will not—he can not—support us as we revolt from such a spectacle," Craig concludes.

2 William Makepeace Thackeray, *Vanity Fair*, ed. Geoffrey and Kathleen Tillotson (Boston: Houghton, 1963). Chapter and page citations refer to this edition and will be included in the text.

3 Von Hendy, 281–83.

4 He probably felt such an aversion, though. See Walter Houghton, *The Victorian Frame of Mind* (New Haven: Yale Univ. Press, 1957), 357, 419. Gordon N. Ray, *Thackeray: The Age of Wisdom, 1847–1863* (London: Oxford Univ. Press, 1958), 123–26, tells of Thackeray's early protests against Victorian prudery and his recourse to innuendo in his later works, but notes that as the editor of *Cornhill* "Thackeray displayed a caution that he would himself have been the first to ridicule earlier in his career" (301).

5 In Chapter 16 Thackeray's self-conscious narrator recognizes the demands of serial publication and the need for deferring certain things until the structurally appropriate time when he explains why, as Becky tried to soften the shock of her marriage, he chose to keep Rawdon away from his aunt: "If Rawdon Crawley had been then and there present, instead of being at the club nervously drinking claret, the pair might have gone on their knees before the old spinster, avowed all and been forgiven in a twinkling. But that good chance was denied to the young couple, doubtless in order that this story might be written, in which numbers of their wonderful adventures are narrated—adventures which could never have occurred to him if they had been housed and sheltered under the comfortable uninteresting forgiveness of Miss Crawley" (153).

6 Thus there is more than coincidence in the fact that Mrs. Bute was educated at Miss Pinkerton's and that mutual admiration between former student and teacher has persisted.

7 As John Dodds has observed in "Introduction" to *Vanity Fair* (New York: Holt, 1955), xvi: "Were it not that she employs her wits against people even less

admirable than herself we might be shocked by our absence of moral qualms about her. As it is, there is a kind of wild justice in her breezy assault upon the citadels of the stupid and the mighty."

[8] The Countess's worldliness is illustrated in Chapter 33, where she, Lady Emily, and Pitt discuss the best means of approaching Miss Crawley. Pitt, fearing that the religious assault proposed by Emily will lose them his aunt's £70,000, insists upon the importance of proceeding cautiously, and Lady Southdown readily defers to his materialistic arguments. Thackeray wryly notes: "Lady Southdown, we say, for the sake of the invalid's health, or for the sake of her soul's ultimate welfare, or for the sake of her money, agreed to temporise" (324).

[9] Concerning the bearing of serial publication on *Vanity Fair*, see Tillotson, *Novels of the Eighteen-Forties*, 25–47, 239–42; and Edgar F. Harden, "The Discipline and Significance of Form in *Vanity Fair*," *PMLA* 82 (1967), 530–41.

[10] While Becky's refusal of the marriage offer by Glauber, old Pitt's physician (Chapter 11), hints at her capacity for snobbishness—"as if I was born, indeed, to be a country surgeon's wife!" she writes Amelia (98)—her share of this fundamental characteristic of the society she invades remains largely latent until much later in the novel.

[11] *The Letters of William Makepeace Thackeray*, ed. Gordon N. Ray (Cambridge, Mass.: Harvard Univ. Press, 1945), III, 570. His essay on George IV in *The Four Georges* offers an even stronger condemnation.

[12] For example, Tillotson, *Novels of the Eighteen-Forties*, 248–49, or Priestley, xxxii-xxxiii.

[13] See Von Hendy, "Misunderstandings About Becky's Characterization in *Vanity Fair*," 281–82.

Drake University

KENNETH E. STORY

THEME AND IMAGE IN *THE PRINCESS*

Concerning the images that appear in Tennyson's poetry, one critic has aptly suggested that "they exist in order to invite sympathy with the mood of the observer."[1] In *The Princess* this observer is the Prince-narrator, from whose point of view the tale unfolds;[2] and the imagery of growth and fruition, which predominates over all other imagery in *The Princess*, complements the literal growth of the Prince toward fulfillment in his quest for relationship. Viewed from the perspective of the Prince-narrator and in its dramatic context in the poem, this imagery operates in two ways: it offers an ironic commentary on the barren efforts of Ida and her companions to forge an existence in a world without men, and it provides a background against which the reader may chart the Prince's own growth. Throughout *The Princess* the imagery of growth and fruition promotes and sustains the serious theme[3] of the poem, an idea treated by Tennyson in many other works: isolation is self-destructive; one can lead a productive life only in relationship with others.

From the beginning of *The Princess* the image of growth is ironically applied to the attempts of Ida and her women to isolate themselves in Ida's academy. Such words as "fruit," "nursery," "seed," "true growth," "grafting," and "grain" abound in the speeches of the women, and in their dramatic context these terms are consistently ironic. When the women prate of "growth," they invariably betray their futile attempts to defy the laws of nature; without exception, the women "grow" in direct proportion to their abandonment of Ida's cause.

The speeches of Psyche, Ida's right-hand woman, are replete with allusions to growth. After the Prince and his two friends disguise them-

50

selves as women and enroll in Ida's university, Psyche lectures the
young "women" on Ida's cause:

> ". . . then commenced a dawn: a beam
> Had slanted forward, falling in a land
> Of promise; fruit would follow. Deep, indeed,
> Their debt of thanks to her [Ida] who first had dared
> To leap the rotten pales of prejudice,
> Disyoke their necks from custom, and assert
> None lordlier than themselves but that which made
> Woman and man."
>
>   (II, ll. 122–29)[4]

Hailing the birth of a new day, Psyche speaks of the outworn attitudes
toward women as "rotten pales" across which Ida has jumped to freedom. Psyche, who is soon to fall in love with the Prince's friend Cyril
and abandon Ida's cause, will discover that Ida has attempted to cross
something more than barriers of prejudice and that, at any rate, the
"rotten pales" are, in the eyes of others besides the women, still quite
substantial.[5] She goes on to refer to the university as a haven where
the women

> ". . . might grow
> To use and power on this Oasis, lapt
> In the arms of leisure, sacred from the blight
> Of ancient influence and scorn."
>
>   (II, ll. 150–53)

This statement is again ironic, for the institution is, in truth, a wasteland which yields none of the promised fruit. The blight is inside these
walls, impairing the growth of Ida into a mature woman, feeding upon
the diseased jealousy of Lady Blanche, and fostering in Psyche an un-
healthy obsequiousness toward her leader (" 'O that iron will, / That
axe-like edge unturnable, our Head, / The Princess' " [II, 185–87]).
When Psyche is alone with the three men she refers to herself as " 'I,
/ Who am not mine' " (II, ll. 204–205) and says,

> "Whate'er I was
> Disrooted, what I am is grafted here."
>   (II, ll. 201–202)

The image is appropriate at this point in the poem: Psyche is at first
loyal to the Princess and her plan; she does not feel that she has a will
of her own. But when she is "disrooted" from her former self (wife,
then widow, living in the Prince's country), she becomes grafted not so
much to Ida's cause as to Ida herself. As Gama relates, they were " 'Two
women faster welded in one love / Than pairs of wedlock' " (VI,
ll. 236–37).[6] Psyche later discovers that this grafting offers little chance

for growth of the scion in relation to the stock. Furthermore it is unnatural for Psyche to be as subservient as she is to Ida's wishes; her
brother Florian refers to her as " 'poor Psyche whom [Ida] drags in
tow' " (III, 1. 87). Although Psyche says that Ida and she were as close
as "elm and vine" (II, 1. 316), her loyalty to Ida is not great enough to
withstand the natural force which betrays that loyalty: love for her
brother, her child, her suitor. Thus she acknowledges the barrenness
of their efforts and disavows the cause.

The growth image is also ironically used in reference to Blanche, the
jealous third-ranking female in the academy. Her self-defense when she
is called before Princess Ida in Canto IV contains several analogies to
growth. Vowing that she was Ida's "second mother" (IV, 1. 278),
Blanche tells her, " 'I fed you with the milk of every Muse' " (IV,
1. 276). Blanche does not, of course, reveal the real reason for her remaining quiet about the actual identity of the intruders. (She has been
persuaded by Cyril's promise that, once the Prince wins his bride,
Blanche will reign the " 'head and heart of all [the] fair she-world' "
[III, 1. 147] of the North.) Pleading that she, not Psyche, is Ida's true
friend, Blanche reminds the Princess,

> ". . . and thus a noble scheme
> Grew up from seed we two long since had sown;
> In us true growth, in her [Psyche] a Jonah's gourd,
> Up in one night and due to sudden sun:
> We took this palace; but even from the first
> You stood in your own light and darkened mine."
> (IV, ll. 290–95)

The "noble scheme" is one which Blanche has already betrayed out of
self-interest, and the "true growth" of which she speaks is another ironic
comment on the barrenness of their grand plan. Blanche's self-defense
focuses on an attempt to discredit Psyche. The "sudden sun" to which
she attributes Psyche's standing with Ida is an extension of an earlier
reference she makes to Ida's life-giving powers: " 'You turned your
warmer currents all to [Psyche], / To me you froze' " (IV, ll. 282–83).
Betraying her bitterness, Blanche objects to the fact that Ida sent all the
best pupils to Psyche, pupils whom Blanche should have had. She further insinuates that Psyche has disgraced herself by being "Long-
closeted" (IV, 1. 303) with the young men. All of these attempts to
discredit Psyche lead to Blanche's statement that Psyche, instead of
being expelled from the university as she should have been,

> ". . . remained among us
> In our young nursery still unknown, the stem
> Less grain than touchwood, while my honest heat

> Were all miscounted as malignant haste
> To push my rival out of place and power."
>
> (IV, ll. 312–16)

This "nursery" is the result of the seeds of the plan which Blanche maintains were sown only by her and Ida. Blanche thinks Psyche is out of place in the scheme, and she views her rival's basic character ("stem") as less sound and less true to the scheme ("less grain") than it is unstable and excitable ("touchwood"). Also, in the use of "touchwood," Blanche is probably hinting at moral decay in Psyche (as fungi decay wood, making it useful for tinder) brought about by her being closed up with the Prince and his friends. (Blanche either does not know or does not acknowledge the fact that one of the men is Psyche's brother.) There is still another connotation to this image, particularly in the light of Blanche's reference to her own "honest heat." Her own energy, or "heat," has been carefully expended in the nurturing of a plan which she claims Psyche had no part in sowing; and, in contrast to Psyche, she has remained true to the cause.

Blanche's self-defense is one vast net of lies, and what she says was "miscounted as malignant haste" to defame Psyche is not at all miscounted. Everyone is aware of her petty jealousy of Psyche; even her daughter disparages her for her attitude (III. ll. 63–78). And no one is fooled here. The rising intensity of her plea (III, ll. 326–39) betrays her awareness that she is not doing well in justifying her conduct. Finally she exclaims:

> "Dismiss me, and I prophesy your plan,
> Divorced from my experience, will be chaff
> For every gust of chance. . . ."
>
> (IV, ll. 335–37)

Here the growth image is taken to ironic heights: without her, the seeds of a plan which she has so carefully sown and tended will grow into nothing more valuable than worthless chaff. All of Blanche's efforts are, however, futile and self-defeating. And for all of her affirmations of her own "true growth," she is unable to hide her self-consuming love of self. It is significant that the Prince, who views these proceedings, uses the word "vulture" to describe Blanche (IV, l. 344); his most damning judgment of the people he encounters is reserved for this woman.[7] The image of fruition as exhibited in Blanche's comments is, in its dramatic context in the poem, an ironic commentary on this unnatural and predatory creature who feeds upon self-interest and dispenses ill will.

The speeches of Princess Ida also allude to growth, and they reveal her own stunted development. She greets the three "women" of the North as the " 'first-fruits of the stranger' " (II, l. 30), and tells them: " 'Ye are green wood, see ye warp not' " (II, l. 61). And the following is a typical speech of Ida's:

> "And Knowledge in our own land [will] make her free,
> And, ever following those two crownèd twins,
> Commerce and conquest, shower the fiery grain
> Of freedom broadcast over all that orbs
> Between the Northern and the Southern morn."
>   (v, ll. 409–13)

Similar use of the growth image occurs in other statements by Ida as she refers to the fertility of her efforts.[8] The various connotations of the image as displayed in Ida's own words are pulled together and accentuated in "Our enemies have fallen," the exultant victory hymn she sings after the tournament in Canto v, and before she yields her love to the Prince.

The lines directly preceding the song describe the scene: "But high upon the palace Ida stood / With Psyche's babe in arm: there on the roofs / Like that great dame of Lapidoth she sang" (VI, ll. 14–16). Not yet knowing that the Prince has been wounded in combat, Ida exults in the victory which her side has just taken in the tournament:

> "Our enemies have fallen, have fallen: the seed,
> The little seed they laughed at in the dark,
> Has risen and cleft the soil, and grown a bulk
> Of spanless girth, that lays on every side
> A thousand arms and rushes to the Sun.
>
> "Our enemies have fallen, have fallen: they came;
> The leaves were wet with women's tears: they heard
> A noise of songs they would not understand;
> They marked it with the red cross to the fall,
> And would have strown it, and are fallen themselves.
>
> "Our enemies have fallen, have fallen: they came,
> The woodmen with their axes: lo the tree!
> But we will make it faggots for the hearth,
> And shape it plank and beam for roof and floor,
> And boats and bridges for the use of men.
>
> "Our enemies have fallen, have fallen: they struck;
> With their own blows they hurt themselves, nor knew
> There dwelt an iron nature in the grain:
> The glittering axe was broken in their arms,
> Their arms were shattered to the shoulder blade.
>
> "Our enemies have fallen, but this shall grow
> A night of Summer from the heat, a breadth
> Of Autumn, dropping fruits of power: and rolled
> With music in the growing breeze of Time,

The tops shall strike from star to star, the fangs
Shall move the stony bases of the world."
                              (VI, ll. 17–42)

The Prince's men have just been defeated by Ida's brother Arac's men in the tournament, and Ida sees herself turning the tables on the Prince and those who have considered her grand plan—the germ from which all the women of the world will be made free—ridiculous. Her project —" 'the seed, / The little seed they laughed at in the dark' "—now " 'Has risen and cleft the soil, and grown a bulk / Of spanless girth. . . .' "

The words Ida uses reveal not only her impassioned state but also her irrationality. She clings tenaciously to a plan whose existence—in spite of what Ida implies here—is now more precarious than ever. The college for women is by no means flourishing: Psyche and Blanche are no longer a part of it; some other women are discontented (witness Violet's song, "Tears, idle tears"). Significantly the plan which was supposedly constructive in its inception has just made use of destructive means to help accomplish its end. Much irony exists in the application of images of fruition to the battle scene. In her notion that the tournament has helped advance her goal, Ida overlooks the fact that her plan has not proved itself worthy of any merit; it has merely had the assistance of a brother—a man within walls from which all men are barred on pain of death—who happens to have an army at his beck and call.

The tree analogy which Ida uses is quite telling and more appropriate than Ida realizes. With their axes the Prince and his men have attempted to chop down the tree representing the female and her hopes. Thus, without Ida's terrific resistance, she might be the tree which would be chopped into pieces for the home-fire ("faggots for the hearth") or molded into other things for the "use of men." But she has triumphed: these woodmen, who have to chop up everything which she holds dear, have been thwarted in their attempt, for the tree is petrified. The word "grain" refers not only to the fiber of the wood, but also to the natural disposition of Ida, which does indeed have an "iron nature" about it.[9] Since the plans of the Prince and his men, in Ida's view, have gone against the grain, the men's hopes (the "glittering axe") have been frustrated. And not only that, but the men have been wounded: " 'Their arms were shattered to the shoulder blade.' " There is irony in Ida's contention that " 'with their own blows they hurt themselves,' " for this is what Ida has done to herself. And her obstinacy works against nature. Just as the tree Ida refers to in the final stanza has grown all out of proportion, so has her noble plan. And as the roots of the tree rock the foundations of the earth, Ida's plan is, at bottom, one which, if followed through, would result in the upheaval of all nature. It is a strike at the fundamental sex drive. Ida's words here are fraught with folly. She is soon to fall in love with the wounded Prince, forsake her university, and agree to a marriage in which she will be an equal partner.

As the women chatter of seeds and growth and grafting, their conduct and circumstances betray the appalling sterility of their efforts. The isolation of the female sex, for whatever reason, is self-destructive; from the first they are in untenable opposition to fundamental laws of nature. As the reader observes ironic application of the growth image to the women's endeavors, he perceives that the Prince, of all the characters of the poem, is the only one who exemplifies true growth, real maturation. (Psyche reverts quickly to her role as loving woman; Ida, who shoulders the banner of error for six cantos, is suddenly transformed in the seventh.) In the course of the poem this extremely sensitive boy succeeds in his earnest quest for manhood.

The early efforts of the Prince to win Ida's love are handicapped by a clash between his ideal of woman (someone like his kind and tender mother who, aware of his weird afflictions, "Pitying made a thousand prayers" [I, l. 21]) and the reality confronting him in the severe and formidable Princess Ida. While disguised as a woman, the Prince cannot elicit pity from Ida for a lovesick boy (III, l. 190–97), convince her of the desirability of marriage and children (III, ll. 225–29), or move her with his song about lasting true love (IV, ll. 75–98).

The first step in the Prince's development occurs in Canto IV, after his rescue of Ida from the river and after the revelation of his identity as a male. No longer able to hide behind women's clothes and plead in the third person for "the Prince," he must now speak as a man and for himself. His boyhood babbling for Ida, " 'as babies for the moon' " (IV, l. 408), now yields, he tells Ida, to something else: " 'Those winters of abeyance all worn out, / A man I came to see you. . .' " (IV, ll. 420–21). Those years of suspended activity during his adolescence must now be replaced by an earnest attempt to fathom his purpose in life. This purpose the Prince sees as a relationship with Ida. In a passage anticipating his later, more mature plea, the Prince tells Ida that his own life, without her, is but half a life. He desires her more " 'Than growing boys their manhood' " (IV, l. 437) and he affirms to Ida that he is " 'but half / Without you; with you, whole' " (IV, ll. 440–41). It is significant that the Prince attempts to counter the Princess's earlier remark that he was nursing a blind ideal, like a girl. He now tells Ida that

" 'it becomes no man to nurse despair, / But in the teeth of clenched antagonisms / . . . follow up the worthiest till he die' " (IV, ll. 44–46). Although the Princess remains unmoved by this new approach, the Prince has learned something. A greater challenge than fulfilling a foolish boyhood dream awaits him: he must shape the ideal to fit reality, a reality which will exist only if he assumes the task of growing toward it.

The tournament in Canto V, which marks the second stage in the Prince's developing self-awareness, is the means by which the idle dreamer becomes the active doer. Ida, her brother Arac, and the Prince's father have all likened the Prince to a girl; his father has told him to " 'make yourself a man to fight with men' " (V, l. 34). When he participates in Ida's tournament, even though he has made it plain that he does not believe in fighting as a proof of manhood (V, ll. 119–43), the Prince is offering a gesture of concession to a world which believes in such attempts at solution. His act of courage in fighting for Ida is an outward manifestation of the manhood within him—manliness which he assumes publicly in order to prove to Ida that he can do more than babble at the "vague brightness" of the princess of his childhood dreams.

This concession to the world is a necessary prelude to the definitive stage in the Prince's growth toward his goal: his acceptance in Canto VII of the demands of the actual upon the ideal. In this final canto, which unites the metaphorical and literal emphases on growth, the Prince experiences a rebirth from the dormant "mystic middle state" in which he lies following his wound in the tournament. Significantly his metamorphosis is viewed in the context of nature taking its course: Ida has been transformed into a loving woman; "Love in the sacred halls / Held carnival at will . . ." (VII, ll. 69–70); and "Like creatures native unto gracious act, / And in their own clear element, [the women] moved" (VII, ll. 12–13). When the Princess, who has been nursing the Prince back to health, stoops to kiss him, the Prince believes that the dream world and the real world are finally reconciled:

> Leapt fiery Passion from the brinks of death;
> And I believed that in the living world
> My spirit closed with Ida's at the lips.
>   (VII, ll. 141–43)

His final speech reflects his newborn recognition that although his ideal of womanhood cannot be realized in the person of the awesome Ida, he can give this ideal some amount of substance by casting it into a mold of reality. Now uppermost in his thoughts is the practical relationship with Ida, a union which will merge to best advantage an effete Prince ("a flower that cannot all unfold" [vii, l. 126] and a formidable Princess ("a stately pine / Set in cataract on an island-crag" [v, l. 335]). Their marriage, he tells Ida, will hail a new day:

> ". . . in the long years liker must they grow;
> The man be more of woman, she of man;
> . . . .
>   . . . each fulfils
> Defect in each, and always thought in thought,
> Purpose in purpose, will in will, they grow,
> The single pure and perfect animal,
> The two-celled heart beating, with one full stroke,
> Life."
>   (vii, ll. 263–64, 285–90)

The Prince, who has been attracted to Ida's masculine strength from the beginning,[10] has matured in his understanding of himself and his needs.[11] Thus, when he tells Ida " 'Yield thyself up: my hopes and thine are one: / Accomplish thou my manhood and thyself" (vii, 343–44), he is affirming that he can achieve manhood only in relationship with this strong partner he has been presumptuous enough to pursue.[12] He needs Ida's strength to compensate for his own weakness, her inflexibility to counteract his physical instability, and her grasp of substance to operate within his world of shadows.

The Princess is, then, a poem about growth: the maturation of one Prince of the North. The metaphorical emphasis upon "growth" in the women provides an ironic counterpoint to the literal growth of the Prince and sustains the reader's sympathy with the mood of the narrator of the poem. In the final canto of *The Princess* the imagistic and literal strands of this thematic motif are merged as the Prince, self-described as "a flower that cannot all unfold," does unfold and peppers his final plea for Ida's love with allusions to the true growth which is to result from his union with Ida:

> And so these twain, upon the skirts of Time,
> Sit side by side, full-summed in all their powers,
> Dispensing harvest, sowing the To-be . . . .
> . . . .
> Purpose in purpose, will in will, they grow . . . .
> . . . .
>   . . . and all the rich to-come
> Reels, as the golden Autumn woodland reels
> Athwart the smoke of burning weeds.
>   (vii, ll. 271–73, 287, 335–37)

The "burning weeds" signal an end to the "barren deeps" from which Ida comes "to conquer all with love" (vii, l. 149); her efforts to forge an existence in a world without men have proven barren and futile. The "golden Autumn" points to the maturation of a special relationship sanctioned by nature and based on the individual claims of the heart. It is a relationship the full meaning of which only the Prince of the North has come to understand.

NOTES

1 David Daiches, "Imagery and Mood in Tennyson and Whitman," in *English Studies Today* 2 (1961), 220.

2 Although the poem proper (which exists within the framing Prologue and Conclusion) theoretically has seven narrators (one for each canto, each narrator in turn assuming the character of the Prince), there is no shift in the point of view of the young Prince of the North; the entire story is told from his perspective.

3 From the time of its publication *The Princess* generally has been viewed as a poetic treatise dealing with female education or women's rights. Far from being a social tract, *The Princess* is a poem recounting a young man's search for love. Had Tennyson chosen walls other than those of the university behind which Ida might hide herself from men, the story would not be greatly affected. Only a few commentators have sufficiently taken into account the relationship between theme and point of view. See Allan Danzig, "Tennyson's *The Princess*: A Definition of Love," *Victorian Poetry* 4 (Spring 1966), 83–89; Gerhard Joseph, *Tennysonian Love: The Strange Diagonal* (Minneapolis: Univ. of Minnesota Press, 1969), 75–101; and Winston Collins, "*The Princess*: The Education of the Prince," *Victorian Poetry* 11 (Winter 1973), 285–94.

4 All citations from *The Princess* are to *The Poems of Tennyson*, ed. Christopher Ricks (London: Longman, 1969).

5 See III, ll. 222–25; IV, ll. 390–95; V, ll. 110–15, 147–60, 435–55; VI, ll. 147–71; and VII *passim*.

6 See also III, ll. 72–73.

7 See also II, ll. 424–28.

8 See II, ll. 83–84; III, ll. 234–39, 250–54, 262; IV, ll. 61, 14–16.

9 The word "iron" is used to describe Ida's disposition by Psyche (II, ll. 185–86), Ida's father (VI, ll. 213), and the Prince (VI, l. 102).

10 See III, ll. 91–100, 160–75, 332–35; IV, ll, 196–98, 252–56, 360–62.

11 Winston Collins, 285, suggests that at the end of the poem the Prince is "a figure of strength, determination, faith, and vision—the kind of hero that from *The Princess* on plays a central role in Tennyson's poetry." The Prince's growth does not, I think, take him to these heroic heights. At the end of the poem he remains an extremely sensitive individual, still more sentimental and tender-hearted than Ida.

12 One passage existing in an unpublished manuscript version of *The Princess* offers a more explicit statement of the Prince's position; in it the Prince tells Ida: " 'if there be / Men-women, let them wed with women-men / And make a proper marriage.' " Quoted in Sir Charles Tennyson, "Tennyson's Unpublished Poems: III. After 1840," *Nineteenth Century* 109 (1931), 631.

Hendrix College

BEGE B. NEEL

THE RULE OF REVERSE IN
"MR. SLUDGE, 'THE MEDIUM' "

Robert Browning's "Mr. Sludge, 'the Medium' " is the object of both biographical and critical interest. Browning's undisputed contempt for Daniel Dunglas Home, the American medium after whom Mr. Sludge is modeled, has been attributed to jealousy resulting from a spiritual accolade recognizing the poetic superiority of Browning's wife, a devoted believer in spiritualism, at one of Home's séances in Ealing during the summer of 1855.[1] In personal letters dated 1863 and 1871 which indicate the extent of the poet's bitterness toward the American medium, Browning called Home a "dung-ball"[2] and a "beast."[3] Browning's portrayal of Sludge as a despicable scoundrel has been considered unfair to Home, who was noted for his openness and good reputation at the time and who remained sufficiently aloof from the scandal produced by the poem to protect his reputation.[4] While there is little question about the biographical foundation of "Mr. Sludge, 'the Medium,' " the poem has been interpreted critically in a number of ways, ranging from a diatribe against the medium and spiritualism, to the psychological study of a scoundrel, to the philosophical investigation of the nature of truth and the imagination. William O. Raymond defines the central issue of the poem as the psychology of the medium.[5] Philip Drew describes Sludge as a combination of "wretchedness" and "glory" making his way through the corrupting society of fools,[6] and DeVane feels that Browning makes a "very sympathetic case" for Sludge at first although he is seen to be despicable in the end through what has been called the "give-away" ending by other commentators.[7] Since some of the medium's arguments parallel those made elsewhere in Browning's poetry, Isobel Armstrong argues that the poem offered Browning a unique opportunity for examining critically some of his own assumptions, such as the integrity of the creative imagination.[8]

Regardless of one's interpretation of "Mr. Sludge, 'the Medium,'" a study of the psychology of the speaker, as reflected in his defense against the accusations placed against him by the auditor, is essential in understanding the poem; however, contrary to the assertions of the Browning scholars mentioned earlier, a close examination of Mr. Sludge's argument reveals the fact that Sludge is not at all glorious, his case is equally unsympathetic throughout the poem, and the ending is very little more of a give-away than any other part of the poem. Furthermore Sludge's statements concerning the negative nature of the creative imagination are disclosed as simply one more part of a despicable speaker's argument, devised in an ultimate effort to redeem himself in the eyes of the auditor and avoid exposure. They must not be interpreted as sincere questions in Browning's own mind.

The key to interpreting the poem in this manner lies in the analysis of one of Mr. Sludge's major devices throughout his defense. This device may be called the "rule of reverse,"[9] a term which Sludge himself uses to designate the tendency of his followers to call his actions the exact reverse of what they are. Mr. Sludge's use of the rule of reverse is characterized by two distinct processes. First he repeatedly changes or reverses the auditor's image of him through the manipulation of language, especially religious terminology, in order to create the most expedient image for exonerating himself at every opportunity. If it is expedient to appear humble, he describes himself as a penitent; on the other hand, if it is expedient to appear righteous, he describes himself as God. Second he applies the rule of reverse to the field of morality, exactly reversing for himself the standards of morality which he defines for his followers. Both forms of the rule of reverse are used extensively in the "truth" section of the argument, the section at which the medium claims to cast aside his dishonest pose.

Mr. Sludge establishes the basis for his later use of the rule of reverse from the very beginning. At the first of his own strategy, when it is essential that he go to extremes to avoid exposure and secure the auditor's willingness to listen, the medium establishes himself as a humble penitent who will "cheat no more" and asks the auditor to be the "salvation" of his "soul" (ll. 55–64). Thus the speaker professes himself a sinner, makes the auditor God, and begins a supposedly sincere confession; however, since Mr. Sludge has already mentioned exposure five times in the preceding lines and the plea for the auditor to "hold [his] tongue" occurs at the very center of his supposed repentance, it is quite obvious that the salvation about which the medium is concerned is in reality the salvation of his reputation, or material rather than spiritual salvation, and the image created is only a disguise. This is evident a few lines later when Sludge momentarily drops his pretense and calls his argument what it really is, a "self-defence" (l. 74).

Having secured the opportunity to present his case further, Mr. Sludge begins his self-defense with an analogy based on a servant boy exploited to substantiate the master's belief in ghosts (l. 98ff.)—equating himself with David, the servant boy, the auditor with David's master, and the séance "circle" with those gathered to view the master's disguised exploitation of the servant. Again Sludge employs religious terminology, now strategically placed to reverse the false and now unnecessary penitent-God image created earlier. Although he does not refer to himself in explicitly religious terms, the medium manipulates the analogy so that he becomes a Christ figure and those who question his spiritual powers are unbelievers. At one point he classifies a doubter as a "doubting Thomas" (l. 221), thus indirectly associating himself with Christ, who had to prove his identity to the skeptical Thomas following the resurrection (cf. John 20.25). After dispensing with the analogy, Sludge goes even further and associates the "skeptic" with Judas (ll. 357–81). From the wording of his argument, the auditor and reader are led to believe that there are thirteen persons, including the medium, attending the séance (three more than Home himself actually included in the circle).[10] Sludge states that the "faithful" should be applauded and "one man's not quite worth twelve," covertly linking himself with Christ, the circle with the twelve disciples, and the doubter with Judas. Thus the scheming medium establishes an ironic image of himself as a Christ figure through his religious allusions, reversing the pose adopted at the beginning of the "confession." Even though this image is openly undercut by Sludge's admission that there is "real truth" in the doubter's accusation (l. 383) and that he himself is taking the people in (ll. 464–67), he achieves his goal of elevating himself in the subconscious minds of the auditor and reader through the manipulation of language.

During the next phase of Sludge's defense, in order both to condemn the stupidity of those who fall for his claims and to present a "religious" image of himself to the auditor in preparation for the "truth" section which follows, the medium again utilizes religious terminology. The subject of religion is now discussed openly. First Mr. Sludge formulates the image of himself as a missionary who has "laid the atheist sprawling on his back, / And propped Saint Paul up" (ll. 666–68), a claim which Daniel Home did in fact make.[11] The use of comic language such as "laid," "sprawling," and "propped," the reference to Swedenborg, and the acknowledgment that the method of converting these atheists is the use of falsehood (l. 671) should, however, indicate that the medium is not religious in conventional terms. Immediately thereafter, reversing the missionary image and showing the degree to which religious terminology permeates his vocabulary as an argumentative device, the speaker creates another image of himself—a confessed anti-Moses who fools the "simpletons" of society into believing he is leading men of "faith" into the "promised land" when he is actually leading them deeper into the "quagmire" of deception (ll. 694–713; cf. Exodus 33). Perhaps realizing that this presents as unfavorable a picture of himself as of his followers, Sludge constructs a new concept to reverse the undesirable image of himself without altering the disagreeable portrait of his foolish followers. By comparing his treatment by these "fools" to the Athenians' mistreatment of Saint Paul (ll. 732–44), he thus atones for his earlier slip of the tongue and strives to conceal the fact that, contrary to being mistreated himself, he is deliberately mistreating his gullible believers. This is the last of the medium's endeavors in the pre-truth section to disguise his dishonorable exploits through the first form of the rule of reverse and the resulting manipulation of religious terminology. Although these early attempts form only a small segment of the whole argument and are usually conspicuously undercut by the context in which they occur, they serve as subtle preparation for the final stage of the strategy.

The second form of the rule of reverse, the application to the realm of morality, occurs less frequently than the first in the initial portions of "Mr. Sludge, 'the Medium.' " The irony involved requires a contrast of two different standards of morality, that which the speaker dictates for others and that which he defines for himself, and the development of such a contrast naturally takes time. There are, nevertheless, at least two examples which anticipate the more extensive application in the concluding sections of the speaker's defense. The first utilizes an image which occurs several times throughout the poem. Sludge's choice of words in stating that the master's guests "shut [their] eyes," "opened [their] mouth[s]," and "gulped down David whole" with "egg-nogg to lubricate the food" (ll. 212–29) certainly implies condemnation of their actions. Such a profane image of humans gulping down another human being is especially derogatory since it suggests a perversion of the pious act of Holy Communion, in which the communicants reverently close their eyes and open their mouths to receive the body and blood of Christ. Yet the medium notes with pride his own imitation of the cobbler's craft:

> His trade was, throwing thus
> His sense out, like an ant-eater's long tongue,
> Soft, innocent, warm, moist, impassable,
> And when 'twas crusted o'er with creatures—slick,
> Their juice enriched his palate. 'Could not Sludge!'
>   (ll. 539–43)

Thus, from Mr. Sludge's point of view, what is wrong for the guests is right for the "innocent," sneaking medium gathering "smut" (l. 502) to entrap others.

In the "truth" section of Mr. Sludge's strategy (ll. 804–1277), the medium attempts to vindicate himself by uniting both forms of the rule of reverse, the manipulation of religious terminology to make his nature appear the reverse of what it is and the reversal for his own use of the moral standards he sets for others. The union is obvious from the very outset of this segment of the poem, and the ironies resulting from the application of the rule of reverse are actually intensified by the "truth" pose. Since the medium is just as insincere as ever, the argument that his questioning of the integrity of the creative imagination represents Browning's own questioning is indeed tenuous.

The first clue to the strong probability that the truth section is just as much a part of Mr. Sludge's strategy as the earlier arguments is the union of both forms of the rule of reverse in the transition to this portion of the poem. Since the medium has not only shown his dexterity in manipulating New Testament passages for his own use, but has shown his knowledge of the Old Testament as well through the prior allusion to Rahab, the harlot who housed Joshua's spies in Jericho (l. 678; cf. Joshua 6.25), and the comparison of himself with Moses (ll. 694–713), it is not unreasonable to assume that Sludge's Biblical reference in the transition is intentional. Having openly admitted that he has cheated whenever possible, Sludge states that the auditor must believe what is to follow although it "seem to set / The crooked straight again" (ll. 805–806), thereby echoing the words of prophecy concerning the coming of the Messiah spoken by God to Isaiah: "Every valley shall be exalted, and every mountain and hill shall be made low: and the crooked shall be made straight, and the rough places plain" (Isaiah 40.4). Thus the medium, at least in his own mind, subtly connects the argument contrived to reverse the impression that he is a cheat with the truth associated with the Messiah, a rather ironic association since Sludge's "truth" is admittedly truth in the midst of falsehood (l. 1277).

Furthermore the fact that the medium's ironic association of false-hood and truth is also an example of the second form of the rule of re-verse verifies the assumption that this association, like all that has come earlier, is just another guise in Mr. Sludge's attempt to justify his dis-honesty. In his former condemnation of the "simpletons" who have fallen for his "lie" through their own "love of a lie,'" the speaker has criticized their mistaken hypothesis that there "must be some truth, truth though a pinpoint big" in "so many tales" (ll. 694–719). Yet he is saying exactly the same thing about his tales here: "This trade of mine—I don't know, can't be sure / But there was something in it, tricks and all!" (ll. 809–10). The medium seems to be up to his old tricks, adapting for his own use opinions which he had formerly criti-cized in his followers. Surely the further use of this trick renders ques-tionable the "honest" intentions of the supposedly sincere medium and the "truth" section of the poem.

Since every stage of Mr. Sludge's defense has involved manipulation of scriptural passages for his own uses and since the transition into this stage involves similar manipulation, the reader should immediately be suspicious of the medium's repeated avowal that his mediumship is based upon "Bible-truth" (ll. 837, 878, 918). This is especially true since his claim that he was born with this natural gift through God's grace (ll. 860–925) is a direct contradiction of his earlier contentions that his stories concerning the spirit world take whatever form the lis-teners encourage (ll. 272–73), that the spiritualists have ruined his soul by confining him to spiritualism (ll. 390–403), and that his trade both is a "game" (l. 633) and can be learned (ll. 434–50). Even here he admits that *he*, not God, has "sharpened up" his sight for his own "profit" (ll. 960–61). Thus the claim that he is a special agent of God and that his mediumship evolves from spiritual power based upon Bibli-cal justification is merely a pose to disguise the true nature of his con-duct. The claim is undermined throughout the remainder of the poem in the same manner. This is evident in Sludge's description of the "cer-tain turn of mind" required for his abilities, a description which is simi-lar in imagery to one of his earlier applications of the rule of reverse:

> Be lazily alive,
> Open-mouthed, like my friend the ant-eater,
> Letting all nature's loosely-guarded motes
> Settle and, slick, be swallowed! Think yourself
> The one in the world, the one for whom the world
> Was made, expect it tickling at your mouth!
> Then will the swarm of busy buzzing flies,

> Clouds of coincidence, break egg-shell, thrive,
> Breed, multiply, and bring you food enough.
>   (ll. 1058–66)

Through the repetition of the anteater imagery, which already has un-favorable connotations because of its prior association with the rule of reverse, and through the underlying intimation that the medium must be an opportunist and manipulator of coincidence, Mr. Sludge totally undermines his previous declarations of the religious nature of his "su-pernatural" powers. This occurs one more time in the "truth" section of the poem when Sludge again employs the rule of reverse. One of the medium's final acts before explicitly abandoning the subject of truth altogether is that of naming himself the "son and heir / Of the king-dom" (ll. 1157–58), an ironic association with the promise given by God to the poor of the temporal world (James 2.5). The medium has no intentions of being anything but rich in material terms, and his de-scription of his "father's house" (cf. John 14.2) is anything but reli-gious; he wants a nobleman to wait on him and a duke "to hold egg-nogg in readiness" (ll. 1188–92). Thus even in the "truth" section, in which the speaker claims that religion is everything to him (l. 1006), the medium's true nature is clearly nonreligious.

The culmination of Mr. Sludge's argument is the declaration and definition of his *own* philosophy and religion, "Sludgehood" (l. 1428). According to his assertions, he cheats and "all the dry, dead, impracti-cable stuff" of the world "starts into life and light again" (ll. 1395–98). Sludge says, "with good help / Of a little lying," the believers "grow mine, / I veritably possess them—banish doubt, / And reticence and modesty alike" (ll. 1428–30). Mr. Sludge's contention that the author of Sludgehood is "at worst your poet," but "does more than they / And acts the books they write" (ll. 1436–43) is hardly credible in light of the deceitful methods of argumentation which the medium has employed throughout the poem, his pronounced endeavors to elevate himself to hide his dishonesty, and the constant reminders of his true con-temptible nature. Certainly Browning himself was aware of the *poten-tial* misuse of the creative imagination, but Mr. Sludge fails to distin-guish between acceptable use and misuse. Earlier, equating his role with that of an actor, the medium conveniently fails to mention that the actor does not hide the fact that he is playing a role from the public. Through-out the poem the scheming Mr. Sludge makes no distinction between his own dishonesty, the works of the cheap novelists who pretend to be-lieve in spiritualism for the sake of cash, and the work of writers such as Shakespeare and Virgil. While his own role clearly does parallel that of the cheap novelist who exploits a pretended belief for the sake of sensationalism, he does not acknowledge the fact that audiences are aware that the work of an artist such as Shakespeare is a representation of reality, not reality itself. Unlike the worldly speaker of "How It Strikes a Contemporary" who views the poet superficially and thus believes the rumors about the poet's conspiracy and smut-gathering simply because he does not understand the poet's role, the contemptible Sludge *knows* that he is twisting the truth. Coming from the mouth of a speaker whom Browning has portrayed as thoroughly scheming and despicable, the medium's contentions certainly cannot be interpreted as the poet's own distrust of the integrity of the creative imagination.

Thus a close examination of "Mr. Sludge, 'the Medium' " reveals the fact that Mr. Sludge's tactics are the same throughout his defense. Yet although the medium makes extensive use of the rule of reverse in the effort to disguise his culpability, the irony of the images he creates and the manner in which they are constantly undermined expose his true nature at each step of the argument. If there is any glory in the wretched Mr. Sludge, it is his ability to manipulate language, but even that fails to exonerate him. The probable lack of success in deceiving even the auditor is disclosed in the speaker's concluding suspicion that the auditor is inside "sniggering" (l. 1502). The medium's care is never sympathetic, for while he succeeds on the surface in shifting most of the blame to the devotees of spiritualism, he simultaneously manipulates the corresponding images of himself through the rule of reverse and makes himself even guiltier. Ironically targets such as materialism, exploitation of the poor by the rich, and the consumer's lack of artistic discrimination are legitimate targets; however, since Mr. Sludge is so interested in money and material possessions himself, since he enjoys being used by the rich and uses them in turn to become rich himself, and since he, too, shows no artistic discrimination, his arguments are merely parodies of the ideas which Browning himself might have held. The last twenty-six lines of the poem, in which the speaker overtly reverses the events included in the dramatic situation of the poem, makes his former auditor the victim of accusation and himself the accusing medium, and expresses his dishonorable plans to continue his deceitful exploits elsewhere, have been classified as the give-away to the character of the despicable Mr. Sludge. If the theory of the rule of reverse is accepted, however, they are merely another example of the medium's manipulation through the rule of reverse, different perhaps in degree from the earlier examples, but not in kind. Finally, since Mr. Sludge is portrayed as a disgustingly dishonest character at every phase of his defense, it cannot be assumed that the thoughts which are expressed as his own are necessarily indicative of the attitudes or questions of Browning.

NOTES

1 Betty Miller, "The Séance at Ealing—A Study in Memory and Imagination," *The Cornhill Magazine* 169 (1957), 317–24.

2 Jean Burton, *Heyday of a Wizard: Daniel Home, the Medium* (New York: Alfred A. Knopf, 1944), 168.

3 William Lyon Phelps, "Robert Browning on Spiritualism," *The Yale Review* 23 (1934), 136.

4 Burton, 44, 78.

5 *The Infinite Moment and Other Essays in Robert Browning* (Toronto: Univ. of Toronto Press, 1950), 142.

6 *The Poetry of Browning: A Critical Edition* (London: Methuen, 1970), 178–79.

7 William Clyde DeVane, *A Browning Handbook* (New York: Appleton, 1955), 311.

8 "Browning's 'Mr. Sludge, "the Medium," ' " *Victorian Poetry* 2 (1964), 3.

9 Robert Browning, "Mr. Sludge, 'the Medium,' " in *The Complete Works of Robert Browning*, ed. Charlotte Porter and Helen A. Clarke (New York: Crowell, 1898), 234. All further references to this poem will be indicated by line numbers within the body of the paper.

10 Burton, 72.

11 Ibid., 33.

University of Tennessee, Knoxville

BOYD LITZINGER

THE NEW VISION OF JUDGMENT:
THE CASE OF ST. GUIDO

Don't open! Hold me from them! I am yours,
I am the Granduke's—no, I am the Pope's!
Abate,—Cardinal,—Christ,—Maria,—God, . . .
Pompilia, will you let them murder me?
(XI, ll. 2424–27)[1]

These are the last lines spoken by Count Guido Franceschini in *The Ring and the Book*, and, like many other passages in the poetry of Robert Browning, they have been the subject of conflicting interpretations. The central problem is whether these lines are a despairing cry for the convicted murderer's life or a sign that, in calling upon the wife he killed, Guido has seen the light, repents, and therefore will be saved. The most sophisticated (and most nearly satisfactory) argument for the latter position is Robert Langbaum's "Is Guido Saved? The Meaning of Browning's Conclusion to *The Ring and the Book*."[2] Professor Langbaum adduces various kinds of evidence to support his case, but it rests finally upon two interpretations: first that lines 1389–1403 of Book X (in which the Pope sees execution as the only possible means by which Guido may see the light) should be read as an accurate prediction of things to come; and second that Book XI shows Guido coming for the first time to a true understanding of his essential nature in a long speech that would be "superfluous if its only function is to elaborate what is sufficiently established without it—that Guido is utterly evil."[3] I find these interpretations unconvincing.

Let us begin with why Book XI exists, why Browning chose to give Guido a second monologue. No one disputes the fact that in his speech

69

to the court (Book V) Guido lies from beginning to end in an attempt to win acquittal and save his life, nor that in his dungeon on the last day of his life he finally speaks the truth. But I discern two reasons (both quite different from Langbaum's) why Browning makes Guido speak a second time. First we must keep in mind Browning's overall purpose in *The Ring and the Book*: to place the reader in the final seat of judgment. According to this plan, it is necessary that each monologist tell the truth *as he sees it*. Good or vicious, bright or dull, knowledgeable or ignorant, generous or self-serving, each speaker through Book X *with the exception of Guido* has done so. Browning's purpose demands, therefore, that Guido speak again, and at last, to tell the truth as he sees it. Second Browning intends not merely to justify Guido's punishment but also to establish Pompilia's innocence beyond shadow of doubt. Browning knew that his source materials admitted of certain interpretations different from his own. He also knew that witnesses and lawyers have been mistaken and have sometimes lied, that magistrates and popes have erred. Simple conviction and subsequent execution were not enough; for Browning, Guido must confess and clear Pompilia from any shadow of infamy. Judged guilty by the court, condemned by the Pope, Guido must undergo a third damnation—his own—thereby assenting to the justice he has received, utterly exonerating Pompilia, and admitting his unrelieved wickedness.[4]

If, as I believe, these are the reasons for Guido's second monologue, then the argument that Book XI exists as an exercise in self-illumination, culminating in repentance, falls. But there is other evidence in the book as well. Throughout his second monologue Guido asserts, indeed boasts, his wolf-nature. He would not and could not be other than he is, a fact with which he is content. His hatred of Pompilia is so fundamental to his being that, he tells us, he would reject heaven if slippng into it meant remitting his hatred:

> I, who with outlet for escape to heaven,
> Would tarry if such flight allowed my foe
> To raise his head, relieved of that firm foot
> Had pinned him to the fiery pavement else!
> So am I made, 'who did not make myself:'
> (How dared she rob my own lip of the word?)
> Beware me in what other world may be!—
> Pompilia, who have brought me to this pass.
> (XI, ll. 2096–2103)[5]

He blames God, not himself, for his wolf-nature; and Pompilia the lamb, not himself the wolf, for the fate he must suffer for killing her. "Vainly," he tells the Cardinal and the Abate who wish to confess him, "you try to change what should not change, / And shall not" (XI, ll. 2223–24). And how does Guido view death? In a passage which Langbaum calls his noblest utterance,[6] he says,

> You never know what life means till you die:
> Even throughout life, 't is death that makes life live,
> Gives it whatever its significance.
> For see, on your own ground and argument,
> Suppose life had no death to fear, how find
> A possibility of nobleness
> In man, prevented daring any more?
> What's love, what's faith without a worst to dread?
> Lack-lustre jewelry! but faith and love
> With death behind them bidding do or die—
> Put such a foil at back, the sparkle's born!
> From out myself how the strange colours come!
>
> (XI, ll. 2375–86)

This, Langbaum interprets, "In seeing the value of death, and in himself, as death approaches, a strange sparkle, Guido bears out the Pope and shows signs of regeneration."[7] Not only do I see no signs of regeneration here, but I also think these lines must be interpreted in quite another way: on the grounds argued by the Cardinal and Abate (the traditional Christian ones), faith, love, and nobleness shine most brightly against the foil of death; but that same background brings out far different and exotic ("strange") colors in Guido. Baseness, hatred, and unbelief shine the more terribly because Guido persists in them in the face of death.

Guido suspects that even he will not go out of existence upon his death. But does he imagine that he will be essentially different then? Hardly, for if he somehow reaches heaven, it will not be through any change *he* has effected:

> Unmanned, re-manned. I hold it probable—
> With something changeless at the heart of me
> To know me by, some nucleus that's myself:
> Accretions did it wrong? Away with them—
> You soon shall see the use of fire!
>
> (XI, ll, 2393–97)

This fire, according to Langbaum, is a purgatorial one which will burn away all but Guido's essential being "that is, as are all essential selves, justified."[8]

Before commenting on this "justification" upon which Langbaum insists, let us turn briefly to the source of the purgatorial experience imagined—the final passage in Book X, where the Pope expresses a hope that sudden death may bring Guido salvation:

> So may the truth be flashed out by one blow,
> And Guido see, one instant, and be saved.
> Else I avert my face, nor follow him
> Into that sad obscure sequestered state
> Where God unmakes but to remake the soul
> He else made first in vain; which must not be.
> (x, ll. 1397–1402)

According to Langbaum, "This hell is really purgatory, where God remakes the soul. But assignation to even so mild a hell 'must not be'."[9] This is misread. What "must not be" is not assignation to the place of remaking, but is that God made any soul in vain. This is no purgatory (where in the usual sense sinners who have repented must still be purged of the effects of sin), for Guido will go there, according to the Pope, if he does *not* see and thereby is not saved. Instead this is a cosmic repair shop where fundamentally flawed souls must, willy-nilly, be made right.

And this is the point. In the Browning version, neither Guido's repentance nor his illumination is a requirement for the universal salvation which God had planned. In that version, no one can be eternally damned simply because damnation of a single soul would violate a system of spiritual economics which dictates that nothing, not even Guido, shall be wasted.

Guido need not change. God will change him in the next world. Book XI is not a speech in which Guido learns at last to recognize the truth about himself (he always knew it but chose to hide it, hoping that the court would believe the lies he told in Book v); instead, it is an admission to us of his true nature—a vicious wolfishness by which he lives and will die, which he cannot and will not change. His final cry proves the point:

> Abate,—Cardinal,—Christ,—Maria,—God, . . .
> Pompilia, will you let them murder me?
> (xi, ll. 2426–27)

This is a cry for life, not forgiveness. Guido wants to avoid death, not damnation. He calls his fate *murder*, not just punishment, simply because he cannot accept execution as the penalty for being what he is. Therefore I cannot agree with Langbaum that illumination "may be understood as occurring either in the last line . . . or in the instant just after."[10] Guido is not transformed. He remains what he always was and knew himself to be, and this will be no bar to his salvation.

The inescapable conclusion is that Browning's eschatology, unlike Dante's and Milton's, does not include a hell. Despite frequent references to hell, devils, saints, and evil warring against good, there is no place of eternal punishment. Indeed the nineteenth-century reader of Browning might have marked some of the stages by which the poet moved to his conclusion. As early as 1841, he could have the simple Pippa declare that, best and worst, we are "God's puppets." Nevertheless in *Pippa Passes* sinners are driven back from the ultimate consequences of their acts by repenting after they hear Pippa's songs. By 1863 Browning can rescue the three suicides in "Apparent Failure" from the consequences of their despair by calling their sins "atoned" by their deaths—and not because of some last-minute repentance but because God, who cannot make evil, made them and therefore

> . . . what began best, can't end worst,
> Nor what God blessed once, prove accurst.

Still, in this poem we can argue that circumstances extenuate these cases. After all, one suicide was blinded by lust, another by a passion for power, the third by a desire to level classes and to establish equality.

But by saving Guido in *The Ring and the Book*, Browning has taken the final step. What extenuates the case of this Iago-like[11] character? No passion moves him, except the naked hatred he admits holding for goodness, purity, and virtue, to wipe which from his sight he murdered Pompilia. Nothing extenuates here, and Browning still cannot see him damned for the simple reason that in Browning's view all are, and must act, as God made them. The fundamental flaw is somehow of God's making, and a man who, like Guido, acts evilly to the end is ultimately not responsible. God seems to be cast in the role of a watchmaker who now and then makes a faulty watch that cannot keep good time and therefore must be repaired at the maker's cost. And this leads—not simplistically, but rather terribly—back to a sense in which Pippa's "God's in his heaven, / All's right with the world" is, for Browning, true. That God will find a use for the evil in this world—to give the Caponsacchis a chance for heroic conduct, the Pompilias a means to sainthood—is simply another mark of God's economy. To quote Bishop Blougram, "And that's what all the blessed evil's for." It is in this sense, then, that one can agree with Langbaum that Guido's essential self is "justified"; Guido is an obstacle in the path of the virtuous, a blackness against which whiteness can shine. Browning, in fact, emphasized this very point when he answered Julia Wedgwood's complaint that he had placed too much emphasis upon evil in *The Ring and the Book*. To her he wrote, "Last, I hold you wrong even in your praise—that is, wrong in thinking that whatever you count white in Pompilia and Innocent could have come out as clearly without the black."[12]

That no one, including Guido, may be damned is a comforting doctrine, a hope that has persisted in one form or another from the time of Socrates (at least), who argued that the good was so beautiful and attractive that those who do evil can do so only if they cannot recognize the good. In these latter days, evil-doing has been explained in other terms, e.g., by the operation of genetic, environmental, economic, and psychological forces beyond man's control. But for whatever reason— whether, as Henry Jones argued,[13] Browning allowed his heart to rule his head, or his own experience led him to the conclusion—man cannot be held eternally responsible for having chosen evil as his good.

This, of course, raises serious problems about the nature of good and evil (are they apparent or real?) and of the will (is it free or not?), problems leading to dilemmas. For example, if evil men are not responsible for their acts, are good men responsible for theirs? Logic would seem to say that Browning cannot have it both ways. No freely chosen villainy? Then no freely chosen heroism. If Guido acts badly because God made him wrong, do Pope Innocent, Caponsacchi, and Pompilia act well because God made them right? Logically, it would seem, no one deserves either blame or praise. And yet Browning lavishes his praise upon his heroes—his soldier-saints and Perseuses and St. Georges. It would seem that, for Browning, evil is apparent, not real; temporal, not eternal. But if this is so, his men and women are not permitted, ordinarily, to recognize the condition, lest they lose their capacity for moral choice and fail to suffer, strive, and grow. For those who grow, there is heaven. For those who fail, heaven again—but only after the remaking process.

Browning realized the complexities of the matter. In poems written after *The Ring and the Book*—notably in *La Saisiaz*, the *Parleyings* ("Francis Furini" in particular), and *Ferishtah's Fancies*—he manfully attempted to tackle these and other philosophical problems. The results gave rise to a small library of commentary. But in dealing more directly with these questions, Browning lost the interest of those readers (clearly the majority) who prefer to experience moral struggles and principled action through the Andreas, Fra Lippos, Blougrams, and—yes—even the Guidos of his golden world of men and women.

And so Guido has a place in Browning's heaven. But if I imagine that heaven correctly, it will be strictly zoned and segregated. With the timid lovers of "The Statue and the Bust," Guido will be somewhat isolated; he will not share the company of God's chivalry who "Burn upward each to his point of bliss." He will certainly not hobnob there with Pompilia and her rescuer, most assuredly not with Elizabeth Barrett and

Robert Browning. But this heaven will be a place of many mansions, and this world's villains and failures will have theirs (after they have been recycled), perhaps in some ghetto on the wrong side of the celestial tracks, where streets are paved with something less than gold. But in heaven they will be. They will never be damned even though, like Guido, they never repented.

NOTES

1 Citations to *The Ring and the Book* are from Vols. v–vi of the Centenary edition of the *Works*, ed. with introductions by F. G. Kenyon, 10 vols. (London: Smith, Elder and Company, 1912).

2 *Victorian Poetry* 10 (1972), 289–305. This essay elaborates upon the stand Professor Langbaum first took in his well-known article, "*The Ring and the Book*: A Relativist Poem," *PMLA* 71 (1956), 109–36.

3 Langbaum, "Is Guido Saved?," 290.

4 In "The Structural Logic of *The Ring and the Book*," *Nineteenth-Century Literary Perspectives: Essays in Honor of Lionel Stevenson*, ed. Clyde de L. Ryals (Durham: Duke Univ. Press, 1974), 105–14, I have tried to show the place and the relationship of each of the books in Browning's scheme.

5 Browning here has allowed Guido to pervert an heroic image, that of the Archangel Michael keeping the serpent beneath his foot and standing calm "just because he feels it writhe." See "Bishop Blougram's Apology," ll. 667–68.

6 Langbaum, "Is Guido Saved?," 304.

7 Ibid., 304.

8 Ibid., 304.

9 Ibid., 297.

10 Ibid., 305.

11 For some reason commentators often find Guido a shade less villainous than Iago, the difference being, apparently, that Guido is "motivated" by hatred of Pompilia's innocence, whereas Iago's perfidy is said to be "unmotivated." With no intention of entering the Shakespearean lists to maintain that "my dog's blacker than your dog," I shall say that the logic of such assertions escapes me. Perhaps the only real difference between the two scoundrels is that Guido snivels.

12 *Robert Browning and Julia Wedgwood: A Broken Friendship as Revealed by Their Letters*, ed. Richard Curle (New York: Frederick A. Stokes Co., 1939), 176.

13 *Browning as a Philosophical and Religious Teacher* (Glasgow: James Maclehose and Sons, 1891), *passim*. Santayana in "The Poetry of Barbarism" had a crack at Browning the thinker too, but as Kenneth L. Knickerbocker (in "A Tentative Apology for Robert Browning") and Philip Drew (in "Henry Jones on Browning's Optimism") have shown, neither philosopher is unanswerable. In *The Browning Critics* (Lexington: Univ. of Kentucky Press, 1965), Dr. Knickerbocker and I have reprinted a chapter from Jones, together with the essays referred to here.

St. Bonaventure University

EDWARD C. MCALEER

EMPEDOCLES, OMAR KHAYYÁM, AND RABBI BEN EZRA

Critics have long suspected that Matthew Arnold's "Growing Old" (1867) is a reply to Robert Browning's "Rabbi Ben Ezra" (1864), basing their suspicion on the contrasting statements of the two poets: Browning's affirmation that old age is the best time of life and Arnold's affirmation that it is nothing of the sort. Recently Conrad A. Balliet has argued convincingly that the old suspicions are valid, basing his conclusion on a comparison of the metrical patterns of the two poems.[1] My own belief is that Arnold was especially prone to reply to "Rabbi Ben Ezra" because Browning's poem is in itself a reply to Arnold's *Empedocles on Etna* (1852). This belief is based both on the content of the two poems and on a comparison of the metrics of Empedocles' chant (Act I, Scene ii) with the metrics of "Rabbi Ben Ezra." We know well that Browning was fond of replying to his contemporaries in disguises more or less faint.

Arnold's stanza consists of four rhymed iambic trimeters followed by an iambic hexameter (3 / 3 / 3 / 3 / 6). Browning's consists of four rhymed iambic trimeters followed by an iambic hexameter with the disguising addition of a pentameter in line three (3 / 3 / 5 / 3 / 3 / 6). Each poet used his distinctive stanza only once, and even a glance at the two poems on the printed page will reveal a striking resemblance. A. W. Crawford has observed that Arnold's stanza may have suggested Browning's, although Professor Crawford did not go a step further and suggest that the rabbi was indeed replying to Empedocles.[2] Swinburne, in an unpublished parody, used the Empedocles stanza to mock the complacencies of both Tennyson and Browning.[3] Here are samples of the stanzas, with added italics.

Arnold

Hither and thither spins
The wind-borne, mirroring soul,
A thousand glimpses wins,
And *never sees a whole*;
Looks once, and drives elsewhere, and leaves its last employ

Browning

Grow old along with me!
The best is yet to be,
The last of life, for which the first was made:
Our times are in His hand
Who saith "*A whole I planned*,
Youth shows but half; trust God: see all nor be afraid!"

Swinburne

This, when our souls are drowning,
Falls on them like a benison;
This satisfies our Browning
And this delights our Tennyson:
And soothed Britannia simpers in serene applause.

It may be that readers have not hitherto noticed the connection because of the frequent and early association of "Rabbi Ben Ezra" with Edward FitzGerald's *Rubáiyát of Omar Khayyám* (1859)[4] and the opinion of some that Browning was actually replying to FitzGerald.[5] Such association is almost inevitable when one considers the strikingly different use each poet makes of the metaphor of the potter's wheel. To Omar the pots are being fashioned from clay that once composed the bodies of living men. To Rabbi Ben Ezra the spinning potter's wheel (the troubled life of man on earth) is machinery designed to shape the cup (man's soul) for the Master's use in heaven.

Whether Browning had encountered this metaphor in the *Rubáiyát*, he had previously encountered it in a dozen places, several of which are listed by W. C. DeVane,[6] although unlisted is what I think to be the precise source of Browning's conception of the figure—Book III, Chapter xi, of Carlyle's *Past and Present*, a presentation copy of which Browning owned.[7] Browning's conception is the same as that of Carlyle before him.

Hast thou looked on the Potter's wheel,—one of the venerablest objects; old as the Prophet Ezechiel [meaning Isaiah] and far older? Rude lumps of clay, how they spin themselves up, by mere quick whirling, into beautiful circular dishes. And fancy the most assiduous Potter, but without his wheel; reduced to make dishes, or rather amorphous botches, by mere kneading and baking! Even such a Potter were Destiny, with a human soul that would rest and lie at ease, that would not work and spin! Of an idle unrevolving man the kindest Destiny, like the most assiduous Potter without wheel, can bake and knead nothing other than a botch. . . .

Rabbi Ben Ezra's confident statement of optimistic faith is indeed antithetical to the courtly hedonism of Omar, as it is to all hedonistic poetry ever written. But we might also say that parts of *Empedocles* constituted a reply to Omar seven years before the *Rubáiyát* was published.[8] The stanza form that Browning chose is quite unlike Fitz-Gerald's, superb as each is for its own purpose; and there are few, if any, verbal echoes.

There has been found no external evidence to indicate that Browning knew the *Rubáiyát* by 1864. The poem was printed in an anonymous little pamphlet that did not sell, gained no public recognition for ten years, and remained publicly anonymous for seventeen. In 1861 a copy came into the hands of D. G. Rossetti, who, immediately enthusiastic, introduced the poem to his friends: Professor DeVane suggests plausibly that Rossetti may have shown Browning a copy when Browning called on him in 1862.[9] (We may not dismiss the possibility that "Rabbi Ben Ezra" had been written before that call, for Browning told Isa Blagden that most of the poems in his 1864 volume had been "written a long time ago" and some seen by his wife, who died in 1861.)[10] Years later, when the cult of Omar was sweeping England and the Continent, Browning did reply. He wrote to George Smith, his publisher, requesting the works of Omar Khayyám,[11] and later published *Ferishtah's Fancies* (1884), in which he used Hebrew quotations "as a direct acknowledgement that certain doctrines may be found in the Old Book which the Concocters of Novel Schemes of Morality put forth as discoveries of their own."[12] Five months before his death he exploded "To Edward FitzGerald" in the *Athenaeum* (July 13, 1889) and, in the stormy aftermath, told his son that he had never heard FitzGerald's name until "a few years ago."[13] Also in the aftermath, he misquoted from memory two lines of FitzGerald's *Rubáiyát*.[14] Certainly Browning knew Omar in the 1880's, but the question remains: Did he when he composed "Rabbi Ben Ezra"?

There is no doubt, on the other hand, that Browning knew *Empedocles*. He owned a copy of the first edition;[15] he referred to the poem several times after 1862 in his letters to Isa Blagden;[16] and it was at his request that Arnold reinstated *Empedocles*[17] in his *New Poems*, the volume that contained "Growing Old." Arnold sent Browning a presentation copy.[18]

In his long, meaty chant in Act I, Scene ii, Empedocles instructs his disciple Pausanius how to deal with the problems that beset Arnold himself. Chief among these problems are first that youth passes, the body decays, pleasures disappear, and hope is lost. (Arnold felt old at thirty.)[19] Second, the age is one of estrangement, disunity, and fragmentation, making it impossible to see life whole. ("I am fragments," Arnold wrote to his sister.)[20] Third, doubt and fear have supplanted the old faith. (Doubt has been called the cornerstone of Arnold's meditative verse.)[21] Rabbi Ben Ezra meets with each of these problems squarely and says, "Wait death!" Empedocles, unable to accept his own advice to Pausanius, plunges into the crater of Etna.

In order to demonstrate the philosophical antitheses between the two poems, my procedure now is to paraphrase Empedocles' chant and to quote significant lines from each passage paraphrased. By way of rebuttal, I follow the same procedure with "Rabbi Ben Ezra," underlining verbal resemblances, while emphasizing that verbal echoes are not requisite for a rebuttal.

Empedocles	Rabbi Ben Ezra

(1)

Man's soul is like a mirror hanging on a cord and spinning in the wind, catching a thousand glimpses but never seeing a whole. (I, 77–86)	Although youth does not see the whole, God planned a whole. Trust God, and you will see all. (1–6)
The wind-born mirroring soul, A thousand glimpses wins, And *never sees a whole*. (83–85)	"*A whole I planned*; Youth shows but half; trust God: *see all*." (5–6)
That man, Howbeit, I judge as lost, Whose mind allows a *plan*, Which would degrade it most. (97–100)	"Perfect I call *Thy plan*: "Thanks that I was a man!" (58–59)
"*You* [the gods] *only* can take in *The world's immense design*." (342–43)	"Praise be Thine! "*I see the whole design*." (54–55)

(2)

Seeing nothing clear, man doubts and fears, causing the gods to laugh at him. (87–91)	I do not object to the hopes and fears of youth; and I welcome the doubt which distinguishes man from the beast. (13–19)

The gods laugh in their sleeve
To watch man *doubt and fear.*
                            (87–88)

Not for such hopes and *fears*
Annulling youth's brief years,
Do I remonstrate . . .
Rather *I prize the doubt*
Low kinds exist without.   (13–17)

(3)

Man's soul is inharmoniously shaken;
his fellow men envy and oppress him;
heaven and earth are at strife; man
feels the burden of himself.   (112–31)

Man should turn the strife of life to
advantage and welcome each rebuff
that forces him to strive.   (31–36)

Thou feelest thy soul's frame
Shaken and rudely hurl'd.
What? life and time go hard with thee
    too, as with us.   (114–16)

Then, welcome each rebuff
That turns earth's smoothness rough,
Each sting that bids nor sit nor stand
    but go!   (31–33)

(4)

The various philosophers attempt to
solve the problems of life by preaching
conflicting doctrines, each according
to his school.   (132–41)

True, there are conflicting opinions.
Other men do not like what I like or
believe. But who shall arbitrate?
                            (127–32)

The sophist sneers: Fool, take
Thy pleasure, right or wrong!
The pious wail: Forsake
A world these sophists throng!
                    (132–35)

Thou, to whom fools propound,
When the wine makes its round,
"Since life fleets . . . seize today!"
Fool!   (154–57)

These hundred doctors try
To preach thee to their school.
We have the truth! they cry,
And yet their oracle,
Trumpet it as they will, is but the same
    as thine.   (137–41)

Now, who shall arbitrate?
Ten men love what I hate,
Shun what I follow, slight what I
    receive;
Ten, who in ears and eyes
Match me. We all surmise,
They this thing, and I that; whom shall
    my soul believe?   (127–32)

(5)

The solution is to "Be neither saint nor
sophist-led, but be a man!"   (136)

It is precisely because I am a man and
not beast that I have to endure the
evils of which you complain. Is the
crop-full bird irked by care?   (24)

(6)

Even when a man leads a virtuous life,
he is not relieved of conflict. The forces
of nature and the ill deeds of other men
make his life dark.   (242–66)

It would be well if man had something
to match the possessions of the brute:
but "we do not get pleasure in proportion to the moral effort which we
make." 22

Yet, even when man forsakes
All sin,—is just, is pure,
Abandons all that makes
His welfare insecure,—
Other existences there are, that clash
    with ours.   (242–46)

Would we some prize might hold
To match those manifold
Possessions of the brute,—gain most
    as we did best!   (64–66)

(7)

In an attempt to solve the problems of life, we turn in vain to science, to history, and to philosophy—to the words and works of dead men.   (316–36)

I believe that the Past has much to offer us. Were not eyes, ears, and brain given us so that we may learn?
    (49–54)

We scrutinize the dates
Of long-*past* human things,
The bounds of effaced states,
The lines of deceased kings;
We search out dead men's words,
    and works of dead men's hands.
    (322–26)

Yet gifts should prove their use:
I own the *Past* profuse
Of power each side, perfection every
    turn;
Eyes, ears took in their dole,
Brain treasured up the whole;
Should not the heart beat once
"How good to live and learn?"
    (49–54)

(8)

In our youth we think that we have the right to the pleasure we desire, but our youth is soon spent and the world fails to impart its promised joy.
    (351–86)

I do not object to the fact that youth seeks pleasure. I do not deny that the body decays and pleasures decrease. But life would not have much to boast of if it consisted solely of joy.
    (7–24)

Pleasure to our hot grasp
Gives flowers after flowers.
With passionate warmth we clasp
Hand after hand in ours;
Nor do we soon perceive how fast our
    youth is spent.   (357–61)

Not that, amassing flowers,
Youth sighed, "Which rose make ours,
Which lily leave and then as best
    recall?" . . .
Not for such hopes and fears
Annulling youth's brief years
Do I remonstrate.   (7–15)

"The world hath fail'd to impart
The *joy* our youth forebodes."
    (374–75)

Poor vaunt of life indeed,
Were man but formed to feed
On *joy*.   (19–21)

Be our *joys* three-parts pain!   (34)

(9)

Even when we see our youth soon spent and our senses decay, we retain the joy-hunger of our youth and our hearts become discontented.   (351–86)

Man should not look back on the lost vigor of his youth, but forward to the joy of immortality. How far can the undecayed body (the "body at its best") project the soul on its lone flight to the Master?   (169–80)

At once our eyes grow clear!
We see, in blank dismay,
Year posting after year,
Sense after sense decay;
Our shivering heart is mined by secret
    discontent.   (362–66)

Our hair grows grey, our eyes are
    dimm'd, our heart is tamed.
                (336)

What though the earlier grooves
Which ran the laughing loves
Around thy base, no longer pause and
    press?
What though, about thy rim,
Skull-things in order grim
Grow out, in graver mood, obey the
    sterner stress?

Look not thou down but up!
To uses of a cup.   (169–76)

(10)

Our bodies, blood, heat, and breath
will return to the elements. But what
will become of the master part, the
mind?   (II, 331–38)

To the elements it came from
Everything will return—
Our bodies to earth,
Our blood to water,
Heat to fire,
Breath to air . . .
But *mind*?   (331–38)

Whatever is at all lasts forever.
Your soul and God endure.
                (157–62)

Fool! All that is, at all,
Lasts ever, past recall;
Earth changes, but *thy soul* and God
    stand sure:
What entered into thee,
That was, is, and shall be . . .
Potter and clay endure.   (157–62)

(11)

When we unwillingly return to earth
reincarnated we shall be the slave of
either flesh or mind.   (364–75)

Or whether we will once more fall
    away
Into some *bondage of the flesh or
    mind*,
Some slough of sense.   (373–75)

Rather, the flesh can help the soul as
much as the soul can help the flesh.
                (67–72)

Let us cry "all good things
"Are ours, nor *soul helps flesh* more,
now than *flesh helps soul*."   (71–72)

(12)

Even in the reincarnated existence we
shall fret and find our efforts fail.
                (373–88)

And each succeeding age in which we
    are born
Will *fret our minds* to an intenser
    play . . . .

And we shall fly for refuge to
    past times . . .

The success of life lies in its apparent
failure. (39–42). Although the world
judges a man by his achievement, his
real worth lies in his aspiration.
                (133–50)

Frets doubt the maw-crammed beast?
                (24)

I own the *Past* profuse . . .   (50)

And we shall feel our powers of
    effort flag,
And rally them for one last fight—
    and fail.   (373–88)

Shall life succeed in that it *seems to
    fail?*   (39)

Browning, then, has met all of Arnold's points and has decisively affirmed the contrary. Just as decisively, "Growing Old" refutes Rabbi Ben Ezra's main point and constitutes a reaffirmation of the youth-age theme of *Empedocles.* The debate continued, quite obviously in Browning's *Agamemnon* (1877) and "Parleying with Gerard de Lairesse" (1887), and subtly elsewhere. In Chapter I of *Culture and Anarchy* (1869) Arnold says, "Culture . . . remembers the text: 'Be not ye called Rabbi!' and it soon passes on from any Rabbi." Conscious of the debate, a wag might be tempted to supply "Ben Ezra" in brackets. Later on, in the Preface to *Agamemnon,* Browning quotes Salmasius' derisive statement about "Hebraisms, Syriasms, Hellenisms, and the whole lot of such bag and baggage." One thinks of Arnold's "Hebraism and Hellenism," another chapter of *Culture and Anarchy.* The same preface to *Agamemnon,* for other reasons, led W. C. DeVane to say of Browning, "Certainly . . . he became more interested in providing an answer to Matthew Arnold than in anything else."[23]

There is one further bit of newspaper gossip. The report was that when the two poets once met in an art gallery Browning turned his back on Arnold because of something that Arnold had said about Browning's poetry, "perhaps *Prince Hohenstiel-Schwangau*" (1871), but before leaving, the two poets chatted "with some cordiality."[24]

NOTES

[1] " 'Growing Old' Along with 'Rabbi Ben Ezra,' " *Victorian Poetry* 1 (Nov. 1963), 300–301.

[2] "Browning's 'Cleon,' " *JEGP* 26 (1927), 485–90.

[3] Georges Lafourcade, *La Jeunesse de Swinburne, 1837–1867* (London: Oxford Univ. Press, 1928), II, 163.

[4] Lafcadio Hearn, *Interpretations of Literature* (New York: Dodd, Mead, 1916), I, 361. (Hearn's lectures were delivered between 1896 and 1902.) E. L. Cary, *Browning* (New York: Putnam's, 1899), 126–131; and many other writers.

[5] W. L. Phelps, *Robert Browning* (Indianapolis: Bobbs-Merrill, 1915), 342. W. C. DeVane follows Phelps in *A Browning Handbook* (New York: Appleton, 1955), 295.

[6] *Handbook,* 293. S. Viswanthian observes that Browning had made similar use of the metaphor five or six years before the publication of FitzGerald's *Rubáiyát.* (" 'Ay, Note That Potter's Wheel,': Browning and 'That Metaphor,' " *Victorian Poetry* 7 (Winter 1969), 349–52.

[7] Sotheby catalogue, *The Browning Collections* (London: Dryden Press, 1913), 86.

[8] E. g., "The sophist sneers: Fool, take / Thy pleasure, right or wrong."

[9] *Handbook,* 293.

10 *Dearest Isa: Robert Browning's Letters to Isabella Blagden*, ed. E. C. McAleer (Austin: Univ. of Texas Press, 1951), 212.

11 Unpublished letter in British Museum.

12 *Learned Lady: Letters from Robert Browning to Mrs. Thomas FitzGerald*, ed. E. C. McAleer (Cambridge, Mass.: Harvard Univ. Press, 1966), viii.

13 *Letters of Robert Browning*, ed. T. L. Hood (London: John Murray, 1933), 311.

14 *Letters of the Brownings to George Barrett*, ed. Paul Landis and R. E. Freeman (Urbana: Univ. of Illinois Press, 1958), 331.

15 Sotheby, 71.

16 *Dearest Isa, passim.*

17 Browning's request may have been influenced by pleasure at recognition of structural echoes of his *Paracelsus* in Arnold's poem.

18 Sotheby, 71.

19 *Letters of Matthew Arnold to Arthur Hugh Clough*, ed. H. F. Lowry (London: Oxford Univ. Press, 1932), 128.

20 W. E. Houghton and G. Robert Stange, *Victorian Poetry and Poetics* (Boston: Houghton, 1959), 547.

21 S. C. Chew and R. D. Altick, *A Literary History of England* (New York: Appleton, 1967), IV, 1410.

22 Lafcadio Hearn's interpretation, I, 355.

23 *Handbook*, 419.

24 On page 27 of a black "Clipping Book" kept by Mrs. Thomas FitzGerald and now in the possession of her granddaughter, Miss Mabel Purefoy FitzGerald of Oxford.

Hunter College of the City University of New York

MICHAEL E. GREENE

ROSSETTI'S "ABSURD TRASH":
"SIR HUGH THE HERON" RECONSIDERED

Dante Gabriel Rossetti did not do a great deal of writing during his childhood and early adolescence, and what he did do, he thought worthless in retrospect. Of the juvenilia, only "Sir Hugh the Heron: A Legendary Tale in Four Parts" was published during Rossetti's lifetime. Rossetti had written it when he was twelve, in 1840 or 1841, and he completed it in 1843 only because his grandfather promised him publication at his private printing press. Rossetti was later embarrassed by the poem and afraid that someone might republish it as a work which had the stamp of his mature approval. "There is no knowing," he wrote in 1881, "what fool may some day foist the absurd trash into print as a production of mine. It is curious and even surprising to myself, as evincing absolutely no promise at all—less than should exist even at twelve. When I wrote it, the *only* English poet I had read was Sir W. Scott, as is plain enough in it."[1] William Michael Rossetti concurs and calls it a "puerile attempt," although "not wholly destitute of spirit in its boyish way."[2]

In the light of Rossetti's statement (and of the poem's undeniable puerility), it is hardly surprising that nobody has had the temerity to republish "Sir Hugh." It has received little attention from critics, consequently—a paragraph in R. D. Waller's *The Rossetti Family 1824–1854*, brief consideration from Robert Cooper in *Lost on Both Sides: Dante Gabriel Rossetti: Critic and Poet*, and only passing mention from other critics.[3] Despite its faults, however, the poem does merit some attention for its indication that the lines of Rossetti's later interests were drawn well before his first work of real merit was written.

"Sir Hugh the Heron" has childish faults—and childish charm. The

85

plot of "Sir Hugh" is primitive, certainly. Sir Hugh rescues a maiden, Beatrice, from pirates; he then leaves her in the hands of his cousin, Sir Aymer, while he goes off to the wars in France. While abroad, Sir Hugh learns through magic that Sir Aymer plans to rape his beloved and returns just in time to kill the villain. The poem's versification is oversimple, the poetic vocabulary is of no great variety or range, and the syntax is often strained and awkward. The purpose of this essay is not, however, to demonstrate that "Sir Hugh" is worthy of serious attention for any intrinsic literary merit: Rossetti's brother is correct in saying that the tale does not show "any express faculty or superior promise."[4] The poem is, however, surprisingly prefigurative of Rossetti's mature style and subject matter, more so than is the juvenile work of most other writers.

Some of the ways in which the poem represents a primitive and apprentice version of Rossetti's later techniques are too clear to require close attention. For example, in the following stanza, Rossetti anticipates his later work:

'What sounds invade my startled ear,
    Borne on the midnight wind?
It is the clang of arms I hear:
    Now shield me, Virgin kind!'
                                (I, st. 9)

The ballad techniques that appeal to Rossetti here—the simple rhythm and rhyme scheme, the question, the invocation of the Virgin—are all exploited in later poems like "Sister Helen" and "Stratton Water." Rossetti's fascination with romance and the ballad is primarily responsible for the self-conscious efforts to make the poem archaic; and his later love of what he called "stunning words" is anticipated in "cumbrous targe," "blithesome mood," "fortalice," "tusky boar," and "dight."[5]

"Sir Hugh the Heron" anticipates Rossetti's later poetry in other ways which are more significant because they show how early some of the modes of perceiving and describing that were to be peculiar to him were formed. For example, Rossetti's lifelong specificity of pictorial and decorative imagery is anticipated in this description of Sir Hugh's attire:

And o'er his burnished hood of mail,
    With pearls encircled round,
The heron plume was seen to trail
    And fall upon the ground.
                                (I, st. 5)

Rossetti refuses, however, to give any description of individualizing physical features. In his later work Rossetti utilizes concrete imagery in conjunction with unspecific settings in exactly the same way, with the result that the reader is unsure whether the poetry is more characterized by concreteness or abstraction. Rossetti's later ability to make specific details define the tone, effect, and drama of a particular situation is also anticipated in "Sir Hugh." In isolated passages Rossetti occasionally attempts to give immediacy to the action by focusing on a single image rather than on the larger panorama of the scene. In one of the battle descriptions, for example, he describes "the soldier's start at the sound of the dart, / As it whistled past his head"—a primitive effort, but nevertheless suggestive of his later technique.

Some of the ambivalences which are operative in Rossetti's later poetry can perhaps be understood as arising from an inability to move beyond a way of perceiving that was already present at age twelve. Signs of Rossetti's later inability to distinguish clearly between the spiritual and the nonspiritual are to be found in "Sir Hugh." For example, at the beginning of the poem, there is a close association between the religious and the secular. Religion is used, as it often is in Rossetti's later poetry, simply to set the scene; it also introduces the hero in a favorable light:

> From yonder chapel on the shore
>   What sounds rise on the air?
> The blessed Virgin they implore;
>   It is the sound of prayer.
> Within there dwelt a gallant knight,
>   And many a vassal bold;
> The baron's armour glittered bright
>   With steel and ruddy gold.
>   (I, sts. 3, 4)

Even as a boy Rossetti delights in contrasting the spiritual and the secular, the saintly and the profane. Although the opening scene offers the reader bloodthirsty pirates creeping up on the chapel, a little later, "the shrieks of the flying" pirates are juxtaposed with "the prayers of the dying."

In Rossetti's later poetry, tension and excitement are frequently produced by the fact that his heroines ambiguously represent both the sacred and the profane. Even so pure a heroine as the lady of "The Staff and Scrip," helpless and threatened by the marauders who killed her father, longs for physical reunion in heaven with the knight who is killed in her defense. A more obvious example of Rossetti's ambivalence in this regard is the Blessed Damozel, incompletely desexualized, virginal but succulent. Rossetti's treatment of the heroine of "Sir Hugh" suggests how little his vision of woman changed throughout his life. It is appropriate that the pure Rossetti heroine should make her debut as

the captive of pirates. When Beatrice makes her first appearance (after
Sir Hugh has killed the pirates), the hero wonders:

> Is it th' illusion of a dream,
>   Or weakness of his sight?
> When from the vessel there doth seem
>   To rise a lady bright.
>
> (I, st. 26)

The "lady bright" (she is addressed as "Lady," and all the ladies in the
poem are "bright") is vulnerable but almost untouchable, and when
she appears on the scene, she seems to Sir Hugh to possess wonderful
magical power and is associated with illusion. She suggests many of
Rossetti's later heroines, mysterious and sacred; and her illusory quality
is possessed by later figures like "Soul's Beauty," who flies ahead of the
hopeless pursuer. In Part IV, Beatrice (the name was suggested as the
type of feminine virtue by Rossetti's father's studies in Dante, as Rossetti himself did not read Dante until he was sixteen),[6] believing that
Sir Hugh may be dead, "felt a sickness at the heart, and a longing after
death." She is cheered by thoughts of a reunion with Sir Hugh in heaven,
and, like her later relative, the Blessed Damozel,

> She prayed that still she might pursue the straight and narrow path,
> Though fallen was her only friend, and desolate her hearth;
> And that she might be brought to *him*, and might with him be blest,
> 'Where the wicked cease from troubling, and the weary are at rest.'
>
> (IV, st. 4)

The similarity to the Blessed Damozel's wish is obvious:

> 'There will I ask of Christ the Lord
>   Thus much for him and me,—
> Only to live as once on earth
>   With Love,—only to be,
> As then awhile, for ever now
>   Together, I and he.'
>
> (ll. 127–32)

The notion of the reunion of earthly lovers in heaven existed in Rossetti's mind well before he wrote "The Blessed Damozel" or "The Staff
and Scrip"; the ideal embodied in it, that of spirit transcending bodily
obstacles, originates in Rossetti's childhood, in the melodrama and excitement surrounding his Beatrice.

Rossetti's idealism, which sometimes leads him to the version of
heaven represented in "The Blessed Damozel" and "The One Hope,"
is not far removed from superstition. He was inordinately superstitious
throughout his life, and he frequently attempts to invest his poetry with
an aura of mystery, sometimes vaguely Christian, sometimes suggestive

of black magic.[7] While Sir Hugh is away, for instance, a minstrel (apparently sent by the devious Sir Aymer) comes to Beatrice to tell how he had issued a warning to Sir Hugh, who supposedly ignored the warning and died as a consequence. The "wild unearthly warning," as R. D. Waller notes—[8]

> Then turn back, ere yet too late:
> Tempt not, rashly bold, thy fate;
> Dread the spell and dread the tomb,
> Warrior of the Heron Plume.
> (II, st. 33)

—anticipates in spirit the warning issued by the old hag to James I of Scotland in "The King's Tragedy," written forty years later:

> 'O King, whom poor men bless for their King,
>   Of thy fate be not so fain;
> But these my words for God's message take,
> And turn thy steed, O King, for her sake
>   Who rides beside thy rein!
> (ll. 196–200)

The most interesting section of the poem is Part III, where, through magic, Sir Hugh learns of the evil designs of Sir Aymer upon Beatrice's virtue. The scene opens in a magician's laboratory on an eerie night:

> 'Tis the time when on the earth
> Oft malignant fiends alight,
> Revelling in demon mirth;
> 'Tis the dread Walpurgis night.
> (III, st. 2)

Sir Hugh enters and demands that the magician show him a vision of Beatrice.[9] In this section Rossetti attempts in several stanzas to create an aura of murky terror; and although he is only marginally successful, he does manage to give the section an intensity that is not unpromising, one which suggests the kind of imaginative morbidity later responsible for the nightmarish darkness of parts of *The House of Life* ("Sleepless Dreams," "Vain Virtues," or "A Superscription," for example).

Much of Rossetti's early reading (despite his disclaimer, he did read writers other than "Sir W. Scott") was of material that any bright, imaginative child might have found attractive; what is unusual is the singleness of direction. "The times of chivalry always furnished his boyish inspiration," says Rossetti's brother; "in fact, he thought of little else about this date" [aet. 12].[10] His reading horizons did later expand. At sixteen he seized upon Dante and the early Italian poets, and a little later was enthusiastic about Malory, Shelley, Keats, Browning, and others.[11] In any case, the tendency toward singleness of interest that his brother notes persisted not over a year or so but throughout his formative years, and to a surprising degree even throughout his life. Up until the time when he wrote "The Blessed Damozel" and "My Sister's Sleep," he read chiefly imaginative literature, and within literature his undisciplined tastes led him only toward the romantic and exotic.

Rossetti's reading reinforced his natural inclinations, and he thus became defined by the fantasy world in which his boyish imagination lived to such an extent that, as here demonstrated, we can find the preoccupations of the adult even in his earliest writings. Rossetti's later poetry exploits the same materials, those which frequently deal in excitement and glamor and refuse to have serious implications or philosophical import or timely significance. "Sir Hugh" emphasizes sentimentally the perceptions and emotions of its main characters much as Rossetti's later poetry does. He yearned throughout his life for a childish land of romance, and the heaven envisaged in poems like "The Blessed Damozel" reflects his poignantly childish dreams. In later work like *The House of Life*, Rossetti would imagine himself pursuing a fleeting, mocking shadow, but that ideal, that shadow, was basically the same as in his childhood, only an ideal given a darker, pathetic tinge by the refusal of experience and the adult world to grant the fulfillment he desired.

One of the vital facts demonstrated by "Sir Hugh the Heron" is that Rossetti's sensibility was already formed by the time of his association with the Pre-Raphaelite Brotherhood. The "patient naturalism" and "flight from actuality into archaic romance" which Graham Hough identifies as defining features of Pre-Raphaelitism were present in Rossetti's juvenilia.[12] The Pre-Raphaelite experience simply reinforced tendencies which were already present, and gave Rossetti a justification for his predispositions.

Any author's first efforts have some bearing upon his future development. In Rossetti's case, however, the degree to which the later work recalls the earlier is startling and generally unrecognized. Rossetti's later work reflects a mind which received its greatest impress and lasting shape at a much earlier age than was the case with many other poets. In Rossetti's case the child was truly father of the man. One reason why Rossetti was so little interested in the march of mind and the course of history was that in a sense he hardly progressed past the concern with exciting stories, sharply etched polarities, and vague idealism that is so refreshingly but crudely obvious in "Sir Hugh the Heron." His fascination with the ideals that found expression in his adolescent work was also responsible to some extent for the unhappiness of his life, which was a continuing search to realize the ideal in the actual and to find a "lady bright" on earth. His accomplishment in any case was not necessarily less because of the narrowness of his background, but any attempt to define him must take into account the fact that his mental and emotional powers were not, and could not be, broadly responsive to the same forces that shaped the poetry of Tennyson, Browning, or Arnold.

NOTES

[1] W. M. Rossetti, ed., *The Works of Dante Gabriel Rossetti* (London: Ellis, 1911), 643, hereafter cited as *Works*.

[2] W. M. Rossetti, *Dante Gabriel Rossetti: His Family Letters, with a Memoir* (London: Ellis & Elvey, 1895), I, 84, hereafter cited as *Memoir*.

[3] See Waller (Manchester: Manchester Univ. Press, 1932), 189–91, and Cooper (Athens: Ohio Univ. Press, 1970), 21–22.

[4] *Memoir*, I, 84.

[5] In "Rossetti's 'William and Marie': Hints of the Future," Benjamin F. Fisher IV prints for the first time the text of another early poem and suggests its usefulness for an understanding of Rossetti's later Gothicism and exploitation of ballad conventions; see *English Language Notes* 9 (1971), 121–29.

[6] *Works*, xiv–xv; *Memoir*, I, 63–64, 102.

[7] The evocative power that the supernatural possesses for Rossetti is suggested by all his juvenile work. For example, in "William and Marie," the same impulse is obviously at work when Sir Richard, a "recreant knight" with a "bloodie sword," is struck down by a bolt of lightning from heaven after he murders both William and Marie.

[8] Waller, 190.

[9] Rossetti's interest in necromancy, and particularly "scrying," is also exploited in "Rose Mary" (1871), where a vision is shown in a crystal. In "Sir Hugh" the vision appears in a mirror, but the situation is basically the same. Rossetti certainly had the earlier poem in mind when he wrote "Rose Mary": as C. K. Hyder notes, the name of Rose Mary's lover, Sir James of Heronhaye, is simply a modification of Sir Hugh the Heron. See Hyder, "Rossetti's *Rose Mary*: A Study in the Occult," *Victorian Poetry* 1 (1963), 199–200.

[10] *Memoir*, I, 106.

[11] See A. M. Turner, "Rossetti's Reading and His Critical Opinions," *PMLA* 42 (1927), 465–91.

[12] *The Last Romantics* (1949; rpt. New York: Barnes & Noble, 1961), 40.

North Carolina A & T State University

ANNA S. PARRILL

PORTRAITS OF LADIES

Although notable exceptions exist, such as Richardson, Flaubert, and Tolstoy, it is essentially true that male novelists feel more at home creating male protagonists than female ones. Male novelists prefer to draw women in supporting roles, where the primary interest lies in how the male protagonist reacts to a female stereotype—wife, mother, lover. This situation may be a result of their ignorance of the nature of the female, or a lack of interest in or respect for the sex. Whatever the reason, it apparently does not apply to two great novelists of the nineteenth century, Henry James and George Meredith, who made women the protagonists of many novels and stories, and created credible, three-dimensional women characters. These two men, contemporaries and friendly acquaintances, admired women for qualities of mind and body, found them different but not inferior to men, and recognized the frustrations and limitations which they faced on every side in their social milieu. Expressing essentially the same ideas about women, ideas foreign or distasteful to most of their contemporaries, they were unique in their day for insight into the nature of women, their strengths, their possibilities, and their repression.

Two novels by these authors serve well to illustrate their very similar perceptions of the sensitive woman's qualities and frustrations. *The Portrait of a Lady* and *The Egoist* were published within a year of each other. Meredith was working on his novel through the year 1878, finished it in February 1879, and saw it appearing serially and in book form in November 1879. James began *The Portrait* in the spring of 1880. He says in his *Notebook I* that he "took up, and worked over, an old beginning, made long before."[1] The novel began appearing

92

serially in *Macmillan's Magazine* in October 1880, and was published in book form in 1881.

Whether Meredith's novel influenced James's conception of his novel is a question without a sure answer. James read and admired Meredith's work, but since they did not meet until 1886 and probably did not correspond before then, they could not have discussed the subject matter of these novels. Isabel Archer of *The Portrait* is surely (after Daisy Miller) the logical next step in James's development of the independent American girl. Clara, in *The Egoist,* however, represents a departure from the soft and yielding heroines of Meredith's previous novels. Lionel Stevenson calls *The Egoist* a "new stage" in Meredith's thinking about the relationship between the sexes.[2]

James and Meredith developed in the characters of Isabel Archer and Clara Middleton admirable and even heroic women. The omniscient narrators in both novels reveal them as not without flaws, but as basically good and intelligent, and contrast them favorably with other female and male characters. They are "heroines," but heroines who do not require heroes. We see them in a social context, in conflict with or in other relationships with men, but they appear as persons exercising their individual wills within their social situations.

Isabel and Clara share certain traits which both James and Meredith apparently deemed admirable in a woman. Both women have intelligence, but it is clearly described as an intuitive perception, a sensitivity, as opposed to a logical, bookish intelligence. Although Isabel and Clara have been reared by their fathers, and thus have been exposed to masculine mental processes, neither is really attracted to logic and to learning. Isabel has among her friends a greater reputation for reading than she deserves, and Clara is obviously capable of, but little interested in, scholarship. Yet both are alert, open-minded about the world, eager to take in new impressions—characteristics totally absent in most of the men in their lives. Early in the novel Ralph Touchett observes how Isabel's "flexible figure turned itself easily this way and that, in sympathy with the alertness with which she evidently caught impressions."[3] It is her receptiveness, her capability of experiencing and enjoying life which so interest Ralph, who is prohibited by temperament and physical disability from enjoying life himself. Clara is also a growing and developing young woman. Her father may blame her for her woman's "mutability," but her realization that marrying Willoughby would be intolerable is a part of her growth in perception. She realizes that she had not seen the whole man during the early stages of their courtship, but even then she had been reluctant to engage herself to him. Since all the world assures her that Willoughby is a great catch, she might justifiably feel that her social set, even her father, is right in encouraging the match. She can never present logical reasons for rejecting Willoughby, since her reasons stem from feelings. She senses, rather than thinks, that marriage to Willoughby would be a mistake, "a horror of swampy flatness."[4]

Neither Clara nor Isabel is a truly creative person or an original thinker, but Isabel is the more assertive. The narrator says of Isabel:

Like the mass of American girls, Isabel had been encouraged to express herself; her remarks had been attended to; she had been expected to have emotions and opinions. Many of her opinions had doubtless but a slender value, many of her emotions passed away in the utterance; but they had left a trace in giving her the habit of seeming at least to feel and think. . . .   (I, 74)

Clara, on the other hand, is witty, but she is restrained about expressing her opinions. This particular difference in the two women mainly points up the difference in the authors' nationalities. James was portraying an admirable American girl; and Meredith, an admirable English girl. James reveals Isabel favorably in contrast to the obtrusively outspoken Henrietta Stackpole and to the excessively restrained sisters of Lord Warburton. Clara is seen as a model damsel in contrast to the gossipy, intrusive Mrs. Mountstuart and Lady Busshe, and to the yes-ladies who are Willoughby's aunts.

Both women have a strong desire to maintain their independence. Isabel considers her inheritance a good thing because it enables her to be financially independent. Even more important than financial independence, however, is what she calls her "personal independence," of which, she explains to Caspar Goodwood, marriage would deprive her. It involves being able to have her own opinions, being able to choose her course of behavior. She is not a radical nonconformist, nor is she even indifferent to public opinion, as is Henrietta Stackpole, but she wants to know what is considered proper, "So as to choose" (I, 93). It is her insistence on "personal independence" which ultimately causes the breach between Isabel and her husband, because she will not think as he thinks or accept his idea of correct conduct. Clara is also strong-willed and independent. This quality is suggested in Mrs. Mountstuart's designation of her as a "dainty rogue in porcelain." Willoughby cannot accept the truth of this phrase, the idea that his fiancée might be a rogue, but it is true. She refuses to acquiesce to Willoughby's opinion of the world, to his idea of a wife's duty to her husband, and to almost everything else he stands for. "My mind is my own, married or not" (63), she thinks. The ironic omniscient narrator states that Clara "preferred to be herself, with the egoism of women" (40).

Of course, too, both characters share an essentially romantic view of the world. Each expects the best from people and rejects others' pessimistic opinions. Isabel cannot accept Ralph Touchett's disparaging assessment of Gilbert Osmond, or of Madame Merle. She later also rejects Osmond's cynical views of the world. Clara absolutely refuses to accept Willoughby's opinion that the rest of the world is selfish, intrusive, and coarse. Isabel and Clara are, however, the more likeable because of their optimism.

Finally, both women are beautiful and charming. Perhaps it is not merely a male-chauvinist requirement that female heroines be beautiful since most people prefer to look upon or hear about physically attractive people. But both James and Meredith conceive of admirable women as made up of soft lines—mental and physical. Meredith waxes rhapsodic on Clara's beauty:

She had a mouth that smiles in repose. . . . Her features were playfellows of one another, none of them pretending to rigid correctness, not the nose to the ordinary dignity of governess among merry girls, despite which the nose was of a fair design. . . . Aspens imaged in water, waiting for the breeze, would offer a susceptible lover some suggestion of her face: a pure smooth-white face tenderly flushed in the cheeks, where the gentle dints were faintly intermelting even during quietness. . . . her eyes wavered only in humour, they were steady when thoughtfulness was awakened. . . .   (35)

Her friends thought Isabel to be beautiful, but the narrator does not dwell on her beauty so much as on other qualities. Henrietta Stackpole forms an excellent contrast to Isabel in physical as well as personality traits. Whereas Henrietta is plump of figure, crisp of manner, and loud of voice, Isabel is slender, charming, and soft-spoken. Both authors apparently feared that with emancipation might come indifference to the social graces and hardness or even coarseness of manner, as is manifested in the case of Henrietta. Clara and Isabel, however, although independent and strong-willed, retain their softness of manner and appearance.

One area difficult to assess because of James's and Meredith's reticence is that of female sexuality. We can safely assume that their heroines are virgins, although Meredith's narrator says, "The capaciously strong in soul among women will ultimately detect an infinite grossness in the demand for purity infinite, spotless bloom" (91–92). This view is very emancipated for the late nineteenth century, more emancipated than one could expect of James. James's heroine apparently feels horror at the thought of the physical contact marriage involves. She recoils in fear from Caspar Goodwood's embrace, from Lord Warburton's proposal, and from marriage generally. She feels that it is vulgar to think too much about marriage. It might be possible, she thinks, for a woman to live alone and be happy without a "more or less coarse-minded" person of the opposite sex. James is, as usual, silent about Isabel's physical relationship with her husband. His moral judgment of Madame Merle and Gilbert Osmond for their affair is severe indeed. One's impression of sex in the novel is that it is either unpleasant, immoral, or both. In *The Egoist* Clara exhibits a horror of physical contact with Willoughby, but it appears as part of her general rejection of his personality and character. His physical overtures are a part of his possessiveness toward her. Other than this revulsion on Clara's part, there is little suggestion of passion or sexuality. Meredith and James were perhaps pandering to Mrs. Grundy, but for James, at any rate, being explicit would be anathema.

Admirers of women and cognizant of their good qualities, James and Meredith could but recognize how society limited women and prevented them from developing their potentials as persons. In the nineteenth century women, especially middle-class women, had little public existence except as appendages to men—wives, mistresses, daughters, sisters, mothers. From infancy they were taught their roles, and to deviate from them was to incur disgrace. Their inhibitions were wide-ranging. For instance, Clara, when planning to flee from Patterne Hall to her friend's home, tells lies to everyone about her plans. She cannot just announce her reasons for going and leave. The narrator explains her necessary deception thus: "young women are trained to cowardice. For them to front an evil with plain speech is to be guilty of effrontery. . . . They are trained to please a man's taste. . . ." (202). Again the narrator comments on how society, dominated by men, causes women to have to operate through subterfuge and then criticizes them for deviousness:

Maidens are commonly reduced to read the masters of their destinies by their instincts; and when these have been edged by over-activity, they must hoodwink their maidenliness to suffer themselves to read: and then they must dupe their minds, else men would soon see they were gifted to discern. Total ignorance being their pledge of purity to men, they have to expunge the writing of their perceptives on the tablets of the brain: they have to know not when they do know. The instinct of seeking to know, crossed by the task of blotting knowledge out, creates that conflict of the natural with the artificial creature to which their ultimately-revealed double-face, complained of by ever-dissatisfied men, is owing.   (167)

In *The Portrait* Isabel admits to Ralph that most girls are ignorant though she goes on to say that some would pursue knowledge, "but the way they're talked to!" (I, 62). As Ralph is musing about what Isabel is likely to do with her life, he reflects, "Most women did with themselves nothing at all; they waited, in attitudes more or less gracefully passive, for a man to come that way and furnish them with a destiny" (I, 87). Ralph and Henry James know that Isabel is an exception to the rule.

Throughout both novels one finds frequent references to the ways society coerces women into docility, but Clara and Isabel, although both prefer independence to society's approval, manage to avoid outraging society at large without losing their self-respect. Clara cleverly escapes from a betrothal, an extremely binding compact in the nineteenth century, with her honor intact and society only slightly scandalized. Isabel finds no honorable escape from marriage; she rejects Caspar Goodwood's offer to carry her away, and she returns to Italy to resume her duties. Her unfortunate marriage and her difficult decision to stay with it result alike, however, not from her yielding to society's dictates, but from her courageously following her own mind and then being morally strong enough to suffer the consequences.

In both novels we find examples of a tyranny over women greater even than that of society at large: the tyranny of the husband. Society shaped women through childhood so that they were properly docile for the ministrations of husbands. Governesses, clergymen, and, worst of all, mothers, taught subservience and obedience. Isabel and Clara happened to escape a mother's guiding hand, were raised by indulgent fathers, who did not realize what sins of omission they were committing, and thus escaped the taming process. They were, therefore, unprepared to accept the kind of treatment that millions of women patiently endured. Both, however, fell prey to a particularly vicious species of the male—the egoist. All persons, even women, may be small-scale egoists, but Meredith defines the authentic egoist thus:

The Egoist, who is our original male in giant form, had no bleeding victim beneath his paw, but there was the sex to mangle. Much as he prefers the well-behaved among women, who can worship and fawn, and in whom terror can be inspired, in his wrath he would make of Beatrice a Lesbia Quadrantaria. (189)

This definition applies not only to Willoughby Patterne but to Gilbert Osmond. Both expect docility, complete submission to their wills. Clara fears Willoughby's power when she sees how he had reduced his aunts to the "state of satellites." She is fortunate that she sees before she marries. Isabel marries, only later to discover Osmond's expectations:

Her mind was to be his—attached to his own like a small garden-plot to a deer park.... He had expected his wife to feel with him and for him, to enter into his opinions, his ambitions, his preferences.... (II, 200)

When Isabel insists on forming her own opinions, especially upon moral issues, Osmond comes to hate and despise her.

Willoughby and Osmond have many characteristics in common. Both express great contempt for the rest of the world, pointing out to Clara and Isabel its many flaws. After their marriage, Osmond tells Isabel of "the stupidity, the depravity, the ignorance of mankind . . . and of the virtue of keeping oneself unspotted by it" (II, 197). Willoughby tries to convince Clara of the errors of the world—"its backbiting, selfishness, coarseness, intrusiveness, infectiousness" (39). He wishes her to blot out everything, live only for him, and even promise not to remarry should he die first. Clara rejects Willoughby's views entirely. Isabel might have been willing to accept Osmond's cynical opinion of the world were it not for the fact that, while disparaging society in general, Osmond actually lives only for society's approval. He collects traditions and forms as he does beautiful possessions. The narrator states,

There were certain things they must do, a certain posture they must take, certain people they must know and not know. When she [Isabel] saw this rigid system close about her, draped though it was in pictured tapestries, that sense of darkness and suffocation . . . took possession of her.... (II, 199)

Willoughby, too, condemns society but lives only for its approval. Binding the unwilling Clara to himself finally becomes mainly a matter of keeping up appearances. He cannot bear for society—represented by Mrs. Mountstuart Jenkinson and Lady Busshe—to see him jilted again. He values Clara's appearance and her health because they are characteristics that the wife of a man in his position should have. His maneuverings to give first Laetitia and then Clara to Vernon Whitford are arrogant, unfeeling attempts to look good in the eyes of the world.

Finally, although both authors assume that intellectual interests and reasoning ability are more common to the male than to the female, they exhibit a gallery of men not nearly so perceptive as their more intuitive female associates. Ralph Touchett's intelligence is sterile, Caspar Goodwood's is keen but obnoxious, Gilbert Osmond's is shallow and his moral sense quite dead. In *The Egoist* Willoughby's intelligence is limited by prejudices of sex and station; Dr. Middleton has no common sense whatsoever; Vernon Whitford is the sole reasoning being among the male population of the novel. In fact, male characters are presented as being entirely too much ruled by emotion in times when their reason is most needed. Meredith's narrator says that women cannot get justice from men: "man's brains might, his blood cannot administer it to them. By chilling him to the bone, they may get what they cry for. But that is a method deadening their point of appeal" (193).

Isabel Archer is only one of James's self-reliant American girls, and Clara Middleton only the first of Meredith's gallery of increasingly confident and intelligent women. Framed within the repressive social milieu of the nineteenth century, these women appear liberated indeed. If we compare them to women of our own times, however, we can see that James and Meredith had visualized only the first steps to freedom, a psychic readiness to defy meaningless authority and to be responsible for oneself. But one cannot reasonably expect that these two novelists could have anticipated the knowledge of female sexuality now available or the freedom of movement and action which women now enjoy. James and Meredith, nevertheless, saw more clearly than almost anybody else at the time how the intelligent woman had to struggle to retain her independence and self-respect in the face of repressive conventions.

NOTES

[1] F. O. Matthiessen and Kenneth B. Burdock, eds., *The Notebooks of Henry James* (New York: Oxford Univ. Press, 1961), 29.

[2] *The Ordeal of George Meredith* (New York: Scribner's, 1953), 229.

[3] Henry James, *The Portrait of a Lady* (New York: Modern Library, 1951), I, 21. Subsequent references to this edition are cited in the text.

[4] George Meredith, *The Egoist* (Boston: Houghton, 1958), 92. Subsequent references to this edition are cited in the text.

Southeastern Louisiana University

WILLIAM W. MORGAN

THE PARTIAL VISION:
HARDY'S IDEA OF DRAMATIC POETRY

One of the more puzzling features of Hardy's statements about his poetic intentions is his frequent use of the designation "dramatic" to describe his work—a body of poetry much of which is transparently personal. In the several introductory statements in his volumes of verse, he states that he does not often speak as himself in the poems, that they are "in a large degree dramatic or personative in conception."[1] Hardy is explicit and insistent about this matter, but he is not very concrete or detailed. It is evident that his principal motivation was to separate himself from some of his personae, but he appears to be claiming much more than the simple prerogative of speaking through the masks of created characters. In the prefaces after *Wessex Poems*, he seems in fact to associate the dramatic persona with the entire issue of systematic consistency in mood, tone, and thought, and he is anxious that we should not expect consistency. Most readers doubtless recognize that Hardy uses masks, but it may appear that his prefaces are claiming too much—that he is not so often dramatic as he says he is. Reading the prefaces analytically and in sequence and observing the various forms in which he speaks of the matters of persona and consistency, we learn, however, that Hardy's conception of dramatic poetry is much broader than the usual and that, for him, the dramatic does not stand in simple opposition to the personal. Once understood, Hardy's conception of dramatic poetry becomes paradoxically a key to understanding the authentically personal voice which characterizes much of his poetry and provides a significant and clarifying context for reading most of his poetic canon.

Hardy published prefaces or introductions in five of his eight volumes of poetry, and in all five he gave the matter of the dramatic persona a position of some prominence. Introducing *Poems of the Past and the Present*, he explained himself in almost the same words he had used for *Wessex Poems*: "Of the subject-matter of this volume—even that which is in other than narrative form—much is dramatic or impersonative even where not explicitly so" (*CP*, 75). One might wish to puzzle over what is meant by "subject-matter" and "other than narrative form," but the thrust of the message is clear: we are not to expect that Hardy himself will speak in all the poems. Eight years later he returns to the same themes and again some of the same words in the "Preface" to *Time's Laughingstocks*:

> Now that the miscellany is brought together, some lack of concord in pieces written at widely severed dates, and in contrasting moods and circumstances, will be obvious enough. This I cannot help, but the sense of disconnection, particularly in respect of those lyrics penned in the first person, will be immaterial when it is borne in mind that they are to be regarded, in the main, as dramatic monologues by different characters.   (*CP*, 175)

Here, however, the emphasis is altered, and the message is much clearer. Hardy is saying that poems which are products of his own moods and circumstances and are therefore in some sense personal utterances "are to be regarded" as the statements of created characters. This is an unorthodox but, as I shall show later, clear and even useful notion of the dramatic persona, and if we remember for now that he has reserved the right to declare a given persona "dramatic" after the fact, we shall find that Hardy's various statements on the matter are much less teasing and obscure.

In the famous "Apology" to *Late Lyrics and Earlier* (1922) we encounter a paragraph which does not at first appear to have much to do with the use of the dramatic persona:

> To add a few more words to what has already taken up too many, there is a contingency liable to miscellanies of verse that I have never seen mentioned, so far as I can remember; I mean the chance little shocks that may be caused over a book of various character like the present and its predecessors by the juxtaposition of unrelated, even discordant, effusions; poems perhaps years apart in the making, yet facing each other. An odd result of this has been that dramatic anecdotes of a satirical and humorous intention following verse in a graver voice, have been read as misfires because they raise the smile that they were intended to raise, the journalist, deaf to the sudden change of key, being unconscious that he is laughing with the author and not at him. I admit that I did not foresee such contingencies as I ought to have done, and that people might not perceive when the tone altered. But the difficulties of arranging the themes in a graduated kinship of moods would have been so great that irrelation was almost unavoidable with efforts so diverse. I must trust for right note-catching to those finely-touched spirits who can divine without half a whisper, whose intuitiveness is proof against all the accidents of inconsequence. In respect of the less alert, however, should

any one's train of thought be thrown out of gear by a consecutive piping of vocal reeds in jarring tonics, without a semiquaver's rest between, and be led thereby to miss the writer's aim and meaning in one out of two contiguous compositions, I shall deeply regret it.   (*CP*, 529)

But of course this statement has a great deal to do with the subject as Hardy so broadly defines it. He is here calling our attention to the variety and "irrelation" which result from his habit of finding numerous isolated moments and incidents worthy of his or our attention. Those "dramatic anecdotes" to which he so casually refers might be supposed, given his definitions, to include such diverse pieces as "Weathers," "The Fallow Deer at the Lonely House," and even the clearly autobiographical "End of the Year 1912." For it appears that one of the important things Hardy means by dramatic is, rather simply, a *temporary* persona, mood, feeling, fancy, or idea.

With this meaning in mind, it is easy to see that throughout his comments on the subject, Hardy was saying the same thing: that his personae, even when they are versions of himself, are often making statements and expressing states of mind which are circumscribed by time and place and are not, in any permanent or complete sense, the attitudes of the poet himself. "I also repeat what I have often stated on such occasions, that no harmonious philosophy is attempted in these pages—or in any bygone pages of mine, for that matter." (*CP*, 796). This weary last paragraph of the "Introductory Note" to *Winter Words*, therefore, may be seen as a brief and dispirited restatement of what he apparently thought to be his clear and simple position on the whole matter. Because his personae are often attending to the moment only, they are neither wholly himself nor mutually consistent with one another. We may, especially the professional critics among us, grumble a bit over Hardy's idiosyncratic adaptation of the language of poetic form, but the message behind the idiosyncrasy remains. For Hardy there are no rigid boundaries between the personal and the dramatic; a poem may be both at once. Hence he may be serious and sincere, even private and personal, in a given poem and still conceive of that poem as a dramatic moment fixed in time and place, a temporary version of himself which need not be consistent with the self he presents in another equally honest and personal poem.

We must, I think, take Hardy at his word when he says that his poems are dramatic in this sense as well as in the more conventional sense. One of the strongest impressions we receive as we read through the *Collected Poems* is that of unity within great tonal and formal variety and even philosophic inconsistency. It is precisely because so many of his poems are dramatic moments that the unity and the variety can coexist. As a thinking, responsive human being, Hardy considered himself free to entertain nonce perceptions and fancies for whatever interest or insight they might yield without censoring them first. Similarly, as a poet, he produced numbers of poems built upon these nonce impressions. The result is a body of work unified by its origins in the experience of a powerfully individualized personality but not consistent in either form or content.

Though he does not emphasize it in the prefaces, Hardy wrote, of course, conventionally dramatic poetry also—that is, poetry which is impersonally dramatic because its perspective prohibits direct self-revelation on the part of the poet, and much of it achieves the same kind of isolation in time and place that he claims for his personal poems. More than 10 per cent of Hardy's poems achieve an impersonal dramatic voice by the simple device of an identified narrator other than the poet. Some of these soliloquies and dramatic monologues are among his best known poems ("The Peasant's Confession," "The Respectable Burgher on 'The Higher Criticism,' " "The Chapel Organist," "One Ralph Blossom Soliloquizes"), and in his fondness for the mask of a created character he has occasionally been likened to Robert Browning. Hardy is a competent character-builder (though he cannot match Browning), but his more interesting and impressive achievements in the impersonal-dramatic are built upon a studied lack of emphasis on the character of the narrator rather than upon the creation of a character whose mind becomes the center of the reader's attention. In a number of his poems, for example, he effaces his narrator so completely that there is not so much as a personal pronoun to give the persona an identity. In the best of these, such as "A Light Snow-Fall After Frost" and "Life and Death at Sunrise," the effect of such effacement is to suggest something like a camera recording without commentary. Such poems are intensely visual and rich with closely observed detail; they are usually written in present tense; they customarily are concerned with a situation or an image of stasis or gradual change; often they present a human figure or figures in some sort of relation to nature or natural forces; most important of all, they make only implicit evaluations of the data they present. This sort of impersonally dramatic poem suggests not so much the absence of the poet's editing mind and eye as it does his modest reluctance to place himself between us and the experience.

> The hills uncap their tops
> Of woodland, pasture, copse,
> And look on the layers of mist

At their foot that still persist:
They are like awakened sleepers on one elbow lifted,
Who gaze around to learn if things during night have shifted.

A waggon creaks up from the fog
With a laboured leisurely jog;
Then a horseman from off the hill-tip
Comes clapping down into the dip;
While woodlarks, finches, sparrows, try to entune at one time,
And cocks and hens and cows and bulls take up the chime.
("Life and Death at Sunrise," *CP*, 692)

Such poetry is not, of course, a mere transcript of sense-data, but it poses rather convincingly as such by its detached impersonality. That is, I think, the point of this particular dramatic technique of Hardy's—to suggest through deemphasizing the persona that the intense experience of sense-data within the frame of a short period of time may be worth the poet's and our attention. He does not profess to know, much less to tell us, the reasons for that worth.

Another dramatic technique of Hardy's—and one which allows him to achieve something like stage drama in short poems—is characterized by an even more thoroughly effaced persona. The technique involves simply presenting the entire poem within quotation marks as if it were being overheard by a silent persona who is part of the poem only by inference. "In the Restaurant" and "In the Moonlight" from "Satires of Circumstance" are typical examples. Both are overheard dialogues—the first between a pair of adulterers contemplating flight and the second between a naively sentimental interrogator and a man who reveals in response to questioning that he has discovered his love for the woman by whose grave he is standing only after her death. Through the simplified perspective of the poems Hardy places us in direct contact with a short period in these anonymous people's lives and forces us to confront the situations and issues of their lives as if we ourselves were overhearing their conversation. (The quotation marks aggressively assert the veracity of that conversation.) It is as if we are being led to eavesdrop, and since the themes of such poems are often unpleasant or at least problematic, it is an unsettling experience to be manipulated into confronting them.[2] Inasmuch as the poems are presented to us nakedly, without a preface or a context, they startle with their immediacy; since thematically they are usually built around some sort of moral conflict (Is adultery wrong? Does one who loves too late deserve pity or contempt?), they press us for moral answers which the poet is unwilling or unable to give. That is perhaps the key to Hardy's motivations in using this technique: he knows that he is presenting materials which are meaningless without a moral context, but by placing us in the position of temporary eavesdroppers, he is making that context our responsibility.

Hardy must have anticipated that his readers would have no trouble recognizing such impersonally dramatic poems, for he gives them little space in his prefaces. His principal intention throughout his discussions of his personae, as I have suggested, was two-fold: to balk attempts to read his poetry as direct self-revelation and to assert the temporary nature of most of his personae so that he might be relieved of the burden of being consistent. Hence he concentrates on the first-person narrators whom we might be tempted to see as the poet himself. In the preface to *Poems of the Past and the Present,* as we have seen, he tells us that much of the "subject-matter" of his poems is "dramatic or impersonative"— by which I take him to mean that the vision of many of his poems (the interplay of the persona's perspective and values with the experience being related or created) is either not his own or is the vision of a particular time only. Without transition he adds:

Moreover, that portion which may be regarded as individual comprises a series of feelings and fancies written down in widely differing moods and circumstances, and at various dates. It will probably be found, therefore, to possess little cohesion of thought or harmony of colouring. I do not greatly regret this. Unadjusted impressions have their value, and the road to a true philosophy of life seems to lie in humbly recording diverse readings of its phenomena as they are forced upon us by chance and change.   (*CP*, 75)

In addition to emphasizing the temporary quality of his "individual" or personal narrators, this passage offers a partial explanation for their temporary quality, for it presents the poet as a rather passive recipient of life's "phenomena"—one radically subject to the influence of time and place, "chance and change." And, most important, this passage tells us what Hardy would have us attend to in his poetry, the particulars of time and place which define the limits of perception for his narrators. Ultimately, then, Hardy's comments on the dramatic nature of his poetry not only warn us away from a certain approach to it, but they point us in a positive direction as well. As he tells us not to look for consistent and direct self-revelation, he also tells us to look for acute sensitivity to the moment and the scene as they create or prohibit the creation of the context of values for his poems.

Hardy's techniques for exploiting the limiting effects of time and space are remarkably varied in their details, but they may be summarized as the restriction of time and the particularization of place. Perhaps his simplest technique is to restrict the persona's consciousness to the immediate present or distant past as he does in "Nobody Comes" and "Childhood Among the Ferns." Without introduction, digression, or conclusion the first poem records a temporal fragment—in straight-forward word order: subject, verb, complement. The fragment of time is perceived as a series of processes whose purposes and terminations are unknown to the persona. Leaves "labour up and down"; the light of the sun fades; the telegraph wire carries messages from others to others; an automobile passes, "in a world of its own," while the persona just watches. The closing line continues the pattern of straightforward, linear word order:

> And mute by the gate I stand again alone,
> And nobody pulls up there.
>   (CP, 705)

The word order, echoing in its form the sense of linear time in the poem, casts "nobody" in the position of subject and gives it an active status as a perceived entity in the persona's consciousness. The last line, then, suggests that the negative quality "nobody" actively enters the persona's consciousness in the wake of silence left behind the passing automobile. Just as the leaves labor, the light fades, the wire carries messages, and the automobile passes, so "nobody" comes. The poem, read thoroughly within its insistently present-tense, linear-time structure, becomes then not a statement or study of loneliness so much as the record of a moment in which the persona—clearly a version of Hardy himself—experienced or apprehended a negative entity. The restriction of time here functions to insist upon the momentary but intensely felt quality of the experience.[3] Similarly in "Childhood Among the Ferns" (and other purely past-tense poems) Hardy insists upon the isolation of the time period by riddling the diction of the poem with adverbial constructions expressing temporal conditions: "one sprinkling day," "as I conned," "I sat on," "then," "as they dried," "till death," "as I sate" (CP, 825). These modifiers, spaced almost evenly throughout a poem written entirely in the past tense, serve to particularize and suspend the time of the poem in the past and to obscure the relation between the persona speaking the poem and the version of himself represented in it.

"Childhood Among the Ferns" also relies heavily upon the piling up of visual and tactile detail, and that is, of course, a part of Hardy's other major limiting technique, the particularization of place. Sometimes Hardy works quite broadly to specify the locations of his poems—with his titles ("Near Lanivet, 1872"), subtitles (Near Tooting Common, the subtitle to "Beyond the Last Lamp"), or subscriptions (BON-

CHURCH, 1910, the subscription to "A Singer Asleep"). More often, however, he works smaller details of place into the temporal structure of his poems. Usually these details are prominent in the initial (and sometimes the closing) lines, as they are in the following opening lines:

> There was a stunted handpost just on the crest,
>   Only a few feet high:
> She was tired, and we stopped in the twilight-time for her rest,
>   At the crossways close thereby.
>
> ("Near Lanivet, 1872," *CP*, 409)

Such details may be themselves more isolated and more sharply etched in order to serve as psychological symbols as in "Neutral Tones":

> We stood by a pond that winter day,
> And the sun was white, as though chidden of God,
> And a few leaves lay on the starving Sod;
>   —They had fallen from an ash, and were gray.
>
> (*CP*, 9)

In the closing quatrain of the poem the persona specifies the quality of psychological permanence which some of the details have achieved:

> Since then, keen lessons that love deceives,
> And wrings with wrong, have shaped to me
> Your face, and the God-curst sun, and a tree,
> And a pond edged with grayish leaves.
>
> (*CP*, 9)

Neither "Neutral Tones" nor "Near Lanivet, 1872," however, is a purely past-tense poem like "Childhood Among the Ferns." Each of them articulates at least a portion of the present—"Neutral Tones" in the last four lines and "Near Lanivet, 1872" in the last two words, "Alas, alas!" It is fairly common in Hardy's past-tense poems for the closing lines or words to reveal something of the persona's present, but as in these two, the revelation is usually only partial and explains only the persona's present relationship to the specific past experience presented in the poem. Even when they speak partially in the present tense, the narrators of such poems focus upon the past as it impinges upon the present rather than upon the present as it is explained by the past. In such poems, then, even the narrators' present-tense utterances are controlled and limited by their roots in the past. The present-tense conclusions merely reinforce the sense of their limited vision.

In both his impersonal and his personal dramatic poems, then, Hardy is at once avoiding complete and direct self-revelation and accommodating the idiosyncrasies of his highly personalized view of the world. In the impersonal poems other than the conventional dramatic monologues and soliloquies, he effaces his narrator to bring the experience to the fore, and in the personal poems he binds his narrator's vision to the moment so as to restrict its relevance to the particulars in the poem. The two types of his dramatic poetry have a shared element: a kind of incompleteness of vision. The impersonally dramatic are incomplete because they are without a context of values, a framework of moral norms; the personally dramatic, because their vision cannot be generalized beyond the temporal and spatial limits specified in them. In neither, then, is Hardy wholly and directly himself. That is, finally, what Hardy means by dramatic—not wholly and directly himself. His insistence upon the dramatic quality of his poetry is not a deception he wished to practice upon the public; indeed, it is far more accurately seen as a measure of his personal and artistic modesty. It is, further, a serious critical statement about his work—and an insightful one.

NOTES

[1] Thomas Hardy, *The Collected Poems of Thomas Hardy* (London: Macmillan, 1962), 3. Subsequent quotations from prefaces and poems are from this volume. Hereafter it will be cited as *CP*, and page numbers will be indicated parenthetically in the text.

[2] At least one of Hardy's overheard dialogues is an exception to the general sordidness of theme which I have noted: "Under the Waterfall." It shares with the others, however, the fact that it presents an experience for which it is difficult to construct the appropriate context. One does not know what value to assign to the principal speaker's almost religious attitude toward that day in the past when she and her lover lost their "chalice" in the stream. Part of Hardy's reluctance to evaluate the experience can probably be explained by the fact that the principal speaker is rather clearly his first wife, Emma.

[3] The momentary quality of the experience is reflected also in the fact that Hardy dates the poem fully and specifically: October 9, 1924.

Illinois State University

LESLIE H. PALMER

THE IRONIC WORD IN HARDY'S NOVELS

Following a newspaper account of a lodging-house keeper's testimony about a Whitechapel murder, Thomas Hardy has a two-sentence comment which demonstrates in action both his denotative and connotative ironies:

> "He had seen her in the lodging-house as late as half-past one o'clock or two that morning. He knew her as an unfortunate, and that she generally frequented Stratford for a living. He asked her for her lodging-money, when she said 'I have not got it. I am weak and ill, and have been in the infirmary.' He told her that she knew the rules, whereupon she went out to get some money." (*Times* report.)
> O richest city in the world! "She knew the rules."[1]

Besides the contrast of the tone, which is also ironic in its lift and drop, several devices make perfectly clear the irony in Hardy's comment, "O richest city in the world! 'She knew the rules.' " Foremost in the first phrase, "O richest city in the world," is the outright falsity of "richest" when juxtaposed with what has gone before. The word simply does not fit. The two thoughts clash, and the reader has to see that the norm is inappropriate. Furthermore Hardy provides as accents (1) an apostrophe, (2) capitalization, and (3) an exclamation point to emphasize his ironic meaning. "Richest" is an inappropriate word, but its presence suggests that such treatment of the "weak and ill" or of anyone else "ought not to be." The economic term highlights the spiritual and emotional deficit of London life. Take away "richest" and Hardy's point has lost its moral sting. Denotative irony, therefore, is an auxiliary to truth here.

Shocked as the reader is by "richest," there still is the equally suggestive repetition in flat, neutral tones of "She knew the rules." Liter-

109

ally, the poor prostitute did "know the rules." The word "rules" has
been stripped, however, of all its favorable connections, and the implication is certainly that such "rules" should not be. Human charity
should outweigh them. Also suggested by "rules" is the idea of the
playing of a game and, on the other hand, the idea of a prison. Both
senses are richly ironic.

Traditionally uses of verbal irony have been thought of as based on
denotation and connotation. These two forms for indirect censure and
praise by blame come close to the popular definitions of irony as "saying
something different" and "saying the contrary."[2] Denotative irony, as
Hardy uses it, is a simple opposite: one word replaces another and is
"the flat substitution of the false word for the true one."[3] Hardy has a
great deal of borderline denotative irony and sarcasm, the difference
being the understanding of the sarcastic speaker *and* the hearer. His
connotative irony shows the distortion of the normal connotations of a
word; it is "literally truthful, but connotatively false."[4] This irony of
connotation is not frequent, at least in an organized sense, but there is
a carry-over from novel to novel. Certain words and ideas are attacked
connotatively again and again, until a reader comes to expect the use
and may even miss some of the sting which surprise and unexpected
subtlety give.

Denotative and connotative ironies are common in Hardy's novels,
but their function as detachable parts means that they serve more en
masse than singly. In Hardy's first published novel, *Desperate Remedies*, two characters upon falling in love discover a natural law as true
as that of gravity: "They rowed that evening; the next came, and with
it the necessity of rowing again" (42).[5] Strictly speaking, the denotation
of "necessity" is false. There is no dire and urgent need. But the suggestion of the word implies their desire to see one another again, and,
as such, the irony is mildly humorous. Dick Dewey is likewise surprised when he sees "the vision of the past night enter the porch-door
as methodically as if she had never been a vision at all" (*UTGT*, 39).
The country girl, alias "vision," is also betrayed by the incongruity of
tone composed by "vision" and "methodically."

For comic effect, Hardy at times mingles tonal irony and other verbal
ironies. *A Pair of Blue Eyes*, one of Hardy's early novels that was quite
popular, contains a lengthy but emphatic display of verbal irony in order
to portray the eccentricity of a new character, Mrs. Swancourt, who
wears thirteen decorative rings that feature such items as "a devil's
head," griffin, dragons' heads, sea monster, and "a gloomy intaglio."

"Beyond this rather quaint array of stone and metal, Mrs. Swancourt wore no ornament whatever" (137). Tone has a part in the irony as the catalogue contrasts with the short summation; there is the irony of what is said ("no ornament whatever") which, although a fact, implies that she has ornament enough already, and finally there is the understatement of "rather quaint array." A point to be remembered is that Hardy uses his ironic techniques interdependently.

The rustics, although "in a degree idealised,"[6] still are ignorant or naive enough to provide an unconscious irony in their speech. Besides their function as a chorus, the rustics provide a stable society which serves as a contrast to the ambitious, self-willed characters. Many of their speeches, however, reflect a quiet frustration. Their romances are thwarted, their marriages are unhappy, and their finances are unsteady. Still, though, their speech in the early novels has its comic side. Hardy's sense of humor is not infrequently used, and irony, especially verbal irony, plays a major part in that humor. One rustic in *Far from the Madding Crowd* claims to have known the Everdene family well, most of all the father, who "became a very celebrated bankrupt two or three times" (69). An auctioneer in the tradition of Chaucer's Pardoner tries to sell a most unusual horse in *The Mayor of Casterbridge*: " 'Tis a very promising broodmare, a trifle over five years old, and nothing the matter with the hoss at all, except that she's a trifle holler in the back and had her left eye knocked out by the kick of another, her own sister, coming along the road" (7–8). That "except" is rather lengthy, and the contrast of "nothing the matter" with the long list of details which follows establishes the incongruity necessary to the ironic attitude.

An example of how indirectly connotative irony works occurs in *A Pair of Blue Eyes*. Hardy shows animals as fellow-sufferers and often gives them personal qualities. One such incident, taken seriously by the rustics, is rich in humor; the group discusses a pig with a personality "who went out of his mind":

"How very mournful!" murmured Mrs. Worm.
"Ay, poor thing, 'a did! As clean out of his mind as the cleverest Christian could go. In early life 'a was very melancholy, and never seemed a hopeful pig by no means. 'Twas Andrew Stainer's pig—that's whose pig 'twas.
"I can mind the pig well enough," attested John Smith.   (261)

The "cleverest Christian" fares rather ill in the comparison. In addition, the use of "attested" stresses the rustics' effort at verifying the incident.

Litotes, or understatement, is a favorite Hardy device which in some ways resembles the effect and function of denotative and connotative irony. Understatement has been a tradition of English irony since the Anglo-Saxon scop; Mrs. Swancourt's "array" is one example of how Hardy uses it. Again, in *A Pair of Blue Eyes* two rivals stare at one another: "Each was troubled at the other's presence" (418). George, the dog of *Far from the Madding Crowd*, "though he understood English but imperfectly, began to growl" (123)—this imperfection may be denotative, but also seems an understatement in form. In *The Return of the Native*, Thomasin frequents the old Roman road: "And it might have been observed that she did not in future walk that way less often from having met Venn there now" (467). In *Tess* a speaker turns to "one of the group who certainly was not ill-defined as plain." In *The Well-Beloved*, a character realized that "Time was against him and love, and Time would probably win" (169).

Overstatement also has a part. Bridesmaids flutter anxiously about to attend to "the will of that apotheosised being—the Bride" (*UTGT*, 199). A visitor meets a family and the family's cat: "He had been expected, and all were glad to see again the sojourner in foreign lands, even down to the lady-like tabby, who was all purr and warmth towards him except when she was all claws and coldness" (*THOE*, 455). Whether understatement, which Hardy prefers, or overstatement, these devices perform in quantitative ways (to say more or less) what connotative irony does in qualitative ways (to say better or worse).[7]

Grim effects as well as comic ones are available to denotative and connotative ironies. As the emphasis on the unsatisfactory and the frustrated in life increases in Hardy's novels, there is a corresponding increase in the verbal irony about those conditions. Starting with *The Return of the Native*, narrator and characters are more vocal in their protests.[8] A father-daughter dialogue from *The Woodlanders* illustrates a Hardy connotative irony about the "good life"; Grace and Mr. Melbury speak:

"I wish you had never, never thought of educating me. I wish I worked in the woods like Marty South! I hate genteel life, and I want to be no better than she!"
"Why?" said her amazed father.
"Because cultivation has only brought me inconveniences and troubles. I say again, I wish you had never sent me to those fashionable schools you set your mind on. It all arose out of that, father. If I had stayed at home I should have married—"
She closed up her mouth suddenly and was silent; and he saw that she was not far from crying.
Melbury was much grieved. "What, and would you like to have grown up as we be here in Hintock—knowing no more, and with no more chance of seeing good life than we have here?"   (266–67)

The truth about "good life" is obvious.

Also obvious is the denotative irony of *The Trumpet-Major* where a girl exclaims, "How I love them!" and prompts another character to ask why she speaks as if she hated them. That irony is flat enough. But the connotative irony with which Chapter XLV of *Far from the Madding Crowd* begins is rather subtle: "When Troy's wife had left the house . . . ." In context, the connotations of "Troy's wife" are extremely ironic. Bathsheba still is his wife, legally, but she is soon to withdraw from him. In the chapter gone before, she has just seen the corpses of Fanny Robin and her child, proof positive that Troy has been Fanny's lover and has wronged her to make Bathsheba his "wife." Thus Hardy's subtle connotative irony places a conscious stress on her ironic position as "Troy's wife." No more can be asked than that verbal irony goes hand in hand with substantive irony.

The Return of the Native employs verbal irony in several important situations. When Clym's mother makes her return trip across the heath, believing that her son and his wife have turned her away, she vents her grief in bitter ironies to a small boy. These follow a ballad pattern; he asks a question, and she gives an ironic answer. After he asks if she has seen something horrible, she replies:

"I have seen what's worse—a woman's face looking at me through a window-pane."
"Is that a bad sight?"
"Yes. It is always a bad sight to see a woman looking out at a weary wayfarer and not letting her in."   (339–40)

Then, as she continues, he says in his childlike way that she must be "a very curious woman to talk like that." She answers bitterly: " 'O no, not at all. . . . Most people who grow up and have children talk as I do. When you grow up your mother will talk as I do too.' "

That grief becomes obsessive grimness, or at least relentless irony, in *Jude the Obscure*. Denotative and connotative ironies in this novel reach an apex. Jude attempts suicide by jumping on the ice of a frozen pond, but here, as in all else, he fails: "It was curious, he thought. What was he reserved for? He supposed he was not a sufficiently dignified person for suicide" (82). Undignified Jude returns home to find Arabella gone; her farewell note says, *"Have gone to my friends. Shall not return."* Jude, who has been tricked into marriage by his sense of honor and her false claim of pregnancy, is not overly sad. He can remember how she broke the news of her "mistake" because women "fancy wrong things sometimes." He can remember the butcher who had warned Arabella that very afternoon about pig-killing "in the delicate state" she supposedly is in, and her raucous laugh, "You needn't be con-cerned about that." As the narrator says of Jude, "There seemed to him, vaguely and dimly, something wrong in a social ritual which made necessary a cancelling of well-formed schemes involving years of thought and labor." The bare-boned term, "social ritual," helps to devalue marriage and to emphasize the arguments against it; its conno-tations are as cold and loveless as the life shared by Jude and Arabella.

After much frustration Jude acknowledges his abject failure "as a law-abiding religious teacher." He had wondered how he could succeed where "the great Phillotson" had failed—an undermining of "great" like that in *Jonathan Wild*. He makes his decision: "At dusk that eve-ning he went into the garden and dug a shallow hole, to which he brought out all the theological and ethical works that he possessed, and had stored here. He knew that, in this country of true believers, most of them were not saleable at a much higher price than waste-paper . . ." (261–62). The connotations of "in this country of true believers," an inserted phrase, have real backlash. When Arabella does return, years later, and she and Jude are reunited, Hardy makes a sardonic effect with his irony: "The landlord of the lodging, who had heard that they were a queer couple, had doubted if they were married at all, especially as he had seen Arabella kiss Jude one evening when she had taken a little cordial; and he was about to give them notice to quit, till by chance overhearing her one night haranguing Jude in rattling terms, and ultimately flinging a shoe at his head, he recognized the note of genuine wedlock; and concluding that they must be respectable, said no more." Now, a part of this irony is substantive, not so much in the words used as their content and meaning—"the note of genuine wedlock" is the sound of an argument and a flung shoe. But "respectable" has been undermined by the previous substantive irony, and humor of a grim kind results.

Sarcasm is frequent in *Jude*. Near irony, it vents a bitter anger under-stood by user and victim. As such, sarcasm is perfectly suited to the Arabella-Jude affair. If Jude is relieved at a pig's merciful death (" 'Thank God! . . . He's dead' "), then Arabella retorts, " 'What's God got to do with such a messy job as pig-killing, I should like to know' " (75). Years later that same pig is a sore subject. Jude loses his temper and threatens to kill Arabella, but relents: " 'I take your word,' he said scornfully as he loosened her. 'But what it is worth I can't say.' " To this jibe Arabella taunts, " 'You couldn't kill the pig, but you could kill me!' "

Hardy's uses of denotative and connotative irony add depth and meaning to situations. These ironies give tone, help interpret character, and provide insight into scenes. They clarify and point out those interpretations which Hardy wants his readers to reach. At times, as when Arabella assures the others that the just-dead Jude is "sleeping quite sound" and "won't wake yet," the situation is dramatized and intensified. The effect is that of a catalyst in chemistry; the irony turns a placid state into one where all things are changed, where the flat surface appearance is shown not to be reality, and where readers' interpretations are shaken and crystallized.

That Hardy began to use denotative and connotative ironies in connection with others is due to their natures. When purely denotative irony is used, it does provide a rough check upon the narrative. Use the real word in "O richest city" and the whole point that "richest" denotes would be missed. Hardy's true meaning might be there in substitution, but effect would be greatly lessened. Overused, however, the device would become tiresome. Connotative irony is somewhat subtler, and it is a good instrument for conveying Hardy's points, especially in bond with substantive irony. As technical devices, the two forms function to provide a moral criticism of the action. Great attention is sometimes required of the reader, but generally Hardy's attempts at these ironies differ sharply enough from the non-ironic to be apparent. Under these conditions and with the obvious irony to alert him, the reader actually is alerted to look for other, and subtler, ironies. The author's norms and morality are therefore made more, and not less, visible in the narrative, and thus the ironic technique reinforces the standards that Hardy wishes to advocate. The narrative passing before the reader is being viewed "objectively" or, more precisely, critically. A distancing effect results from this definite viewpoint. As Hardy uses them, within the limitations of their natures, denotative and connotative ironies are helpful auxiliaries to the creation of the world of fiction.

A third branch of Hardy's verbal irony is irony of tone which defines itself by a characteristic difference of sound and content or sound and sound. Punctuation and syntax help establish it, but tonal irony is seldom dependent upon diction. Thus the contrast in Hardy's vocabulary, which produces an odd tension, is not a true part of tonal irony. Tonal irony functions as a shift of voice. It has been compared by Eleanor Hutchens with denotative irony (98), but the effect of the shift need not be that abrupt. Tonal irony does with sounds to the reader's ear what denotative and connotative ironies do to his eye.

The various types can enjoy a symbiotic relationship, and several of the examples given earlier combine ironies of denotation and connotation with irony of tone. For instance, the ironic description of Mrs. Swancourt gains from the difference in tone of the catalogue of her rings with the one-sentence comment that follows.

Tone does depend upon sound, and readers can interpret sounds differently. For that reason, Hardy frequently qualifies his dialogue in order to point out his ironic tones. Mr. Spinks, one of the choir to be replaced in *Under the Greenwood Tree*, speaks in a manner which requires a pointer: " 'Really, I think we useless ones had better march out of church, fiddles and all!' said Mr. Spinks, with a laugh which, to a stranger, would have sounded mild and real. Only the initiated body of men he addressed could have understood the horrible bitterness of irony that lurked under the quiet words 'useless ones,' and the ghastliness of the laughter apparently so natural" (42). Since one of the two major parts of the novel dwells on the question of "usefulness" and progress, the tonal stress of the irony here points out a central issue of this "idyll." Whether or not the choir is "useless" in a modern, changing world too sophisticated for fiddles, tonal irony has helped one have his say—and in doing so points out a standard to judge by. The irony helps support old ways and old traditions. To help point out ironies of tone to the reader, Hardy soon learns to use the qualifying adverbs "drily," "bitterly," and "wryly." Of the three, "drily" is used most:

"You mistake: I'll remind you of particular," he said drily. And he did remind her at some length.   (*The Trumpet-Major*, 153)

One afternoon the daughter was not indoors when Henchard came, and he said drily, "This is a very good opportunity for me to ask you to name the happy day, Susan."   (*The Mayor of Casterbridge*, 93–94)

"That excuse has been made a little too often in this school to be effectual in saving our souls," said the head girl of the year, drily.   (*Jude the Obscure*, 167)

Contrasts of sound-sense and sound-sound are frequent throughout the novels. In *Under the Greenwood Tree*, a passage about a butcher's bill clashes sense and sound in an ironic way: "Perhaps it was the first time in the history of commercial transactions that the quality of shortness in a butcher's bill was a cause of tribulation to the debtor" (171). Likewise clashing is an extended metaphor of *Far from the Madding Crowd* where love and commerce are compared: "Love being an extremely exacting usurer (a sense of exorbitant profit, bodily or materially, is at the bottom of those lower atmospheres), every morning Oak's feelings were as sensitive as the money-market in calculation upon his chances" (26). Aesthetic distance of still another sort, this time from the characters and their problems, comes in *The Trumpet-Major*, Hardy's historical novel about the Napoleonic scare in England:[9] "Widow Garland's thoughts were those of the period. 'Can it be the French?' she said, arranging herself for the extremest form of consternation. 'Can that arch-enemy of mankind have landed at last?' It should be stated that at this time there were two arch-enemies of mankind—Satan as usual, and Buonaparte, who had sprung up and eclipsed his elder rival altogether. Mrs. Garland alluded, of course, to the junior gentleman" (6). The contrast of the widow's excitement with the narrator's calm about the "junior gentleman" is heightened by the different pace and rhythm—that is tonal irony.

A lengthy circumlocution followed by a snappy phrase produces some of Hardy's best tonal irony. Rhythm, pace, and timing are manipulated. First there is the build-up, and then the drop-off. Hardy uses this device in his minor or lesser novels and also in the better ones. *Far from the Madding Crowd* tells how "Oak had nothing finished and ready to say as yet, and not being able to frame love phrases which end where they begin, passionate tales—Full of sound and fury—Signifying nothing—he said no word at all" (p. 26). From Shakespeare to "he said no word at all" is an ironic drop. *The Mayor of Casterbridge* also develops irony of tone by this laconic drop:

What Henchard saw thus early was, naturally enough, seen at a little later date by other people. That Mr. Farfrae "walked with that bankrupt Henchard's step-daughter, of all women," became a common topic in the town, the simple per-ambulating term being used hereabout to signify a wooing; and the nineteen superior young ladies of Casterbridge, who had each looked upon herself as the only woman capable of making the merchant Councilman happy, indignantly left off going to the church Farfrae attended, left off conscious mannerisms, left off putting him in their prayers at night amongst their blood relations; in short, reverted to their natural courses.   (355)

Tonal irony, in short, exposes those "nineteen superior young ladies" for what they are. The periphrasis and parallelism punctured by the summation drop sound against sound.

Over a quarter of a century Hardy's style, and his ironic tone as well, changes. Two ironic passages from an early novel, *Far from the Madding Crowd*, give an idea of his early irony of tone. Under the impression that his job was to run the sheep, Oak's young dog has driven the flock over a cliff to their deaths:

George's son had done his work so thoroughly that he was considered too good a workman to live, and was, in fact, taken out and tragically shot at twelve o'clock that same day—another instance of the untoward fate which so often attends dogs and other philosophers who follow out a train of reasoning to its logical conclusion, and attempt perfectly consistent conduct in a world made up so largely of compromise.   (42)

In a second ironic passage, a dog described as ideal supports dying Fannie Robin in her desperate attempts to reach shelter. Patient, unable to comprehend more than that she is a human being who is acting strangely, the dumb beast stays with her and, as she holds on, carries her to a house. The people take her in and ask, "How did she get here?" Then Fanny asks where the dog is who helped her. " 'I stoned him away,' said the man" (309). The quiet, restrained tone makes this effective irony, and not bathos.

The same tone, with less humor and less possibility for hope as balances, is the center of *The Return of the Native* and *Tess of the D'Urbervilles*. In the latter, for example, irony of tone seldom arrives at humor. As Hardy says of "Sir John's" drunken trip home, the trip "produced a comical effect, frequent enough on nocturnal homecomings; and, like most comical effects, not quite so comic after all" (30).[10] Although he has already described the Durbeyfield parents as irresponsible by means of his dramatic action, Hardy pauses to make a dire point:

All these young souls were passengers in the Durbeyfield ship—entirely dependent on the judgment of the two Durbeyfield adults for their pleasures, their necessities, their health, even their existence. If the heads of the Durbeyfield household chose to sail into difficulty, disaster, starvation, disease, degradation, death, thither were these half-dozen little captives under hatches compelled to sail with them—six helpless creatures, who had never been asked if they wished for it on such hard conditions as were involved in being of the shiftless house of Durbeyfield. Some people would like to know whence the poet whose philosophy is in these days deemed as profound and trustworthy as his song is breezy and pure, gets his authority for speaking of "Nature's holy plan."   (24)

Even though a Victorian thinker was apt to substitute Nature "red in tooth and claw" for "Nature's holy plan," the slap at Wordsworth is gratuitously snide. At this point the didactic commentary is obtrusive, offensive, and unnecessary. The wringing of hands and handkerchiefs, the plea for the six little passengers in the H.M.S. Durbeyfield, are lugubrious. Sentimentality, not sense, results.

Juxtaposition creates in *Jude the Obscure* an irony of tone that sets up an aesthetic distance and sets off the reader from both the dreamer and the pragmatist. On two occasions, for example, Jude's idealistic dreams are rudely broken into. As a boy, he neglects his job of scaring birds because his heart grows "sympathetic with the birds' thwarted desires." Following Jude's idealistic speech of brotherhood to his "dear little birdies" (and Hardy's comment that "puny and sorry as those lives were, they much resembled his own"), Jude is surprised with blows and these words: "So it's 'Eat my dear birdies,' is it, young man? 'Eat, dear birdies,' indeed! I'll tickle your breeches, and see if you say, 'Eat, dear birdies,' again in a hurry!"

The blows echo from the church, "towards the building of which structure the farmer had largely subscribed, to testify his love for God and man." Jude goes home disgraced, not perceiving "the flaw in the terrestrial scheme" by which "what was good for God's birds was bad for God's gardener."

Again, Jude dreams of his future, going to Christminster, whether he will be a bishop, what he will study, all the while unaware of some flirtatious young women and their cries. At this high point, full of lofty thoughts and noble phrases which alter Biblical ones, ("I'll be her beloved son, in whom she shall be well pleased," [41]) Jude is smacked "sharply in the ear" with a "soft cold substance"—a pig's pizzle. The sharp contrast is skillfully engineered by Hardy and brings onstage with that ironic calling card Arabella Donn, who is symbolized throughout by the pig.[11] By the end of *Jude*, tonal irony has served to complement the ironic theme of the whole. It is no longer inert, separable from the mass. Take away tonal irony in *Jude*, and the amputation mars the whole tone and the whole novel. It is that important.

Tonal irony eventually became integral to Hardy's style. From the first it was used to comment upon situation, character, and action, but that comment by a contrast of sounds or sound and sense was external, a trick of the narrator, somewhat detachable from the rest of the novel. The effect of ironic tone was that of a drop of ink in a glass of water. By the last novels, however, where Hardy's philosophy colors all, the ironic is all—there is a glass of ink, a drop of water. Irony of tone can lend an air of objectivity; it can place the audience at a distance from characters (even the best ones), from accepted beliefs, and from observed actions. The weakness of tonal irony in the later novels is that it can be overused to the point that there is either a predictable or an unprofitable contrast of sound and sound or sound and meaning.

Referential irony defines its presence more readily than does tonal irony and can be more easily agreed upon among Hardy's readers. The device involves Hardy's manipulation of references to produce incongruity. These comparisons in large part are allusions, but metaphor, simile, image, and naming are other subdivisions that might become

ironic. A = B, or A is like B—but the reader can see that the identification or the comparison is untrue or unlikely. Either reference will
cause the reader to reconsider the true nature of A. Two rival, dis-
junctive categories can establish humorous effects or tragic, but always
critical reappraisal.

Hardy's references are to literature, the classics, philosophy, and art.
Some seem mere pedantry. While giving Hardy his due, Douglas Brown
says that one need not worry about the passages in a "learned, pontifical
or patronizing style": "Least of all about the pretentious phrases and
the passages of classical or biblical allusion, the self-conscious similes.
They ring false, they seem to have been put in to make the prose
resonate."[12] Undoubtedly, many of the additions are meant to add an
aura of learnings to the architects's prose. A number of changes in
diction for *The Mayor of Casterbridge* after serial publication "unmis-
takably add literary tone."[13]

Not all of Hardy's references are ironic, even in *Jude the Obscure*,
his most carefully plotted use of ironic reference. In large measure even
those references that are ironic are meant to perform all the other
duties of normal reference. Therefore, even though the Biblical reference which compares Henchard to Saul can be seen as having ironic
tendencies, by no means is it a one-dimensional reference. It is possible
to see its activity as building up character, adding to the form and tone
of the novel, tending toward symbolism, and carrying out other aspects
of reference. Not all of Hardy's references in the community of any one
novel are meant to be incongruous; a great deal of descriptive scene
painting which is basically passive goes on. As Hardy develops his
talent, however, these scenes and their metaphorical language become
more effective. Evelyn Hardy says of his figurative language, "When
Hardy is emotionally stirred and writing at white-heat the inspired
similes pour from him like sparks from a chimney on a frosty night, or
they form and re-form like beaded bubbles breaking at the brim of a
glass-full of heady wine, as many as five or six similes appearing in a
single paragraph. It is well to seek these out in his early work and then
to see how, as his talent develops and he gives his imagination rein, the
similes mature in depth and range."[14] So do all Hardy's references
mature, of course, including referential irony.

Of the ironic references, one wishes that Hardy's description of a
Dutch clock could be included, with its "entrails hanging down beneath
its white face and wiry hands like the faeces of a Harpy" (*Desperate
Remedies*, 366). That simile is "of the poorer sort."[15] But another in

the same novel, while also inferior, does have an ironic effect; refused permission to accompany Cytherea to her door, Springrove "looked at her as a waiter looks at the change he brings back" (34). A metaphor which follows also helps set off the reader from Springrove and his emotions; the young lover sees Cytherea disappear behind the blinds with "a hopeless sense of loss akin to that which Adam is said . . . to have felt when he first saw the sun set, and thought, in his inexperience, that it would return no more" (35).

Titles, chapter headings, and character and place names also may suggest irony. *Under the Greenwood Tree* and "Dick Dewey" and "Fancy Day" in the context of the novel hint at a slightly ironic attitude toward them; these names are not, however, pure stock names like those of Restoration comedy. *Far from the Madding Crowd* turns out not to be so far. Character names like Joseph Poorgrass, Gabriel Oak, Bathsheba Everdene, Fanny Robin, Boldwood, and Troy allude to characteristics of the owner or make comparisons of the character to the original "Gabriel" or "Bathsheba." Joseph (73–74) quotes scripture, "beginning to feel like a man in the Bible"! Like the Biblical Bathsheba, who caused David to sin, Bathsheba Everdene causes Boldwood and Troy to sin. She sends Boldwood the valentine which turns him from a dignified country farmer into a passionate, impulsive lover who murders Troy. Troy sees her, as David saw Bathsheba, and falls in love. In doing so, he wrongs Fanny Robin. "Menlove" is an appropriate name for a housemaid in *The Hand of Ethelberta*; this "fisher of men," to use the Hardyan phrase, snares all sorts, including a boy in his early teens. Names like Jude Fawley, Arabella Donn, and Sue Bridehead are similarly suggestive; the references hint at ironies within the characters, and are adumbrations of the problems within each.[16]

When Hardy first used allusion, it was a sparing, nonintegral addition to his technique. The allusion was an added thought, a reference to his reading, isolated, and not a part of any larger patterns of reference. By the time of the later novels though, the allusion to the Bible or Greek myth is a thread in a larger pattern and can be drawn tight to stress the irony of situation, character, and tone.

Literary and Biblical allusions are wide-ranging, from Old Testament to New, from Defoe to the *Whole Duty of Man*. In one of the minor novels, *The Trumpet-Major,* old Mr. Derriman sighs that he is put upon and mistreated (all an act) : " 'I am a poor put-upon soul; but my "Duty of Man" will be left to me when the newspaper is gone.' And he sank into the chair with an air of exhaustion" (46). Such a humorous reference gives way in time to bitterly ironical allusions like the one to Wordsworth and "Nature's holy plan" in *Tess of the D'Urbervilles.*

Referential irony has the primary function of extending meaning in an ironic way by allusion, sometimes by metaphor, simile, image, or naming. The irony may be aimed at even those characters who are sympathetic, and the distancing effect that is obtained helps to lend balance to the novel. The direction of the emotion is thus away from sentimentality and toward objectivity. Nevertheless the referential irony can be aimed at pointing out that an ironic situation parallels that of a noble figure, and may not be based so much upon the ironic differences of the two as upon the similarities of the ironies the two have suffered. In that case, as in *Jude,* the effect is toward a sympathetic view of the character and his problems, and the reader is drawn closer to the character. A weakness of Hardy's early referential irony is that the comparison is not a part of the substance, but is extraneous and detachable. But these references later can help to establish scene, character, tone, and symbolism, and are vital to the shape the novel is to take. It is true that in the earliest novels not very much would be lost by the absence of referential irony; the Cushi-King David allusion of *Desperate Remedies,* while useful, really does not have the continuous, intertwined significance of the Samson reference in *Jude the Obscure.* Both references point out ironic aspects of character, but the two are not equally functional. As should be expected, Hardy refines his technique in a quarter-century so that his art becomes more of a unity.[17]

In brief, the various branches of verbal irony which Hardy uses in his novels all show a growth in (1) frequency of occurrence, (2) maturity, and (3) artistry. There is a developing mastery of technique. In the beginning Hardy threw in denotative, connotative, tonal, and referential ironies as accessories to his art. The four were individual, unrelated, and detachable from his spectacular plots. Insular and narrow, the verbal ironies become broader, more interwoven, more dramatic, and more a part of the pattern of Hardy's work. At last all four devices are functioning at maximum efficiency; they contribute to Hardy's substantive irony as it conveys his themes. Denotation, connotation, tone, and reference: the four devices of Hardy's verbal irony cease to be accessories and instead are auxiliaries.

NOTES

[1] Florence Emily Hardy, *The Early Life of Thomas Hardy, 1840–1891* (New York: Macmillan, 1928), 280. Hardy dictated most of the "life" to his second wife.

2 Norman Knox, *The Word Irony and Its Context, 1500–1755* (Durham: Duke Univ. Press, 1961), 13.

3 Eleanor Newman Hutchens, *Irony in Tom Jones* (University: Univ. of Alabama Press, 1965), 69.

4 Hutchens, 68.

5 All references to Hardy's novels in the text are to *The Works of Thomas Hardy in Prose and Verse* with Prefaces and Notes. 24 vols., The Wessex Edition (London: Macmillan, 1912–31).

6 H. C. Duffin, *Thomas Hardy, A Study of the Wessex Novels* (London: Longmans, 1916), 95.

7 Hutchens, 121–22.

8 Carl J. Weber, *Hardy of Wessex* (New York: Columbia Univ. Press, 1940), 70.

9 For a contrast of novelist techniques, consider the irony of Thackeray's panoramic vision in *Vanity Fair* and Hardy's.

10 By now Hardy can say of Meredith that he, while showing the comic spirit, would not "let himself discover the tragedy that always underlies comedy if you only scratch deeply enough." Florence Emily Hardy, *The Later Years of Thomas Hardy, 1892–1928* (New York: Macmillan, 1930), 257.

11 Her sensual animality is thus stressed. Norman Holland, Jr., "*Jude the Obscure*—His Symbolic Indictment of Christianity," *Nineteenth-Century Fiction* 9 (June 1954), 51, has a thesis which converts Arabella into the unclean animal of the Hebrews.

12 *Thomas Hardy, The Mayor of Casterbridge* (Great Neck, N.Y.: Barron's Educational Series, 1962), 40.

13 Mary Ellen Chase, *Thomas Hardy from Serial to Novel* (Minneapolis: Univ. of Minnesota Press, 1927), 58.

14 *Thomas Hardy, A Critical Biography* (London: Hogarth, 1954), 104.

15 Ibid., 104.

16 Robert F. Fleissner, "The Name Jude," *Victorian Newsletter*, No. 27 (Spring 1965), 24. He sees the name Jude as offering a faint gleam of hope through its reference to historical Judes.

17 Near the end of the novel Jude compares Arabella with the whore of Babylon in a magnificent ironic reference: " 'Don't say anything against my honour!' enjoined Jude hotly, standing up. 'I'd marry the W— of Babylon rather than do anything dishonourable. No reflection on you, my dear. It is a mere rhetorical figure—what they call in the books, hyperbole' " (461).

North Texas State University

EDMUND GOSSE, WILLIAM ARCHER, AND IBSEN
IN LATE VICTORIAN BRITAIN

In a review of a recent study on Henrik Ibsen in the *Times Literary Supplement* (May 26, 1972), the reviewer (1) criticized the editor of the work for failing to clarify "the nature of the crucial roles played by William Archer and Edmund Gosse in the establishment of Ibsen in England" and (2) cited the need for "some light . . . on what still remains a dark corner: the complex personal relationship between the two men who more than anybody else were responsible for creating Ibsen's reputation in the English-speaking world. . . ."[1] The following essay, based in part on some unpublished correspondence between William Archer, Edward Tyas Cook, and Edmund Gosse, sheds some light on the complex relationship of Archer, the dramatic critic, and Gosse, the literary critic and essayist.

William Archer, a Scot, was also a playwright and a close friend of George Bernard Shaw. Educated at the University of Edinburgh, Archer settled in London in 1878 and became a dramatic critic for several newspapers including the *Pall Mall Gazette*. In addition to his interest in Ibsen's plays, Archer worked sedulously for the abolition of censorship of the theater and the establishment of a national theater.[2] In a large sense Archer was "the father of modern dramatic criticism" in Britain[3] and, to a great extent, responsible for making the Victorian era "the undoubted golden age of the dramatic critic."[4] He had known Gosse since the early 1880s and, during the "season" in London, was often a guest at the home of Gosse and his wife.[5]

Edmund Gosse, the son of the well-known zoologist, Philip Henry Gosse, worked as a cataloguer in the British Museum from 1865 to

124

1875. While at the museum, Gosse achieved some notice for his poetry and reviews in *The Spectator* and other periodicals. On the basis of his knowledge of French, German, Italian, and some Swedish, Gosse obtained an appointment in 1875 as a translator in the Board of Trade's commercial department, but it was a position which he disliked and from which he hoped to escape by enhancing his reputation as a literary critic.[6] During the decade after 1875 Gosse advanced his literary career by publishing, by assiduously cultivating the friendship of such eminent writers as Robert Browning, Thomas Hardy, Coventry Patmore, Henry James, and William Dean Howells, and by projecting himself as an authority on Scandinavian culture as a result of his essays on Henrik Ibsen.[7] He had discovered the work of Ibsen in 1871 and always claimed to have been the first to introduce Ibsen into England during the autumn of 1871.[8]

Gosse was encouraged by his colleague at the British Museum, the folklorist W. R. S. Ralston, to undertake a systematic study of the Dano-Norwegian language in order to become the museum's specialist on Scandinavian literature and languages. Since this suited Gosse's ambition to be accepted as a literary critic, he taught himself Danish and Norwegian and achieved a sufficient reading knowledge of these languages. While Gosse was on a cruise in Norway during the summer of 1871, a book dealer in Trondheim introduced him to Ibsen's *Brand* and the *Digte* poetry collection, and from this time onward Gosse was the first great advocate of Ibsen in Britain.[9] The two men began to correspond, and Gosse flattered Ibsen, who sought to become well known in Britain, by posting copies of his published reviews of Ibsen's work to the playwright and by assuming the role of "Ibsen's prophet to English readers."[10]

In the spring of 1872 Gosse made the acquaintance of the Primate of Denmark, Dr. B. J. Fog, and the Danish linguist, Jakob Lokke, and through these men established important contacts with literary figures, scholars, and artists in Denmark and Norway. Lokke, a close friend of Ibsen, facilitated Gosse's visit in the summer of 1872 to Denmark, from whence he journeyed to Norway where he met influential Norwegian writers. As a result of his visit in Scandinavia, Gosse returned to Britain ever more determined to make himself "a missionary in the cause of Scandinavian literature in England."[11] During 1873–74, Gosse became a regular contributor on Scandinavian literature and especially on Ibsen to several English periodicals, but some of these articles contained some serious errors which were noted in Norway. The most important of Gosse's essays on Ibsen was an article on "Ibsen, the Norwegian Satirist" in the June 1873 issue of the *Fortnightly Review*, which predicted that Ibsen was a "world poet" whose art would eventually win the respect of Europe.[12]

Although Gosse again visited Denmark in May 1874 and expanded the circle of his friends and acquaintances, there was a marked decrease in his publication of articles on Scandinavian literature during the years 1875–80. Nevertheless he continued to maintain his correspondence with Ibsen and George Brandes and to comment on every new work they produced.[13] Then, in 1879, Gosse published his first book on Scandinavian literature, *Studies in the Literature of Northern Europe*, which was basically a reprint of several essays he had previously published on the subject in English periodicals, with one of the largest sections of the volume devoted to Ibsen and his work.[14] But while Gosse was praised as the most competent English authority on the literature of Scandinavia, his great ambition was to become a leading literary critic in Britain.[15]

During the first half of the 1880s, Gosse's reputation as a critic was much augmented by his biography of *Gray* (London, 1882) in the "English Men of Letters" series and by his *Seventeenth Century Studies: A Contribution to the History of English Poetry* (London, 1883). He was invited to lecture in the United States during 1884–85 on English literature "From Shakespeare to Pope"[16] and, through the good offices of Sidney Colvin, was appointed in 1885 to the Clark Lectureship at Trinity College, Cambridge, where he repeated his American lectures and, during the year, published the lectures in a volume entitled *English Literature from Shakespeare to Pope: An Inquiry into the Causes and the Phenomena of the Rise of Classical Poetry*. Elected to the Clark Lectureship for an additional term of three years, Gosse suddenly found himself assailed from an unexpected quarter and the object of a barrage of criticism from which his reputation never recovered.[17] His book was subjected to "a devastating chapter-and-verse attack" in the October 1886 issue of the *Quarterly Review* by a former friend, John Churton Collins.[18]

Collins was "a hustler, a trouble-maker," whose major "contribution to critical history belongs in the 'no-holds barred' tradition of the rugged polemician."[19] Unlike Gosse, who possessed "width of knowledge and interest in languages and letters," Collins was a solid scholar with "a prodigious and exact memory for facts and sources."[20] Burdened with the necessity to support a large family, Collins worked tirelessly to sustain his brood by producing books and articles and "by the laborious and poorly paid industry of 'Extension Lectures.' "[21] Despite his learning and scholarship, he was unable to achieve a university appointment largely because he irritated academics by his inveterate habit of tracking down sources to expose their errors of fact and interpretation.[22] During the early 1880s, Collins began to exhibit a "paranoiac envy and irascibility" when he attacked Lord Tennyson (who replied by scorning Collins as "A louse on the locks of literature").[23] He was especially aroused by those who professed to be authorities in literature and whom he regarded as frauds, and by 1885 Collins' victims included not only Tennyson but also John Addington Symonds and Algernon Swinburne. Then, in October 1885, Collins turned on Gosse in a virulent attack "which left in its wake greater reverberations than any he had previously set in motion."[24]

Collins' assault on Gosse was motivated by a blend of envy and contempt for Gosse's pretentious and careless scholarship. For years Collins had urged the teaching of English literature in the universities and, when the Clark Lectureship in English Literature was established and accorded in 1885 to that "amiable dilettante" Gosse, who had never attended a university, Collins could hardly conceal his ire. When Gosse published the Clark lectures in *From Shakespeare to Pope*, Collins exploded and attacked Gosse more like "a brooding assassin than the judge" of his work.[25] Yet, Collins was quite right in his criticism of the book as "a mass of error and inaccuracy" in which centuries and even poetry and prose were confused and garbled. Gosse, charged Collins, was guilty of "ephemeral literal journalism" and an offense to sound scholarship.[26] In many ways Gosse had invited trouble because he had become "cocksure and bumptious" and, as he confided to William Dean Howells, "to easily successful."[27] Indeed, as James Sutherland asserts, "If John Churton Collins was a louse on the locks of literature, Gosse was something of a flea on the skirts of scholarship."[28]

Bewildered and indignant, Gosse counterattacked in *The Athenaeum* (October 23, 1886), accusing Collins of envy and malice and refusing to admit the veracity of Collins' charges.[29] A week later Collins replied in *The Athenaeum* (October 30, 1886), further documenting Gosse's errors, denying that he had been motivated by jealousy of Gosse's appointment to the Clark Lectureship, and citing Swinburne, who had previously accepted his criticism with "silent dignity," as a worthy example for Gosse to emulate.[30] When this remark evoked a stinging rebuke from Swinburne and a weak rejoinder from Collins in *The Athenaeum* during November,[31] the periodical closed its columns to the dispute between Collins and his victims.[32]

Meanwhile the Collins-Gosse vendetta was also being carried on in the daily *Pall Mall Gazette*, whose editor, W. T. Stead, and assistant editor, Edward Tyas Cook, exploited the affair as long as it remained good copy.[33] In a leading article on "The Literary Duel and Its Lessons" on October 30, Cook alluded to a recent statement in the *St. James's Gazette*[34] accusing Collins of seeking to inherit "Macaulay's Mantle" and of failing to understand that "to emulate Macaulay something is necessary besides the great essayist's worst tricks of style and manner," but declared that the real issue in the Collins-Gosse dispute was what it revealed of the "Log-Rolling" which the *Pall Mall Gazette* had previously charged was rampant among the "Litterateurs." Cook wrote:

there are far more important matters in the dispute than the reputation of one of the lesser lights of ephemeral literature. *The Quarterly Reviewer* [Collins] . . . was not attacking Mr. Gosse at all, he was attacking Mr. Gosse first as the darling of the literary journals, and secondly, as a teacher of the most important College in Cambridge. . . . If anyone wants to gauge the value of the criticism which a certain clique of LITTERATEURS pass upon each others' work, let him first read the review of Mr. Gosse's book in the *Quarterly*, and then what the reviews say in the *Athenaeum* and in the *Saturday Review*. Neither of these journals had a single hole to pick in Mr. Gosse's work, which the *Saturday* welcomed . . . [as] . . . 'good Madeira wine from across the sea,' and which the *Athenaeum* advised the student of English poetry to 'read twice and consult often.' . . .

Moreover, added Cook, while such errors made by a Latin or Greek scholar at the universities would surely spell his "ostracism" from the community of scholarship, Gosse and his defenders dismiss his mistakes as "trivialities." Why, asked Cook, should thoroughness and accuracy in scholarship be demanded in the classics and other subjects and "English Literature . . . [be] . . . treated as a kind of school girl's accomplishment in which a smattering will do instead of scholarship?"[35]

On October 31 Cook's friend William Archer wrote a letter which not only presented Archer's view of the Collins-Gosse controversy, but also revealed Archer's low opinion of Gosse's literary talent. After stating that Cook's "slap at the *St. James's*" was "perfectly justified," Archer asserted that "Collins clearly and grossly misunderstands Gosse (and hasn't the grace to admit it) . . . [and] . . . shows himself either an unfair or a malevolent critic." Archer averred:

He makes little or no mention of Gosse's *English*—objects (pedantically in my opinion) to one or two words he uses such as 'acutality' 'alembricated' etc., as though the development of the English language had stopped short of Macaulay —but leaves his *composition* untouched. Now there is on the third or fourth page of Gosse's book a sentence so unspeakably, incredibly bad as to reflect far more discredit on Trinity College and the Savile Club than five hundred wrong dates; and throughout one sees that Gosse really wrote so ill as to be scarcely responsible for what he says. Well then, Collins either didn't notice this, in which case he is a mighty poor critic of style; or, noticing it, he suppressed the fact because it suited him to make Gosse out an ignorant charlatan instead of what he really is—a helpless, shambling, inaccurate, 'piffling' little person. . . . Gosse really doesn't know the rules of English grammar and in this case, as in several others, I believe he has said what he did *not* mean. You may say that this is a more serious accusation than that of inaccuracy as to dates or even that of rolling two Shafteburys into one—and I quite agree with you. But it is less serious than that of deliberately pretending familiarity with books he knew nothing about—and *my argument is that Mr. Collins has omitted the attack which he shd. have made against Gosse's style in order to strengthen the attack wh. he shd. not have made against Gosse's honesty. . . .*[36]

Archer's critical comments were undoubtedly also motivated by his lack of respect for Gosse's essays on and translations of Ibsen and some feelings of rivalry. Indeed, despite "the pioneer efforts" of Gosse on behalf of Ibsen, his social dramas were still almost completely unknown in Britain by the early 1880s.[37] Moreover, although Gosse had expanded and republished his essay on Ibsen as a satirist (in the January 1873 *Fortnightly Review*) in his *Studies in the Literature of Northern Europe* (1879), his comments dealt almost solely with Ibsen's historical and poetical works. The production of Ibsen's *Pillars of Society* in late 1880 and *A Doll's House* in 1884 in London had made little impression on the British.[38] It was not until 1888 that some serious interest was aroused in Ibsen's drama, largely as a result of the persistent enthusiasm and publicity of William Archer. As a youngster, Archer had learned Norwegian during his visits with relatives in Norway and, as he later reminded Gosse, he had first learned of Ibsen's work at his uncle's home in Laurvik "in [the] summer of 1873."[39] During 1879–80, Archer translated Ibsen's *Pillars of Society* and had it privately performed in December 1880, but was unable to have it published until 1888. He had visited Ibsen in Rome during the winter of 1881–82 and again at Jutland in 1887, and by 1888 was recognized as "the acknowledged leader of the Ibsen movement in England."[40] But by the late 1880s, the social and intellectual ferment and the rise of socialism in Britain provided a favorable environment for the acceptance of Ibsen's social dramas. Thus, in 1888, the publication by Walter Scott in London of a collection of Ibsen's plays, *Pillars of Society* and *Ghosts*, translated by Archer, and *An Enemy of the People*, translated by Eleanor Marx-Aveling, was quite successful and greatly increased the number of Ibsen enthusiasts in Britain. The production of Archer's translation of *A Doll's*

House in June 1889 was a success in spite of criticism that Ibsen's realism was offensive to British sensibilities.[41]

And so, while Gosse was the first to write about Ibsen in English and helped prepare the way for the acceptance of Ibsen's "social dramas" in Britain,[42] Archer, "who became Ibsen's translator *par excellence* in Britain, did not appear as a champion of Ibsen until . . . after Gosse had made himself the advocate of Ibsen's poetic and dramatic genius in England."[43] Indeed both Gosse and Archer placed their reputations in jeopardy by espousing the cause of Ibsen in Victorian Britain.[44]

In November 1889, three months after Archer had published a trenchant article on "Ibsen and English Criticism" in the *Fortnightly Review*,[45] Walter Scott announced that he would publish a complete edition of Ibsen's prose plays under the direction of Archer, who would translate several of the plays and assume responsibility for the accuracy of the entire project.[46] During 1890–91, with the assistance of his brother Charles and his sister-in-law Frances, Archer produced the first English collection and edition of Ibsen's dramas, which had Ibsen's approval, and the first collection of his works published in the world, under the general title, *Ibsen's Prose Dramas*.[47] It was such a great and lasting success that "Archer's versions [of Ibsen] assumed an authority very rare among translations; people came to speak of them as if they were the actual work of Ibsen, very much as they quoted the Authorised Version of the Bible as if it were the immediate word of God."[48]

In 1890, as Archer was preparing the edition of Ibsen's collected plays, Gosse published his *Northern Studies* which featured two chapters on Ibsen[49] with some errors that irritated Archer. Then, immediately after the presentation of Ibsen's new play, *Hedda Gabler*, in Copenhagen during December 1890, the London publisher, William Heinemann, made arrangements with Ibsen for the publication of the play translated into English by Gosse.[50] On receiving the proofs of the play, Gosse published a review of *Hedda Gabler* in the January 1891 issue of the *Fortnightly Review*,[51] shortly before his translation of the play was published by Heinemann on January 20, simultaneously in Britain and the United States.[52] However, a misunderstanding now occurred because Heinemann's acquisition of the translation rights for *Hedda Gabler* conflicted with arrangements previously made by Archer to include the play in the edition of Ibsen's prose dramas scheduled for publication by Walter Scott. Worse yet, Archer not only felt that Gosse had behaved dishonorably toward him by preventing *Hedda Gabler* from being incorporated in his (Archer's) edition of Ibsen's plays, but, more significantly, he was convinced that Gosse was incapable of rendering an accurate translation of Ibsen's work from the Norwegian because of the serious errors in his previous translations of Ibsen's plays.[53] Thus, on reading a prepublication copy of Gosse's translation of *Hedda Gabler*,[54] Archer erupted with indignation and on January 19 dispatched a letter to E. T. Cook, now editor of the *Pall Mall Gazette*, requesting "space . . . for a *signed* exposure of this awful bungling—either in the form of a letter or of an article." Archer wrote:

I have just gone through Gosse's translation of *Hedda Gabler* and find it perfectly *awful*—by far the worst translation that has ever been made of Ibsen, and a cruel injustice to the old man. There is scarcely a sentence of tolerable English in the whole thing—but apart entirely from questions of style and taste, how many positive, glaring mistranslations,—absolutely crying blunders—do you think he has managed to cram into it? Between 80 and 90! And in these I don't count mere inadvertences—singulars for plurals, or vice versa, immaterial mistakes of tense, and so forth—but only blunders which prove that he did not in the least understand what he was doing, and which stultify the text.

Will you give me space—and how much?—for a signed exposure of this awful bungling—either in the form of a letter or of an article? I shall allude briefly to the fact that he has taken advantage of an act of courtesy of mine to set up a claim of monopoly of this play and then to say that while he was, in his way, doing something to spread a knowledge of Ibsen in England, I said nothing about the blunders he fell into (*e. g.* in *Northern Studies*)—but that now, when he pens Ibsen into a corner and then massacres him, he goes a trifle too far and has to be shown up.

You may understand that, just because of the personal quarrel between us, I would not say anything about his translation if there were not an absolutely crushing case to be made against it. But the thing is really incredible—and it would be a gross injustice to Ibsen to allow it to pass unchallenged. If you don't see your way to giving me space enough—1½ to 2 columns—I must try some one else; but of course I should much prefer to do it in the *P.M.G.*

I see a man in the *Evening News* [Jan. 19], who evidently knows nothing about Norwegian or Ibsen, calls the translation 'crude, clumsy, silly, jejune, inane . . . and inept'—but he accepts it as literally accurate. What would he say if he knew of the 85 blunders!

Of course, when I send you the copy, if you think the case not strong enough to be given prominence, you have only to say so. What I want to know just now is whether, *assuming* the case to be as I represent it, you can afford me the requisite space?

Would you mind telegraphing me—yes or no—as early as possible; for if it is to be done at all, ' 'twere well 'twere done quickly.'[55]

Cook deemed Archer's case against Gosse strong enough and, sensing good copy, published Archer's attack upon Gosse as a signed article entitled "A Translator-Traitor. Mr. Edmund Gosse and Henrik Ibsen" in the *Pall Mall Gazette* on January 23, 1891. In his critique of Gosse, Archer declared that Gosse's translation was "so inconceivably careless and so fantastically inaccurate as to constitute a cruel injustice to . . .

Ibsen." "I cannot pretend to be an impartial critic," admitted Archer; "I have long known that Mr. Gosse's Norwegian is sadly imperfect." Although in the past Gosse had made serious errors in Norwegian translations, he (Archer) had refrained from criticizing a man who was doing a real service in bringing Norwegian literature to the notice of English readers, but now the case was different. Then, referring to his pique with Gosse over the publication of *Hedda Gabler*, Archer explained:

> Some months ago, I waived in Mr. Gosse's favour a position of advantage which I held with regard to 'Hedda Gabler.' This I did out of pure courtesy, and on the explicit understanding that the privilege I thus transferred to him could not and would not be used to impede Mr. Walter Scott in completing his edition of Ibsen's Prose Dramas under my editorship. In flat contravention of this understanding . . . Gosse now asserts a monopoly in the play. This being so, I hold it incumbent on me to point out that the version on which, if Mr. Gosse has his way, the English-speaking world will have to depend exclusively for its knowledge of 'Hedda Gabler,' is one of the very worst translations on record, and reproduces the . . . original about as faithfully as a fourth-form schoolboy, translating . . . a page of Tacitus. . . .

To further emphasize his point, Archer concluded the article with a long list of errors which he had found in Gosse's rendition of *Hedda Gabler*.[56]

Although Archer's article evoked two replies from William Heinemann (and two spirited retorts from Archer),[57] Gosse, fearing a repetition of his unpleasant encounter with Churton Collins in 1886, remained silent but hurried to reconcile Archer and to settle their dispute amicably.[58] Heinemann gave permission to Archer to produce another translation of *Hedda Gabler* and to include it in Archer's edition of Ibsen's prose dramas in 1891,[59] and Gosse, acknowledging the superiority of Archer's translation over his own, included it in the volume of his (Gosse's) edition of *The Prose Dramas of Henrik Ibsen* which was published in the United States during 1891.[60] Later, in his revised edition of *The Collected Works of Henrik Ibsen* in 1906–12, Archer published a version of *Hedda Gabler* which was listed as *jointly translated* by Gosse and himself.[61]

Good relations were restored between Gosse and Archer by autumn 1892, when they agreed (with the approval of Ibsen) to collaborate in a translation of Ibsen's *Master Builder Solness*; they published the play in January 1893.[62] In early 1898, Archer and Gosse organized a private appeal for a subscription among the British friends and admirers of Ibsen to finance the presentation of a gift of silver to Ibsen on his seventieth birthday (March 20, 1898).[63] Archer also shared Gosse's dislike of Bernard Shaw's attempting to make himself "the self-appointed exponent of Ibsen's message to the British public." In fact, as early as 1889, Archer warned against Shaw's interpretation of Ibsen as something of "a social prophet" and later criticized Shaw's *Quintessence of Ibsenism* (1891) as a good example of "misguided Ibsen criticism."[64] During the late 1890s, Archer and Gosse were much irritated by Shaw's comments on Ibsen in *The Saturday Review*.[65] Thus, in reply to a complaint from Gosse concerning a recent effusion by Shaw on Ibsen's dramas, Archer wrote to Gosse on March 29, 1898:

> I haven't read Shaw's article—I have long ago given up reading Shaw, more especially on . . . Ibsen—for I quite agree with you as to the harm he does to Ibsen and the higher drama in general, while at the same time I am unwilling to be perpetually at loggerheads with him. . . . I thought of sending a line to the *Saturday* [*Review*] . . . , but [I] am not sure that it would be wise to let it *appear* as though I had read his article.
>
> I quite agree with you that it doesn't matter a jot what Shaw or anyone else says—the Old Man [Ibsen] has been gratified [by the reception of his work in Britain], and England has played a creditable part in the [recent] celebration. . . .[66]

But Archer was always quick to correct some of Gosse's errors and misconceptions. Thus, when Gosse asserted that Archer had stated that he was first attracted to Ibsen by Gosse's article in the *Fortnightly Review* in 1873, Archer gently informed Gosse on March 23, 1898:

> As a matter of historic fact, . . . though it isn't of the slightest importance—you must be under some misapprehension as to my having said that it was your Fortnightly article that 'directed my notice' to Ibsen. I first learned Ibsen's name through seeing his books in the booksellers' windows in Norway, and what lead [*sic*] me to buy and read one of them was—as I remember most distinctly—a conversation on the balcony of my uncle's house in Laurvik one summer afternoon . . . in summer of 1873 . . . . What I think I must have said . . . was that it gave me great pleasure and encouragement years afterwards to find my boyish admiration of Ibsen was shared by so eminent a critic as yourself. So far as I remember, I did not read your Fortnightly article until it was republished in *Northern Studies* [1879]. I wish I had come across it earlier, for I could then have hurled you at the feet of the sceptics who used to jeer at my raptures over this incomprehensible Hyperborean.[67]

Similarly, on the publication of Gosse's book, *Two Visits to Denmark: 1872, 1874* (London, 1911), Archer was quick to detect an error of fact concerning Ibsen's relationship with Bjornstjerne Bjørnson which he immediately reported to Gosse on October 20, 1911. Archer wrote:

> In reading your TWO VISITS TO DENMARK I was rather 'took aback' by the story at p. 174 of Ibsen and Bjørnson[68] in Rome; for I was pretty sure that they had never been there together. Just to make certain I wrote to Sigurd Ibsen [Ibsen's son]; and I have this morning received a letter from him in which he quite pos-

itively confirms my impression. The story is perhaps all the more interesting on this account, as it shows that already in 1874 there was inaccurate gossip about these two men in the air. Molbech[69] must have misunderstood something that some one had told him—he may have transferred to Rome the gossip of Christiania [Oslo]. Perhaps in another edition you will give us a footnote on the growth of the Ibsen-&-Bjørnson legend.

One thing I can enjoy in reading your book is the feeling that I am not, after all, quite the oldest man in the world. *This book shows that you had the start of me by several years—which otherwise no one would suspect....*[70]

Until his death in 1924, Archer continued to maintain friendly relations with Gosse. After serving as librarian to the House of Lords from 1904 to 1914, Gosse was honored with a knighthood in 1925 and during the last decade of his life (1918–28) was a regular contributor of weekly literary articles to *The Times*. He survived Archer by four years and died in May 1928. It was not only their "acrimonious behind-the-scenes battles" in 1890–91, but also their subsequent collaboration which had "far-reaching consequences for the manner in which Ibsen's works ultimately reached the English public"[71] and indeed the world.

NOTES

[1] See "Anglo-American Ibsenists," rev. of *Ibsen: The Critical Heritage*, ed. Michael Egan, *TLS*, May 26, 1972, 601.

[2] On the life and career of William Archer (1856–1924), see Lt. Col. Charles Archer, *William Archer. Life, Work and Friendship* (New Haven: Yale Univ. Press, 1931).

[3] Holbrook Jackson, *The Eighteen-Nineties. A Review of Art and Ideas at the Close of the Nineteenth Century* (Harmondsworth: Penguin, 1939), 186.

[4] See rev. of *Victorian Dramatic Criticism*, by George Powell, *TLS*, June 18, 1971, 712.

[5] Clara and Rudolf Kirk, eds., "Letters to an 'Enchanted Guest': W. D. Howells to Edmund Gosse," *Journal of the Rutgers University Library* 22 (1959), 2.

[6] On the life and career of Edmund W. Gosse (1849–1928), see Evan Charteris, *The Life and Letters of Sir Edmund Gosse* (London: Heinemann, 1931); D. S. MacColl, "Edmund Gosse," *London Mercury* 24 (1931), 152–59; Edmund Gosse, *America. The Diary of a Visit, Winter 1884–1885*, eds. Robert L. Peters and David G. Halliburton (West Lafayette, Ind.: Purdue Univ. Press, 1966); Michael Meyer, *Ibsen. A Biography* (Garden City, N.Y.: Doubleday, 1971).

[7] See Edmund Gosse, "Ibsen, The Norwegian Satirist," *Fortnightly Review* 19 (1873), 74–88; Gosse's essay on Ibsen in Edmund W. Gosse, *Studies in the Literature of Northern Europe* (London: C. Kegan Paul, 1879), 35–69; Malcolm Elwin, *Old Gods Falling* (New York: Macmillan, 1939), 202.

[8] Gosse to William Archer, Mar. 9, 1888, Charteris, *Life and Letters of Gosse*, 223–24; MacColl, "Edmund Gosse," 155.

[9] Halvdan Koht, *Life of Ibsen*, trans. Einar Haugen (New York: Benjamin Blom, 1971), 295.

[10] Elias Bredsdorff, *Sir Edmund Gosse's Correspondence with Scandinavian Writers* (Copenhagen: Gyldendal, 1960), 3.

[11] Ibid., 4–5.

[12] Gosse, "Ibsen," *Fortnightly Review* 19 (1873), 74–88; also Koht, *Ibsen*, 295.

[13] Bredsdorff, *Gosse's Correspondence*, 6–10.

[14] See Gosse, *Studies in the Literature of Northern Europe*, 35–69; and Bredsdorff, *Gosse's Correspondence*, 11.

[15] Ibid.

[16] See MacColl, "Edmund Gosse," 156; Gosse, *America, passim.*

[17] Charteris, *Life and Letters of Gosse*, 196ff.; Kirk, "Letters to an 'Enchanted Guest'," 15; John Gross, *The Rise and Fall of the Man of Letters. A Study of the Idiosyncracies and the Humane in Modern Literature* (New York: Macmillan, 1969), 159.

[18] See John Churton Collins, "English Literature at the Universities," *Quarterly Review* 163 (1886), 289–329.

[19] Gross, *Rise and Fall*, 175; Phyllis Grosskurth, "Churton Collins: Scourge of the Late Victorians," *University of Toronto Quarterly* 34 (1965), 254.

[20] MacColl, "Edmund Gosse," 156.

[21] Grosskurth, "Churton Collins," 257; MacColl, "Edmund Gosse," 156.

[22] Gross, *Rise and Fall*, 175–77.

[23] See Charles Tennyson, *Alfred Tennyson* (London: Macmillan, 1949), 490.

[24] Grosskurth, "Churton Collins," 258–60.

[25] Ibid., 260–61; Gross, *Rise and Fall*, 177.

[26] Collins, "English Literature," *Quarterly Review* 163 (1886), 289ff.

[27] Grosskurth, "Churton Collins," 262; Gosse to William Dean Howells, Nov. 30, 1886, Kirk, "Letters to an 'Enchanted Guest'," 20.

[28] James Sutherland, "Dealing with Correspondences," *TLS*, Jan. 26, 1973, 75.

[29] Edmund Gosse, "The *Quarterly Review* and Mr. Gosse," *The Athenaeum*, Oct. 23, 1886, 534–35.

[30] See John Churton Collins in ibid., Oct. 30, 1886, 534ff.

[31] See Swinburne's "The Literature of the 'Quarterly Review'," ibid., Nov. 6, 1886, 601ff.; and Collins' reply in ibid., Nov. 13, 1886, 636ff.

[32] Grosskurth, "Churton Collins," 264.

[33] See *Pall Mall Gazette*, Oct. 15, 1886, 11; Oct. 18, 1886, 13; Oct. 21, 1886, 6; Oct. 22, 1886, 4; Oct. 23, 1886, 6; Oct. 25, 1886, 6; Oct. 29, 1886, 6; Oct. 30, 1886, 1. Thus Gosse wrote to a friend: "The degree to which I am still made the victim here of pails of journalistic slops is really extraordinary...." Gosse to William Dean Howells, Nov. 30, 1886, Kirk, "Letters to an 'Enchanted Guest'," 20.

[34] See *St. James's Gazette*, Oct. 30, 1888, 4–5.

[35] *Pall Mall Gazette*, Oct. 30, 1886, 1.

[36] William Archer to E. T. Cook, Oct. 31, 1886, Sir Edward Tyas Cook Papers (courtesy of the late Mrs. D. G. Duff). My italics in the last sentence.

[37] Koht, *Ibsen*, 337.

[38] Ibid., 307.

[39] Archer to Gosse, Mar. 23, 1898, Sir Edmund W. Gosse Collection, The Brotherton Library, University of Leeds (courtesy of The Brotherton Library).

[40] Koht, *Ibsen*, 382, 407; Bredsdorff, *Gosse's Correspondence*, 166.

[41] Koht, *Ibsen*, 407; Bredsdorff, *Gosse's Correspondence*, 42.

[42] Cf. Gosse, "Ibsen's Social Dramas," *Fortnightly Review* 51 (1889), 107–21.

[43] Bredsdorff, *Gosse's Correspondence*, 24.

[44] Karl Litzenberg, "The Victorians and the World Abroad," *The Reinterpretation of Victorian Literature*, ed. Joseph E. Baker (Princeton: Princeton Univ. Press, 1950), 188, 194.

[45] See William Archer, "Ibsen and English Criticism," *Fortnightly Review* 52 (1889), 30–37.

46 See *Athenaeum*, Nov. 30, 1889, 751; also Bredsdorff, *Gosse's Correspondence*, 42.

47 (London: Walter Scott, 1890–91), 5 vols.; see also Koht, *Ibsen*, 408; Bredsdorff, *Gosse's Correspondence*, 42.

48 "A Poet, Not Just a Practitioner," rev. of *The Oxford Ibsen*, III, ed. James Walter McFarlane, *TLS*, Sept. 1, 1972, 1014.

49 (London: Heinemann, 1890), Ch. i & ii, 38–76, 77–104.

50 Bredsdorff, *Gosse's Correspondence*, 42; Charles Archer, *William Archer*, 174–75.

51 See Gosse, "Ibsen's New Drama," *Fortnightly Review* 55 (1891), 4–14.

52 Bredsdorff, *Gosse's Correspondence*, 42, 44; see also Archer's Introduction to *Hedda Gabler* in 1907, William Archer, ed., *The Collected Works of Henrik Ibsen*, X (London: Heinemann, 1907), 9.

53 Bredsdorff, *Gosse's Correspondence*, 45; Charles Archer, *William Archer*, 175.

54 See Henrik Ibsen, *Hedda Gabler*, trans. Edmund Gosse (London: Heinemann, 1891).

55 Archer to Cook, Jan. 19, 1891, Sir E. T. Cook Papers.

56 William Archer, "A Translator-Traitor. Mr. Edmund Gosse and Henrik Ibsen," *Pall Mall Gazette*, Jan. 23, 1891, 2; see also Bredsdorff, *Gosse's Correspondence*, 45–46.

57 See Heinemann's article and letter in the *Pall Mall Gazette*, Jan. 24, 1891, 2; Feb. 4, 1891, 2, and the replies of Archer and Alfred Feist in ibid., Jan. 27, 1891; Jan. 29, 1891, 2; and Feb. 4, 1891, 2.

58 Bredsdorff, *Gosse's Correspondence*, 47; Charles Archer, *William Archer*, 175; see also G. Bernard Shaw to T. Fisher Unwin, April 22, 1891, Dan H. Laurence, ed., *Bernard Shaw. Collected Letters, 1874–1897* (London: Max Reinhardt, 1965), 292–93.

59 See William Archer, ed., *Ibsen's Prose Dramas* (London: Walter Scott, 1891), v.

60 See Archer's translation of *Hedda Gabler* in Edmund Gosse, ed., *The Prose Dramas of Henrik Ibsen* (New York: United States Book Co., 1891), III.

61 See Archer, ed., *Collected Works of Henrik Ibsen*, X, 3–18.

62 See Henrik Ibsen, *The Master Builder. A Play in Three Acts*, trans. Edmund Gosse and William Archer (New York: Tait, 1893); Bredsdorff, *Gosse's Correspondence*, 48; Charles Archer, *William Archer*, 197.

63 Bredsdorff, *Gosse's Correspondence*, 48; Charles Archer, *William Archer*, 237.

64 Daniel Charles Gerould, "George Bernard Shaw's Criticism of Ibsen," *Comparative Literature* 15 (1963), 130; also Miriam Franc, *Ibsen in England* (Boston: Four Seas Co., 1919), 34–35, 41.

65 For some of Shaw's pronouncements on Ibsen in *The Saturday Review* (1895–98), see Bernard Shaw, *Our Theatres in the Nineties* (London: Constable, 1932), I, 164–65, 195, 278–79; II, 84, 248–49ff.; III, 32ff., 125ff. See also a very convincing defense of Shaw in Gerould, "George Bernard Shaw's Criticism of Ibsen," 130–45.

66 Archer to Gosse, Mar. 29, 1898, Gosse Collection.

67 Archer to Gosse, Mar. 23, 1898, ibid.

68 Bjornstjerne Bjørnson (1832–1910), Norwegian poet, novelist, and dramatist, was at one time Ibsen's friend. On Ibsen's fear and suspicion of Bjørnson and "the basic insecurity of their relationship," see Koht, *Ibsen*, 243–44, 252.

69 Chr. K. F. Molbech, poet and reader for the Danish Royal Theatre, facilitated the production of Ibsen's play, *The Vikings of Helgeland*, at the Royal Theatre in Copenhagen during 1875. Ibid., 291.

[70] Archer to Gosse, Oct. 20, 1911, Gosse Correspondence. My italics.
[71] See "Anglo-American Ibsenists," rev. of *Ibsen: The Critical Heritage*, ed. Michael Egan, *TLS*, May 26, 1972, 601.

Georgia State University

MAURICE HUNGIVILLE

EPITHETS AND EPITAPHS:
RUDYARD KIPLING'S REPUTATION AS A POET

In 1919 T. S. Eliot referred to Rudyard Kipling as a "neglected celebrity" and regretted that the minds of contemporary critics were not "sufficiently curious, sufficiently brave" to examine Kipling's poetry.[1] The fact that the examination of Kipling's poetry required inordinate amounts of curiosity and bravery was due to the violent forces which had transformed Kipling's reputation as a poet into a bitter battleground of conflicting political and artistic ideologies.

By 1900 Kipling's readers had divided themselves into two irrevocably hostile camps—the critics and the cultists. The more aggressive camp contained the cultists, whose enthusiasm for Kipling was often as intense as it was extraliterary. The cultists, with a few notable exceptions, were people whose interest in poetry was both incidental and indirect. Their real interests were elsewhere—in politics, religion, business, or sports—and they tended to value poetry only as it sanctioned and solemnized these other interests. Poetry of the sort Kipling wrote served to put the stamp of solemnity on such normally unpoetic pursuits, and the cultists responded with an enthusiasm which they rarely displayed for poets.

One such normally unpoetic pursuit was war, and during World War I the cultists regarded Kipling's poetry as a national resource to be mobilized in the war effort. Kipling, to the cultists who reviewed *The Years Between* in 1919, was "the Roosevelt of Poetry" and a fitting rebuke to the literary slackers who failed to respond to the war effort. W. B. Yeats's insistence that a poet "should keep his mouth shut" was denounced as "drivel," and the example of Kipling was invoked to show that "a poet can be a man of action too." [2]

138

Some results of the Kipling cultists' activities on behalf of their poet can be seen in the unprecedented public recognition accorded Kipling throughout his lifetime. The Nobel Prize, awarded in 1907, the Gold Medal of the Royal Society, awarded in 1926, and the founding of the Kipling Society in 1925 all attest to the zeal of Kipling's enthusiasts.[3] Yet behind the public honors there was widespread critical contempt for Kipling, and the cultists contributed, albeit indirectly, to this extreme reaction. The cultists, with their uncompromising enthusiasm, were all too often inclined to use Kipling's poetry as a rebuke to other writers of different, less congenial poetry. Kipling's poetry, as his admirers were fond of pointing out, was "masculine," practical, and patriotic in a way that made other, purer poets appear effeminate, impractical, and suspiciously internationalist.

The Kipling cultists and the Kipling critics were essentially in agreement about what they found in Kipling's poetry—imperialism, journalism, didacticism—and they differed only in their attitudes towards these extraneous subjects. The critics, outraged by Kipling's aggressive political poems, seemed to regard Kipling's imperialism as a menace to public health as well as to poetry. Thus the liberal member of Parliament, C. F. Masterman, railed against "the apostles of the new imperialism" and a conception of war "carried out in the spirit of music-hall comedy." Such a spirit of war, it seemed to Masterman, presented an obscene spectacle of "men at the close of the struggle wiping their hands which have successfully gouged out the eyes of their enemies while they hum the latest popular song."[4] In America, where passions still ran high over the Philippine intervention, critics seemed to react even more violently to the infectious imperialism of Kipling's poetry. Michael Monahan, writing in *The Philistine*, vividly described how America, surfeited with Kipling's views, "vomits its rage upon the laureate of slaughter" and rejects at last the "homicidal genius" and his poisonous poetry. "The dear American public," Monahan wrote in 1901, "gagged at last on the blood-bolted gospel of Ruddy Kipling. After so much raw meat, the d.a.p. is now expiating its gluttony by a humble attack of indigestion."[5]

The issues that divided the critics and the cultists remained relatively fixed, and throughout Kipling's lifetime his poetry received only two original and independent reviews. And these, significantly, were not written by professional reviewers, but by his peers, his fellow professional poets. Robert Bridges' observations on Kipling's style and diction were casual comments made in an article reviewing Lane Cooper's concordance to the poetry of Wordsworth. Wordsworth and Kipling,

Bridges noted at the outset, were poets of immense differences who shared a common conviction that the moribund poetic diction of their times "was capable of dialectical regeneration." Kipling's use of cockney dialect was motivated, Bridges believed, by a Wordsworthian sense that the linguistic tools at the poet's disposal had been blunted and debased by artificial traditions.

Kipling's dissatisfaction with the decayed diction of his age was, then, a familiar poetic predicament. Wordsworth, Bridges recalled, had attempted to recapture the speech of common people, and, more recently, Synge had questioned whether "before verse can be human again it must not learn to be brutal?" Kipling's achievement was unique, though, because his "dialectical regeneration" of English diction was combined with a concomitant, distinctly modern regeneration of verse forms. This latter achievement was especially interesting to Bridges, who analyzed Kipling's portrait of Queen Elizabeth in "The Looking Glass" as an example of the poet's extraordinary sensitive orchestration of allusions. Bridges observed, first of all, that the opening line of this poem, "The Queen was in her chamber, and she was middling old," was a variation on the nonsensical nursery rhyme, "The Queen was in her parlour eating bread and honey." The echo of the familiar nursery rhyme and the expression "middling old" had the immediate effect of placing the Queen "down among the homeliest of her subjects." The result of these images and allusions, Bridges explained, was masterful: the variation of the familiar, the clash of discordant imagery and associations combined the heroic and the homely to dramatize "the vain woman's vanity and the tyrant's bad conscience."

The incongruities of imagery in this poem were of a kind that previous critics, conditioned by romantic expectations, had viewed as serious flaws. To Bridges, however, these very incongruities gave the poem a deeper dimension and precipitated a creative conflict of forces. "In spite of these things," Bridges wrote, "the whole has an irresistible force, so that our dislike of the incongruities, if we feel any, is overpowered; and this force, though it may be due to the apparent obstacles, may seem the greater for its victory over them."

Kipling's sensitive orchestration of allusions, evidenced in this and other poems, convinced Bridges that Kipling's poetry, regardless of its unpleasant politics, had much that was instructive to offer the practicing poet. Kipling, Bridges concluded, "has so true a feeling for the value of words and for the right cadences of idiomatic speech and so vast a vocabulary, that his example is generally useful to a generation whose cultured speech rhythms are so slovenly and uncertain."[6]

Robert Bridges' conclusion that Kipling's poetry had something to offer the practicing poet was confirmed in 1919 by another practicing poet of great talent. T. S. Eliot, reviewing *The Years Between* for the *Athenaeum* in an article entitled "Kipling Redivivus," suggested that Kipling was "a laureate without laurels" and a "neglected celebrity." Eliot did not undertake to provide the laurels, but he did, at least, muster the curiosity and bravery to take a fresh and relatively unencumbered look at Kipling's poetry. Eliot insisted that Kipling was no isolated phenomenon; he had antecedents, most obviously Swinburne, and he had methods which had never been sufficiently analyzed. Kipling and Swinburne, Eliot went on to note, were alike in their use of sound. Both, that is, neglected the sound value of music and attempted to employ "the sound value of oratory." Kipling and Swinburne wrote what Eliot called "the poetry of oratory," and their words were music "just as the words of the orator or preacher are music; they persuade, not by reason, but by emphatic sound." "Swinburne and Mr. Kipling," Eliot continued,

have, like the public speaker, an idea to impose; and they impose it in the public speaker's way, by turning the idea into sound, and iterating the sound. And like the public speaker's their business is not to express, to lay before you, to state, but to propel, to impose on you, the idea. And, like the orator, they are personal, not by revelation, but by throwing themselves in and gesturing the emotion of the moment. The emotion is not "there" simply, solidly independent of the author, of the audience, there and forever like Shakespeare's and Aeschylus's emotions; it is present only as the author is on the platform and compels you to feel it.

In addition to sharing the orator's stratagems, both Kipling and Swinburne were poets of ideas. In Eliot's view, a poet who had ideas, even a few simple ideas such as liberty or empire, was distinctly inferior to that higher order of poets who had larger points of view or "worlds." Shakespeare, Dante, and Villon had "'worlds," but Kipling had only ideas, and his poetry consequently appeared "to lack cohesion, to be, frankly, immature."

Kipling's ideas were inadequate, then, and so, it seemed to Eliot, were his manner and his audience. Kipling's manner, characterized by "an abuse of the English Bible," seemed to be hopelessly debased by "its touch of newspapers, of Billy Sunday, and the Revised Version filtered through Rabbi-Zeal of The Land Busy." Above all, the Biblical style seemed to resist any significant modern content. Kipling's audience, the large audience of the orator, was also scorned by Eliot, who preferred "an audience of one hypothetical intelligent man who does not exist, and who is the audience of the artist." And yet, in spite of all these specific reservations, Eliot seemed convinced, in a vague and uncertain way, that there was some indefinable greatness in Kipling's poetry. Kipling, Eliot insisted, is not an "artist," but by virtue of an "unconsciousness about him" he is "very nearly a great writer." There was, moreover, "an echo of greatness in his naive appeal to so large an audience as he addresses."[7]

Eliot, as usual, had managed to assert far more than he had demonstrated, and his 1919 review of *The Years Between* was a peculiar combination of asserted praise and documented deficiencies. Eliot, groping for definitions, seemed to sense that Kipling, if not an artist, was, in some sense, great. His readiness to measure Kipling by the standards of Shakespeare, Villon, and Dante certainly attests to the seriousness with which he grappled with Kipling's poetry. Eliot would not attempt to define Kipling's achievement with precision until his 1941 anthology of Kipling's verse,[8] but in 1919 he had already demonstrated a rare curiosity about Kipling's unique achievement.

Kipling's poet-critics, Eliot and Bridges, represented the best, that is the most original, concrete, and authentic responses to Kipling's poetry since Richard Le Gallienne's *Rudyard Kipling: A Criticism* had appeared in 1900. Originality, concreteness, and authenticity were rare qualities amidst the smug certainties of Kipling criticism, and the best critics, like Eliot and Bridges, often distinguished themselves by asking rather than answering significant questions.

Neither the Kipling critics nor the Kipling cultists were inclined to ask questions about Kipling's final volume of poetry, *The Years Between*. In 1919 Kipling was a known quantity, and most reviewers seemed satisfied that his poetry could be adequately reviewed with the platitudes of the past. Aside from T. S. Eliot's review, *The Years Between* stimulated with almost Pavlovian predictability the same stock responses that had been made twenty years earlier. Ronald Macfie, writing in *The Bookman*, praised *The Years Between* in cultist terms as "a virile volume,"[9] and the critics likewise made the familiar political objections. J. C. Squire, writing under the pseudonym Solomon Eagle, could recommend Kipling's "opinionative songs" only "to a man who thoroughly shares Mr. Kipling's opinions."[10] The anonymous reviewer of the *Dial* briefly dismissed Kipling as "reaction's most vehement spokesman,"[11] and the *London Times Literary Supplement* merely reminded readers that "the poetry of Kipling has long been anathema with field sports, Imperialism, and public schools."[12]

Yet *The Years Between* was not the standard Kipling product, and it was, in many ways, a dramatic departure from the one-dimensional homiletic poems which were customarily associated with Kipling. The new volume did contain the expected war poetry, but it was, for the first time, a war poetry which found its inspiration in a truly universal world war which had, unlike the Boer War, unified the British people in a great national crisis. The war seemed to provoke in Kipling a larger patriotism which embraced England's allies—and at times all humanity—and led to a more sensitive and specific awareness of menaced values. Kipling, as many critics have observed,[13] always expressed an almost paranoiac sense of anxiety, and his fearful insights almost always translated into angry indictments. In World War I Kipling seemed to have found an event which was at last equal to his anger. The result can be seen in the new breadth and intensity of emotion which seemed to distinguish *The Years Between* from Kipling's earlier works. Such poems as "The Covenant," "France," "The Choice," and "For All We Have and Are" certainly express far more than the narrow militarism, specialized hatreds, and petulant partisanship which characterized *The Five Nations*. Other poems such as "A Death Bed," "En-dor," "Hyenas," and the Goyaesque "Epitaphs of War" exhibited a grim, new realism. This realism, at times bordering on the morbid, completely avoids the romantic falsifications of war which C. F. Masterman and other critics had condemned in *The Five Nations*. Kipling's references to "our dead" who "twitch and stiffen and slaver and groan / Ere the eyes are set in the head"[14] place him in the forefront of the young war poets who developed a new realistic tradition of war poetry.

In addition to this new realism and the larger, saner patriotism, *The Years Between* reflected a more mature and contemplative poetic mood which Kipling had rarely been able to articulate in his more youthful verse. The new mood is perhaps most evident in "Mesopotamia." This strange poem, written two years after Kipling lost his son in the war, was designed as a protest against the incompetence of the Indian government and the mismanagement of the first Mesopotamian campaign.[15] But because of its intensity of rage and novelty of sentiment, "Mesopotamia" transcends protest and becomes an almost pacifist poem.

Mesopotamia
1917

They shall not return to us, the resolute, the young,
    The eager and whole-hearted whom we gave:
But the men who left them thriftily to die in their own dung,
    Shall they come with years and honour to the grave?

They shall not return to us, the strong men coldly slain
    In sight of help denied from day to day:

> But the men who edged their agonies and chid them in their pain,
>   Are they too strong and wise to put away?
>
> Our dead shall not return to us while Day and Night divide—
>   Never while the bars of sunset hold.
> But the idle-minded overlings who quibbled while they died,
>   Shall they thrust for high employments as of old?
>
> Shall we only threaten and be angry for an hour?
>   When the storm is ended shall we find
> How softly but how swiftly they have sidled back to power
>   By the favour and contrivance of their kind?
>
> Even while they soothe us, while they promise large amends,
>   Even while they make a show of fear,
> Do they call upon their debtors, and take counsel with their friends,
>   To confirm and re-establish each career?
>
> Their lives cannot repay us—their death could not undo—
>   The shame that they have laid upon our race.
> But the slothfulness that wasted and the arrogance that slew,
>   Shall we leave it unabated in its place?

Although *The Years Between* reflected profound and dramatic changes in both the poet and the nation, most critics remained in essential agreement that Kipling was a force to be resisted and that his poetry, above all, should be scorned. Over four decades of Kipling criticism had been, with a few notable exceptions, designed to discount and discredit Kipling's reputation as a poet. The success of these hostile Kipling critics was at no time more evident than at Kipling's death in 1936. When Kipling had lain gravely ill in New York in the winter of 1899, the whole world seemed poised in anguish and anxiety while his doctors issued hourly bulletins to the huge crowds which gathered outside his hotel.[16] Now thirty-seven years after his alarming illness, Kipling's death caused scarcely a ripple in literary circles.

Few were surprised at Kipling's death, for Kipling, the poetry he wrote, and the world he had celebrated had long ago been buried beneath decades of critical contempt. Edmund Wilson had written in 1932 that Kipling "was as much a part of a definite period that came to an end with the war as Theodore Roosevelt was, and he did not, as did Roosevelt, die appropriately when it was over."[17] As early as 1924, Philip Guedalla had already undertaken to embalm Kipling in Strachey-esque irony. Kipling, Guedalla wrote, seemed "to belong to an age of fabulous antiquity. His flag, his Queen, his soldiers, are the vague figures of a mythology that is rapidly fading into folklore." Kipling's subjects had passed into deserved oblivion, and, for most critics, there was nothing in his poetry to redeem him. His widely touted contributions to poetic diction failed to impress Guedalla as they had impressed Bridges, and Guedalla, concluding with a final *bon mot*, wrote that Kipling as a poet "found the English language marble and left it stucco."[18]

Many seemed to sense that Kipling had lived beyond his time, and most of the brief and perfunctory obituary notices reflected the conviction that Kipling's poetry had long been moribund. Indeed several obituary writers, apparently unaware that Kipling had lived and worked for thirty-six years of the new century, eulogized him as a Victorian. William McFee wrote of Kipling's death as one of "the last echoes of the Victorian age,"[19] and Herbert Palmer, praising Kipling as "the father of modern outspokenness," reminded readers that Kipling had used "livid, raw-hide words where all the other Victorian writers used dashes."[20] Henry Seidel Canby consigned Kipling to the stagnant status of a "sterile" classic who was read "only in the underworld of readers whose imaginations still lived in the Nineteenth century."[21] R. A. Scott-James recognized the modern elements in Kipling's poetry—the "mass emotion," the colloquial language, and the violent rhythms which served "like jazz music to stir the community of feeling of the audience." It was these very elements of modernism, though, that prevented Kipling's poetry from being "a lonely adventure of the spirit, as it had been for most of the Victorian poets" and convinced Scott-James that few of Kipling's poems would be remembered.[22]

Many of the obituaries reflected the years of harsh, uncompromising conflict between the Kipling critics and the Kipling cultists. The critics repeated once again the standard clichés which had been handed down through the years since Richard Le Gallienne, Francis Adams, and Robert Buchanan had first dealt with Kipling as a menacing force in British literary life. Malcolm Muggeridge, for example, recalled Kipling's vulgarity—a vulgarity which had become in a more enlightened age "the vulgarity of the many causes he espoused."[23] Similarly, Douglas Jerrold remembered Kipling as "a voice out of the past" who served as the "sometimes inspired and always effective spokesman for a kind of imperialism no longer in fashion."[24]

The cultists, like the critics, mourned Kipling in the most predictable terms. Arthur Hood, in an angry article entitled "The Laureate of the People," summed up the feelings of those who valued Kipling as the last remaining voice of decency amidst triumphant decadence. To Hood, Kipling was, above all, a spokesman for wholesome sanity "in a world of lounge-lizards, rat-minded, would-be poets exulting in sewers, musicians imitating the savagery of banged tom-toms, and so-called artists emulating the drawing of children and bedlamites." The death of Kipling to angry idolators like Hood was obviously far more than the death of a poet; it was a social and cultural calamity which left England defenseless at a time "when the red ants of communism are untiringly busy in undermining all the long established standards of morality and honest manliness."[25]

Surprisingly enough, there were some who mourned Kipling the poet more than Kipling the imperialist or Kipling the prose writer. The *Spectator* predicted that Kipling's poems, neglected by the critics, would outlast the prose. The prose, it seemed, was already dated, but the *Spectator*'s anonymous writer noted that "there is a substantial corpus of Kipling's verse that can scarcely be forgotten."[26]

Rebecca West, the novelist, also eulogized Kipling as a poet. Writing in the *New Statesman and Nation*, Miss West berated Kipling's admirers "among the rich and the great" who had promoted the poet "as an oracle of wisdom; as Shakespeare touched with grace and elevated to a kind of mezzanine rank just below the Archbishop of Canterbury." By using Kipling as a "literary fetish," his admirers, Miss West wrote, had obscured his authentic achievements as "a sweet singer" who interpreted the mind of his age. Kipling, to Rebecca West, remained above all a "shy and delicate lyricist," and only the distortions and exaggerations of his admirers had prevented the world from recognizing that "all his life long, Kipling was a better poet than he was a prose writer."[27]

Paradoxically, it was the creative writers and the practicing poets, deeply immersed in the modern movements, who tended to eulogize Kipling as a poet. One of the most perceptive and sympathetic of these obituary assessments of Kipling was written by the promoter of avantgarde poetry in America, Harriet Monroe. Although she did register "utter amazement at the smug superiority so complacently revealed" in some of Kipling's poems, Miss Monroe was less inclined than her British counterparts to let political passions interfere with her evaluation of Kipling's poetry. Rudyard Kipling, she wrote, was "a master of rhymed eloquence" and the possessor of some enviable poetic gifts. In the "Barrack-Room Ballads" he had perfected "a variety of double quick short lines" which moved with a continually fresh "muscular facility," and Miss Monroe acknowledged that in this kind of rhyming Kipling was "pre-eminently the modern master."

In addition to the admirable metrical talents displayed in his "rhymed eloquence," Kipling was also recognized for his artistic assimilation of heretofore unacceptable topics. After quoting "McAndrew's Hymn," Miss Monroe wrote of Kipling as "one of the few modern poets (I am another) to feel the imaginative appeal of all the super power magnificence which creates a miracle every day, and to resent the narrow vision which sees in it nothing but mechanics." Yet it was Kipling's more conventionally beautiful songs which seemed to show the essence of his poetic achievement. Citing the "tragic" "Danny Deever," the superbly elegiac "Recessional," and the "delicately wistful" "Mandalay," Miss Monroe concluded that "it is upon a few songs such as these that Kipling's fame as a poet will ultimately rest."[28]

The obituaries which recorded Kipling's passing from the literary scene reflected the inability of nearly half a century to deal with Kipling's unique achievement as a poet. It was a failure due, in part, to the inherent inadequacies of the critical methods of the times. Close analysis of the text, in fact all the methodology of modern criticism, had not yet been popularized, and the many notable critics who commented on Kipling's poetry were limited to impressionistic generalizations and the search for slogans which might paraphrase rather than explicate Kipling's poetry. Consequently the best Kipling criticism from 1900 to 1936 consisted, for the most part, of isolated, undeveloped insights. Critics praised Kipling's poetry as an expression of the British character or *zeitgeist*, but none saw in Kipling's verse the more immediate product of a more specific spirit. No one, that is, looked beyond the vague generalities of the British spirit to see Kipling as a representative writer of Edwardian "invasion literature"[29] or a pioneer in the new, realistic tradition of war poetry.

But beyond the inherent inadequacies which impoverished the criticism of all writers there were certain unique and powerful forces which made Rudyard Kipling's reputation a special case. Kipling's reputation as a poet had never been based entirely on literary considerations. From the very beginning of his poetic career in 1890 Kipling was hailed as a new star in a singularly dim literary universe, denounced as an unexpected and alarming claimant for Tennyson's hallowed mantle as poet laureate, and condemned as a vulgar upstart who appealed to the basest and most prosaic interests of the newly literate reading public. As a writer of patriotic and "masculine" verse Kipling was popularly promoted as an anodyne to the disease of decadence which seemed to infect British letters at the time of Oscar Wilde's scandalous trials. Finally, Kipling as a promoter of imperialism in general and the Boer War in particular was soon ensnared in a variety of extraliterary irrelevancies.

Rudyard Kipling's reputation as a poet never recovered from these extraliterary forces which aroused such violent hostilities at the very beginning of his career. The reviewers from 1903 to 1919 perpetuated the anti-Kipling tradition of the nineties and succeeded in exiling Kipling to the popular culture, where his poetry remained unexamined—immune to the new critical methods which might have rescued him from uncritical idolatry. As a result, it was to the common readers that Kipling owed his continued popularity. It was a popularity unsanctioned by taste, undisciplined by critical intelligence, and, in many eyes, totally unmerited. Paradoxically it was also a popularity which contributed a major impediment to critical approval, for many critics, feeling perhaps that they were pursuing the more astonishing enigma, preferred to ignore Kipling's poetry and to explain, instead, his popularity.

Yet in spite of the critics Kipling was read, and his poetry was a pervasive, if sometimes unwelcome, presence in the poetic atmosphere of his age. It was a presence which was rarely approved and scarcely acknowledged, but it was, nevertheless, not to be ignored. For some, it was certainly a force to be resisted, and many poets, no doubt, regarded Kipling's poetry as D. H. Lawrence regarded Ben Franklin's proverbs—as "thorns in young flesh."[30] In any event, Kipling's presence and usefulness made it impossible for the major poets of his age to ignore him with the smug self-assurance of the critics. It is perhaps no accident that the best criticism of Kipling's poetry written during his long lifetime was invariably written by poets, rather than critics, reviewers, or scholars. Unlike the reviewers, those harried retailers of literary opinion, Kipling's poet-critics tended to ignore both immediate political problems and ultimate Arnoldian issues and instead approached Kipling's poems with pragmatic, technical curiosity. Such an approach, concerned with specific strategies, made Kipling a useful arsenal of artistic techniques at a time when most critics regarded him as a museum of archaic and irrelevant ideas. It was apparent to these poet-critics that Kipling's reformation of diction was not unlike Ezra Pound's more flamboyant revolt against "Tennysonianisms" and "literaryisms,"[31] nor, as Robert Bridges recalled, was it unlike Synge's suggestion that "before verse can be made human again, it must first learn to be brutal."[32] Kipling's allusiveness, his assimilation and ironic orchestration of elements from the popular culture was not lost on Bridges, nor we may assume on Eliot. Certainly Kipling's mastery of verse exercised an evident fascination for Eliot, whose poetic dramas attempted to realize an ideal union of public and private utterance by combining the intensity of poetry with the continuity of verse.[33]

T. S. Eliot's promotion of Kipling's poetry and W. H. Auden's solemn prediction that Yeats, like Kipling, would be forgiven for his language are not, then, expressions of inexplicable eccentricity. In the context of Kipling criticism, Auden's enigmatic prophecy and Eliot's generous praise can be seen as a surfacing of a professional interest in Kipling's artistry which developed during the darkest decades of critical indifference.

NOTES

[1] T. S. Eliot, "Kipling Redivivus," *Athenaeum*, May 9, 1919, 297–98.

[2] Charles H. Towne, "The Vanished Yeats, The Never-Vanishing Kipling, and Some Others," *The Bookman* (New York) 49 (July 1919), 618–19.

[3] C. E. Carrington, *The Life of Rudyard Kipling* (New York: Doubleday, 1955), 310, 381.

[4] Charles F. Masterman, "After the Reaction," *Contemporary Review* 86 (Dec. 1904), 815–34.

[5] "The Kipling Blue Pill," *The Philistine* 13 (Oct. 1901), 129–36.

[6] "Wordsworth and Kipling," *TLS*, Feb. 29, 1912, rpt. in *Collected Essays, Papers, etc.* (London: Oxford Univ. Press, 1927), 27–38.

[7] T. S. Eliot, "Kipling Redivivus," 297–98.

[8] The reception of this anthology is chronicled in my "A Choice of Critics: T. S. Eliot's Edition of Kipling's Verse," *Dalhousie Review* 52, No. 4 (Winter 1973), 572–87.

[9] Ronald Macfie, "The Years Between," *The Bookman* (London), 56 (May 1919), 76–77.

[10] "The Years Between," *New Statesman* 13 (April 12, 1919), 48.

[11] "Notes on Books," *Dial* 66 (May 31, 1919), 571–74.

[12] "Mr. Kipling Condemns," *TLS*, April 10, 1919, 196.

[13] W. H. Auden, "The Poet of the Encirclement," *New Republic* 109 (Oct. 25, 1953), 579–81, and Edmund Wilson, *The Wound and the Bow* (Boston: Houghton, 1941), 105–81.

[14] "En-dor," *Rudyard Kipling's Verse* (New York: Doubleday, 1940), 363.

[15] Carrington, 339.

[16] *The New York Journal,* reprinted in "Kipling in America," *The American Monthly Review of Reviews* 19 (April 1899), 419–22, and Carrington, 235, 225.

[17] "The Post-War Kipling," *New Republic* 71 (May 25, 1932), 50–51.

[18] *A Gallery* (New York: Putnam's, 1924), rpt. in *Contemporary Essays*, William Hastings, ed. (Boston: Houghton, 1928), 174–79.

[19] "The Kipling who was more than the Poet of Empire," *New York Times Book Review* (Feb. 9, 1936), 2, 28.

[20] "Rudyard Kipling," *Cornhill Magazine* 155 (Jan. 1937), 24–31.

[21] "Kipling—The Great Colonial," *Saturday Review of Literature* 12 (Jan. 25, 1936), 3–4, 14, 16.

[22] "Rudyard Kipling," *London Monthly* 32 (Feb. 1936), 373–75.

[23] "Men and Books," *Time and Tide* 18 (Feb. 20, 1937), 241.

[24] "Current Comments," *English Review* 69 (Feb. 1936), 139.

[25] "The Laureate of the People," *Poetry Review* 27 (March-April 1936), 97–102.

[26] "Rudyard Kipling," *Spectator* (Jan. 24, 1936), 118–19.

[27] "Rudyard Kipling," *New Statesman and Nation* 11 (Jan. 25, 1936), 112–14.

[28] "Kipling as a Poet," *Poetry* 48 (April 1936), 32–36.

[29] Samuel Hynes, *The Edwardian Mind* (Princeton: Princeton Univ. Press, 1968), 15–53.

[30] *Studies in Classic American Literature* (New York: Thomas Seltzer, 1923), 21.

[31] Ezra Pound, a letter to Harriet Monroe as quoted by Richard Ellman, *Eminent Domain* (New York: Oxford Univ. Press, 1967), 67.

[32] Bridges, "Wordsworth and Kipling," *Collected Essays, Papers, etc.*, 28.

[33] Northrop Frye, *T. S. Eliot* (New York: Grove Press, 1963), 24–46.

Michigan State University

CONTRIBUTORS

JOSEPH O. BAYLEN, Regents' Professor of History and Chairman of the Department of History at Georgia State University, has published extensively on late Victorian and Edwardian British history. Scheduled for publication during 1975 is his biography of the journalist and advocate of world peace, W. T. Stead. An earlier book of his on Stead, *The Tsar's "Lecturer-General": W. T. Stead and the Russian Revolution of 1905*, appeared in 1969.

MICHAEL E. GREENE, Assistant Professor of English at North Carolina A&T State University, teaches courses in Victorian literature and has published in *The English Quarterly* and *Ball State Forum*. He is presently working on Dickens and on William Allingham.

HOWARD H. HINKEL, Assistant Professor of English at the University of Missouri, has written book reviews and has published in *Papers on Language & Literature*.

MAURICE HUNGIVILLE, Assistant Professor in the Department of American Thought and Language at Michigan State University, has published articles on Ezra Pound in *American Literature* and the *Texas Quarterly*, an article on Emily Dickinson in *The Dickinson Bulletin*, and an article on Rudyard Kipling in *The Dalhousie Review*.

FLORENCE P. KRAUSE, Associate Professor and Acting Chairman of the Department of English at William Woods College, Fulton, Missouri, has written a short story, book reviews, and several bits of verse, but her study relating Keats and Shakespeare is her first published scholarly article.

BOYD LITZINGER, Professor of English at Saint Bonaventure University in New York, completed a dissertation on Browning under Kenneth L. Knickerbocker in 1956 and has since published widely on Browning and other major Victorian poets. In 1965 he and Professor Knickerbocker collaborated on *The Browning Critics*. His latest undertaking is an edition of Browning's letters to the Frederick Lehmanns, which will be published in the Baylor Browning Interests Series.

EDWARD C. McALEER, Professor Emeritus, Hunter College of the City University of New York, has published extensively on nineteenth- and twentieth-century English literature, including *Dearest Isa: Robert Browning's Letters to Isabella Blagden* (1951), *The Sensitive Plant: A Life of Lady Mount Cashell* (1958), and *Learned Lady: Letters from Robert Browning to Mrs. Thomas Fitzgerald* (1966).

BRUCE K. MARTIN, Assistant Professor of English at Drake University, has published articles on George Eliot and John Steinbeck and is working on a study of the poetry of Thomas Hardy. He teaches Victorian and modern British literature and also literary criticism.

WILLIAM W. MORGAN, Associate Professor of English at Illinois State University, has previously published an essay on Shakespeare and three articles on Hardy. He was also a contributor to Helmut Gerber and Eugene Davis' *Thomas Hardy: An Annotated Bibliography of Writings About Him* (1973).

BEGE B. NEEL is a doctoral candidate and graduate teaching assistant in the Department of English at the University of Tennessee, Knoxville. This is her first published article.

LESLIE H. PALMER, Assistant Professor of English at North Texas State University, has published essays on Matthew Arnold and Ezra Pound (in *Paideuma*) and on T. S. Eliot (in *Forum*). His poems have appeared in *Green River Review* and in *Patterns*.

ANNA S. PARRILL, Associate Professor of English at Southeastern Louisiana University, is currently doing research in the nineteenth-century novel. This is her first published article.

KENNETH E. STORY, Associate Professor of English at Hendrix College in Arkansas, is working on a book-length study of Tennyson's *The Princess* and on articles about the fiction of Flannery O'Connor and Carson McCullers. This is his first published article.

JAMES B. TWITCHELL, Assistant Professor of English at the University of Florida, has published on Byron in *Studies in English Literature, 1500–1900*, on Coleridge in *Psychoanalytic Review*, and on Shelley in *The Keats-Shelley Journal*.

CHARLES R. WOODARD, Professor of English at the University of Alabama in Huntsville, has published articles in *College English* and in the Hodges-Thaler special issue of *Tennessee Studies in Literature*. He has also written poems which have appeared in numerous journals and little magazines.